IF BLINDNESS STRIKES: DON'T STRIKE OUT
A Lively Look at Living with a Visual Impairment

IF BLINDNESS STRIKES: DON'T STRIKE OUT

A LIVELY LOOK AT LIVING
WITH A VISUAL IMPAIRMENT

By

MARGARET M. SMITH

Detroit Receiving Hospital and University Health Center
Detroit, Michigan

With Forewords by

Fred Girard
Staff Writer
The Detroit News
Detroit, Michigan

and

Edward S. Thomas
President
Detroit Receiving Hospital and University
Health Center
Detroit, Michigan

CHARLES C THOMAS • PUBLISHER
Springfield • Illinois • U.S.A.

Published and Distributed Throughout the World by

CHARLES C THOMAS • PUBLISHER
2600 South First Street
Springfield, Illinois 62717

© *1984 by* CHARLES C THOMAS • PUBLISHER

ISBN 0-398-04937-8

Library of Congress Catalog Card Number: 83-18239

Printed in the United States of America
SC-R-3

Library of Congress Cataloging in Publication Data

Smith, Margaret M.
   If blindness strikes: don't strike out.

   Bibliography: p.
   1. Blind—Rehabilitation—United States. 2. Visually
handicapped—Rehabilitation—United States. I. Title.
HV1795.S64 1984   362.4'183   83-18239
ISBN 0-398-04937-8

THE BOOK THAT
HAD TO BE WRITTEN

I did not, I say with no little pleasure, nick my Adam's apple while shaving this morning. This, after an entire adult lifetime spent walking about with a bright red spot glinting from that unshaveable protruberance like the misplaced forehead jewel of some poor rajah.

What wrought this astonishing change? I learned to swallow. The simple act of swallowing makes the Adam's apple disappear for the space of a few brisk razor strokes, leaving behind nothing but flat, open, shaveable space. I did not know this simple little maneuver because no one ever told me about it. I had a gap in my education . . . a blind spot.

Protection of the Adam's apple from sharp surfaces is one of a countless number of ways and means Margaret M. Smith has compiled in IF BLINDNESS STRIKES: DON'T STRIKE OUT.

Her book is not merely for the blind, or the soon-to-be-blind, or their families, friends, and co-workers. It's for all of us with blind spots. It's for all of us here on Spaceship Earth who haven't yet realized that some of our fellow crewmembers are men; some are women; some are black, some are white; and some are blind.

Blindness, I have come to realize through knowing Margaret Smith, is a state of constant awareness, an ongoing intellectual effort to fix one's place in space and time, a never-ending need to plan a step—or several steps—ahead. Margaret blindfolded me once, and walked me through city streets to a restaurant for lunch. A few techniques came easily, such as ordering food for manageability rather than taste ("I'll pass on the English peas, thanks,"), but what struck me most was the constant and necessary busyness

This chess game has a multiplicity of rules. You need to learn them from a good teacher. Margaret Smith has absorbed them not only during a lifetime as a productive person who happens to be blind but in her career in rehabilitation for the blind, on the national cutting edge of technology and method. It is this storehouse of experience she opens to us in her book.

Some ground Margaret covers is unavoidably technical: She is on intimate terms with mind-bending machinery such as the Optacon, a minicamera that reads individual letters and reproduces them through vibrations on a fingertip, and specialized lenses, telescopic, microscopic, and prismatic, that maximize any precious sight left. But mostly Margaret's book provides what can't be found anywhere else: the actual how-to's of daily life for the blind and those around them. How to keep clothes matched. How to label everything you'll need to touch. How to ask for help with dignity. How, even, to get that pesky Adam's apple out of the way while shaving.

This is, above all, a book of hope. If blindness strikes, it says, don't strike out. Strike back.

FRED GIRARD
Staff writer
The Detroit News

I have to write another book, Mr. Thomas." I wasn't really surprised when Margaret Smith blurted out those words as she sat on the other side of my desk one brisk fall morning. I didn't remind her of the grueling hours to be crowded into her life already full with a job, home, and social activities. I took her at her word. She meant what she said.

"We're reaching so few people," said Margaret. I nodded in silent agreement, caught myself, and chuckled. Then I reflected for a few moments. Our emergency/trauma hospital and outpatient services, located in the Detroit Medical Center, are the heart of one of the largest medical complexes in the country. Visually Handicapped Services, with its seven-member staff, is a small department which makes a big impact. I've seen students starting their rehabilitation with trepidation, even fear. As their self-confidence takes hold, it's almost as if they emerge from a cocoon of uncertainty. When I stop by the area, I'm likely to see several students preparing lunch, somebody else learning to sew, while others tackle typing or Braille. While behind the wheel, I often see blind folks being taught to cross busy streets or waiting at bus stops.

Families and friends share a student's successes and disappointments. The staff encourages them to visit and to talk about their feelings and reactions to a loved one who has a serious vision problem.

"We still haven't reached enough professionals who have contact with blind people," Margaret continued. I couldn't quibble with that frustration either.

The staff frequently provides in-service training to ophthalmologists, optometrists, nurses, social workers, psychologists, psychiatrists, and physical and occupational therapists. Because this is a teaching hospital, affiliated with Wayne State University, students here and from nearby hospitals and universities learn a lot about blindness.

As a hospital administrator, I'm used to dealing with statistics. But I needed no figures to convince me. Efforts to reach and teach visually impaired people and those who touch their lives miss vast numbers who need such support and information.

Although Margaret crams a lot of suggestions and information into this book (she covers things I never even thought about), it doesn't seem like a text. Sometimes you, the reader, will laugh, cry, and identify with victories and shortcomings told through annecdotes. You will gain more than an insight into blindness. It leaves you with a different outlook on life.

Rising to leave my office, Margaret gripped my hand firmly. "Just be around for moral support, Mr. Thomas. I'll need plenty before this is over."

Now I can say that the word is out, or shall I say that the words are down on paper. It is with joy and pride that I urge you to join me in discovering why THIS IS THE BOOK THAT HAD TO BE WRITTEN.

EDWARD S. THOMAS

President
Detroit Receiving Hospital and
University Health Center

ACKNOWLEDGMENTS

T he words *thank you* fall flat and short when it comes to recognizing the many people who were so much a part of this book. To those who are named and unnamed goes my gratitude. They never said no when I asked for help. I extend special appreciation to Fred Girard, who gave the precious gift of his expertise and patience in editing this manuscript. As a newspaperman to the core, Fred's mastery of the written word made this book possible. It was Edward Thomas, President of Detroit Receiving Hospital and University Health Center, whose encouragement never wavered, even when my spirits were flagging. To all of you, people behind the pages, a trite but heartfelt THANK YOU.

Jane Jordan Browne
Terry Donovan
Douglas Dossin
Patrick Greaves
Kenneth Hanninen, Ph.D.
Philip Hessburg, M.D.
Leamon Jones
Leota Keenan
Shirley Koerber
Donald Lakin, O.D.

Peter Lederer, D.V.M.
Linda Leggs
Dorothy Norton
Michael Patten
Alice Raftary
Larry Sell, M.D.
Suzanne Sippola
Erine Theodorou
Lyle and Lee Thume
J. Patrick Wright

CONTENTS

IF BLINDNESS STRIKES: DON'T STRIKE OUT
A Lively Look at Living with a Visual Impairment

Chapter 1

YOUR WORLD FALLS APART

S everal weeks ago a sixty-two-year-old woman sat across the desk from me. As a professional worker in rehabilitation of the adult blind, I had heard stories such as hers before. She had suffered drastic loss of sight in the past four months. Giving up driving was her first concession. Reading print became impossible. Daily existence developed into nightmarish dimensions—dressing, cooking, shopping, meeting job demands, handling money.

Shortly before seeing me, she sat in an opthalmologist's office, hearing him speak words that would alter her life: "Kay, your vision will never return. It will only get worse. If you want to learn more about your eye disease, here's a book you can read."

Through tears she managed, "But, Doctor, I can't read!" and walked out of his office.

Hundreds of clients have sat in the same seat, telling me similar stories—of lives that have shattered with the onset of blindness.

Kay, a social worker, had helped others pick up the pieces of their lives during her forty years of practice, but like the physician who could not heal himself, neither could the social worker help herself. She was facing the most devastating emotional blow of her life. Besides being unable to look upon her loved ones, to appreciate natural beauty, to enjoy the freedom of driving, to wander through art galleries and delight in the glory of the sun rising or setting, another dilemma confronted her. How would the significant others in her life look upon her as a blind person? Would family and friends shower her with pity or avoid her as if she carried a communicable disease? Facing colleagues, superiors, her own clients, and their families in her work world when she herself was so afraid was another obstacle she almost dared not contemplate. How would she get to the three different public schools at which she served as social worker? Once at her work place, how was she to move safely but unobtrusively from one office to the next, to the rest room, lounge, cafeteria? Reading files, filling out forms, and writing reports are a major part of a social worker's routine. She could not read print.

In addition to coping with the psychological impact of blindness, Kay, always a self-sufficient woman who lived alone, lacked practical solutions to problems of daily living. Her concerns were real and reasonable. How would she identify colors of clothing to be sure outfits matched or complemented? She had always been fashion conscious and meticulous about her appearance. Were there ways of being certain that she was presentable? Frankly admitting that she liked to eat, how would she prepare even the simplest meal? Could she handle food when dining in public without being a star distraction? Going over her daily mail, keeping track of personal records, handling money, maintaining her checking account—these were questions for which she had no answers.

Bob's life as a sighted person ended without even a moment's warning. He was a twenty-four-year-old divorced father with a three-year-old son. He had drifted in and out of college, trying several jobs before working in a brewery. His indecision at that point in his life was like that of many young people. He hadn't found himself and did not fit into the demands of higher learning; marriage had not worked out for him; he was uncertain about a career.

A conveyer belt that moved cases of beer had jammed. Not bothering to stop the conveyer mechanism, Bob leaned over to see what was causing the back-up. Twelve cases of beer fell on his head, rendering him nearly unconscious, totally severing his optic nerve, instantly causing total, irreversible blindness.

"I could hear somebody screaming to stop the machinery and someone else shouting to call the plant doctor," he says. "I knew something terrible, something really serious happened to me. I just couldn't talk." It wasn't until several weeks later, while still in the hospital recovering from his injuries, that Bob heard those words from his doctor that he refused to believe: "You will always be totally blind. Nothing we can do will make you see again. I'm sorry."

It was almost a year before Bob allowed himself to confront some of the decisions he couldn't make before. Should he continue living with his parents—having been on his own almost since high school graduation? It's hard to "go home again." His job in the industrial plant was out of the question. Could he handle college? How can a blind father be a complete parent to a child? What careers would be open to him as a blind man? Would he need to learn new skills to convince would-be employers and fight discrimination against himself because of his handicap? How would he fit into social situations when so much is said with a glance? He suffered self-doubt about women taking a second look at a man who is blind.

Severe loss of vision most frequently strikes persons over sixty-five—at least 50 percent of those who are legally blind are in this age bracket. At seventy-five, Winny was sprightly, busy in senior citizen activities, a frequent and welcome visitor to the home of her son, his wife, and their four children. She occasionally cared for her older sister, who, at age seventy-eight, was nearly an invalid because of arthritis. It was while driving to her son's home that Winny noticed that she wasn't reading street signs clearly. She ran a red light and almost hit another car coming through the intersection. "Must be these glasses," she thought, vowing to be checked for new glasses as soon as possible. Her optometrist (trained to measure visual acuity and to prescribe lenses) sent her immediately to an opthalmologist, a medical doctor specializing in treatment of the eyes.

After several visits and repeated examinations, the opthalmologist delivered the fateful news: "I can't do anything for you. New glasses won't help, not even surgery. You won't become totally blind, but your degenerative eye disease is beyond treatment."

Winny was angry and depressed, struck by the seeming injustice of her situation. She had raised her family well and worked hard all her life. Wasn't she entitled to enjoy her last few years in peace? Sure, she felt the usual aches and pains that come with old age, but she wasn't alone. She feared her son and daughter-in-law would insist upon taking her into their own home. Yet she had her own home—a cozy apartment in a senior citizen building. Although a bus took residents to the supermarket once a week, she wondered if she could find what she needed among those confusing, dazzling displays in the aisles. She took pride in mending for herself and helping out by sewing for the grandchildren. Being unable to thread a needle would put an end to that. Her son lived twenty-five miles away. She would have to wait for him or his wife to come after her. If the kids wore on her nerves, she couldn't just jump into her car and leave. She was still in better shape than her sister Helen. But was her vision enough to care for someone as ill as Helen?

I must admit being tempted to write a preface. That seems to be the acceptable way to begin many how-to books. Knowing full well that some readers often pass by such introductions, I wanted to catch them before they did. So I skipped it and plunged right in by telling a few stories, true stories, some of which may hold a familiar ring for you.

These accounts are bare outlines of what has happened to real people, clients I have met in my eighteen years of working with adults who have lost their sight. You will meet them by first name only. Although first names may sound a bit chummy and perhaps too personal, I have taken this liberty to ensure their anonymity. I don't intend to imply lack of respect or overfamiliarity because of their blindness. The first-name approach will continue throughout the book as we meet some of these people again.

There are a few moments in a lifetime that remain permanently, sharply etched in memory. Composed of words, sensations and emotions that surround these times—of joy, sorrow, or shock—they will live with you forever. You could have been sitting in the examining chair of your opthalmologist's office as he/she spoke those fatal words, "I'm sorry, but there is nothing we can do about your sight." The same message might have been borne to you by a loved one—husband or wife, son or daughter, dear friend—seated by your hospital bed. An optometrist, fitting you for new glasses, may have hinted that something far more serious was causing your poor vision, a progressive loss that frequent changes of glasses couldn't stop. Whoever pronounced those words and however they were said—gently, reluctantly, clinically—cannot still their life-shattering impact.

Your reaction likely was shock, disbelief—even denial, "This must have happened to somebody else," you insisted to yourself, "but it couldn't happen to me." You rejected the thought of a diagnosis of blindness by rationalizing that the doctors were wrong. After all, medical scientists are always making mistakes. Hospitals can goof, too, you further reasoned. A nurse could have mixed up the chart with someone else's. Another subterfuge: "My eye disease is different. It won't follow the same course as predicted. Somehow I'll be the exception." The dawn of realization doesn't occur overnight. You were not ready to accept the sentence. You sought a second opinion, a third and perhaps a fourth. For endless hours you waited in ophthalmologists' reception rooms, not even bothering to pretend to thumb through months-old magazines stacked on end tables. You couldn't divert your mind from the one thought that, somewhere, someone was going to prescribe a treatment—medication, surgery, procedure—that would either stop your sight from deteriorating further or, better still, restore normal vision.

Your frantic, futile search for a cure may have been led by relatives or friends who had heard or read about a doctor with a record of previous successes. Why couldn't you be one of these? Desperation can drive a person to seek macabre and questionable care. An artist about whom I read would not resign himself to failing vision from retinitis pigmentosa. He learned about a program in England that advocated venom from bee stings to regenerate the deterioration of retinas irreversibly damaged by this disease. He subjected himself to repeated stings from swarms of bees day after day before giving up this futile agony.

Some people, either from religious conviction or last-ditch effort, reach out to faith healers.

Despite routes you have followed, hopes built only to be dashed, ultimately you faced the verdict, repeated and confirmed by all the specialists: You are legally blind, and the prognosis is poor. The medical consensus is that your vision, bad as it is, won't get better. In the case of many patients, it can go from bad to worse.

To hear such bad news is probably among the most painful experiences you will ever encounter. To bear the bad news is also a dreaded mission. One eye specialist, in a thriving practice for many years, confided to me, "I find that telling a patient there is nothing to be done, that his condition will not improve, actually hurts me. I think about it all day, worry about how to break it gently, even rehearse and rehash how I'll put it to the patient. Deep down inside I want to rush through the consultation, get it over as quickly as I can and leave. Doctors are just as human as anyone else. It's natural to wish to avoid that which is hurtful."

DeWitt Stetten, himself a medical doctor, addressed medical colleagues, particularly ophthalmologists, in the *New England Journal of Medicine*. With his gradual sight loss, Dr. Stetten learned through persistence and accident how to cope with blindness. He wrote that his road to recovery, making his life more than a living hell, could have been much smoother if eye specialists had not considered his case as a failure, dropping him in the cold and alone because the science of ophthalmology could not supply a solution.

Dr. Stetten's dilemma probably resembles your own. After hearing repeatedly that no more stops could be pulled, your world fell apart. You felt alone and isolated, walled in and cut off from a society that operates and interacts within a framework designated and executed by and for fully seeing people. After recognizing that what could not happen to you did, in reality, happen to you, you may have withdrawn, dropping out by turning off the world. Retreat can take many forms, one of the most common being that of going to bed.

Isabel began losing her sight in the early fifties. She and her single son, aged thirty, shared a large house. "I would stay in bed until one o'clock in the afternoon," she candidly admits. "Blindness forced me to take an early retirement. I had worked in an office most of my life. Work was my whole existence. When I couldn't file any more and decipher handwritten messages, I threw in the sponge. Since I couldn't go to the office every day, I found that contact with friends became less and less frequent. I had nothing to talk about on those occasions when I met with friends. They stopped coming to see me, and I quit calling them. It was easier to stay in bed most of the day, get up to throw together a little lunch, listen to the TV soaps, and go back to bed again."

A few despondent people react more strongly. Larry was in his midthirties, living with his family—his wife of ten years and two small children. Having been a successful salesman, he recalls, "I had never given sight much thought. It's just like breathing. We take it for granted. I couldn't face impending blindness. How would I cope with absence of vision as a husband, father, and breadwinner? I tried to commit suicide. Thank God I wasn't successful. I ended up in a mental hospital for a few months, long enough to pull myself together."

A few people, when struck by blindness, never make any inroads to recovery. A friend speaks sadly of his aunt, now dead. She had been an upper echelon executive in an advertising agency. At the peak of her career, she had the world by the tail. Her total loss of vision not only ended her professional life but markedly changed her daily existence. She went from a confident, assertive business-woman into the role of a whining, embittered hermit. She severed all ties with relatives and friends, thwarting their attempts to reach her. Allowing herself to become a recluse, she died a hostile old lady.

The old saying "Misery loves company" may or may not hold solace for you. You are not alone in your plight. Over a half-million Americans suffer a serious visual impairment. It is impossible to tally their number because there is no way of keeping track, no means of reporting by ophthalmologists or optometrists who declare a patient legally blind.

Most occurrences of blindness can be traced to eye diseases such as diabetes retinopathy, glaucoma, cataracts, macular degeneration, and retinitis pigmentosa, to name the most common. Accidents—auto, industrial, explosions (from firecrackers to land mines)—and acts of intentional violence also account for sudden loss of vision. People who are congenitally blind (born with a serious visual defect) constitute about 20 percent of this population. In some instances, such as retinitis pigmentosa or retrolental fibroplasia, vision was seriously impaired at birth, developing into total blindness in adolescence or adulthood. Children who are born totally blind, or with only enough vision to perceive light, don't realize their handicap until they are four or five years old. They cannot observe that others avoid obstacles, identify colors, and recognize people and objects far away.

So, a mountain looms in your distance. Will you work out ways to climb it, go around it, or through it? Or will you stand at its foot in utter frustration and desolation, contemplating but not even trying to conquer its peaks? If you choose climbing that mountain, count on falling sometimes or hanging on with barely a toehold. After dropping over some cliffs, you may feel as if you can't get up again. Rise you must. The alternative is turning your back and burying yourself at the foot of that mountain. Unlike that mountain, life doesn't wait—it won't stand still for anyone.

Chapter 2

PICKING UP THE PIECES

W hile having dinner one evening with a good friend, Sean, the conversation turned to psychology. Since she herself is a psychologist, we usually avoid shoptalk. (Sean is one of those vibrant, interested-in-everything people, so shoptalk isn't hard to avoid.) Apparently she had been on one of her reading binges and blurted out, "Margaret, so much has been written on the so-called psychology of blindness, how it molds the personality, its effect on learning and emotions. I hope your book will at least mention these schools of thought, but personally I don't believe in the psychology of the blind."

Sean is right. This book concentrates on some of the common problems that confront a person upon losing his/her sight. It is a practical, problem-solving approach that deals with cooking a meal without burning down the house, rather than overcoming depression. If you can figure out how to keep track of various denominations of bills, how to pour a cup of coffee without caus-ing a mini-Youngstown flood (or scalding yourself), or methods of labeling clothes so that your color combinations won't stop a clock—then much of your apprehension and depression will disappear. Although I'm not a psychologist, I don't subscribe to the theory of a "blind personality" either. Deprived of what most people consider the most vital and valuable of the senses, any human being would be expected to react strongly. Self-help books that range from primal-scream therapy to Freudian psychoanaly-sis flourish today. Blind people, like their seeing counterparts, conceivably could profit from some of these popular psychology books, if appropriately chosen. Seeking professional counseling from someone qualified in treating those who must adjust to a disability can be an immeasurable aid.

Besides attacking the nitty-gritty of daily living, another battle lurks in the foreground: interaction with sighted people—from a spouse to a stranger on the street. Because this book will be published first in print, my hope is that whoever reads it to you first will gain insight. Well-meaning but ill-informed family and friends are just as unfamiliar with blindness as you once were. Waitresses will ask, "Does she want dessert?" A pedestrian loses his command of speech when you ask the location of the cleaner's. He points instead of telling you that it is at the next corner. I shall try to smooth the wrinkles from these potential situations so that you, the blind reader, will retain the dignity of any human being, receiving respect regardless of visual acuity. You, the sighted reader, will feel more comfortable if you know specifically what to do and not do—the way to guide a blind person, the appropriate times to offer help, and the words to use, i.e. that it's perfectly okay to use words such as *look, see,* and *blind* in your conversation.

Let's hit the word *blind* head-on. This is an age of euphemisms. We call garbage collectors sanitation engineers, teachers are known as educators, old age is softened to the sunset years. The fancier or more glib the term, the better it sounds. High-blown or witty phrases disguise meanings. Thus, we have to be attuned to jargon to understand what is going on. Absence of sight is no exception. *Visual impairment, visually handicapped,* and *sightless* are common terms. Many people never say "blind" because it has a harsh ring or negative connotation—such as blind alley, blind drunk, blind luck, or robbed blind. (Even love is blind.) But this five-letter word, easy to say and write, sums it up completely. It includes those who have no sight, or just enough to see light from dark, to people who, although seriously restricted, can walk unaided by cane or dog, read print, and see some detail—a handsome man or ravishing woman, for instance! I shall use the word *blind* without apology, although other terms will pop up for the sake of variety.

Without being technical, what is legal blindness as defined by law throughout the United States? It simply means that a person with normal vision can see in 200 feet what a person with limited vision can see in 20 feet or less, with the best of correction. Correction refers to eyeglasses or contact lenses. Therefore, someone who is legally blind has a visual acuity of 20/200 or less. Legal blindness also includes people whose visual field is restricted to 20 degrees or less with the best of correction. Your visual field, or peripheral vision, is that which you see from the side of your eye. It is possible for someone to have 20/20 vision by looking straight ahead but to be able to detect very little from either side. I know a man who can read a title on a bookshelf from across the room. Yet he will trip on a tricycle on the sidewalk or bump his head on a low-hanging awning because these obstacles are out of his range. Such a restriction is aptly named "tunnel" or "gunbarrel" vision.

Like many, you may think that most legally blind folks are totally blind. Not so. Only 20 percent of the legally blind see nothing. The remainder fall somewhere between light perception and counting fingers at 2 feet, enough sight to perceive large objects, up to the borderline of legal blindness. Some people who are close to the limit of the definition function more closely to the norms of the fully sighted. Only a fraction of the 500,000 legally blind Americans have never seen.

Now that you know what legal blindness is and what degrees of sight that it encompasses, let's dispel some of the notions and misconceptions about blindness and its victims that you yourself may have held when you were sighted. These wrong ideas may cause anxiety and can create expectations and ideals that you can never meet. Melodramatic movies and TV programs, as well as stories in print media, sometimes foster such misunderstandings. You may have gleaned them from a chance acquaintance with someone who is blind—for example, because the blind man on the next block can cut his lawn doesn't mean every blind person could.

Or, suddenly the other senses take over, compensating for the malfunctioning eyes. Not true. When a blind person hears a sound not noticed by others, it's a sign he/she is paying more attention to the information brought by the ear. It's a case of being audibly observant, honed by lots of practice and effort. Hearing doesn't automatically become sharper when the eyes fail. Touch, taste, and smell don't undergo instant awakening either. A person who lost his/her sight last week cannot learn,Braille any more easily than a seeing friend. This recently blind individual would be equally at a loss if expected to sniff out a faint scent or detect an unpronounced flavor. Remaining senses require time for training and development. Degree of improvement depends upon other physical limitations. Someone with a hearing loss will never become adept at using auditory cues. Age and motivation are also factors that determine extent of awareness through the other senses.

Another false idea goes beyond the senses to the intellect. Blind people, according to this myth, fall into two categories: genius or mental defective. IQ studies of the blind show as much variation as with their sighted counterparts. People tested from both groups, for the most part, fall into the middle range: 90 to 110, which is considered normal. Perhaps the fact that some blind people attain high academic achievements, such as a chemistry professor and a mathematics professor, each having a Ph.D., to name only two of many, gives the impression that all belong in the genius category. David Hartman graduated from Temple University, the first blind medical doctor to be graduated in over 100 years. (He continued by specializing in psychiatry.) On the other hand, the assumption is sometimes made that there is a link between lack of sight and lack of intelligence.

Another mystique is that blind people have a sixth sense — whatever that is. The sixth sense is wrongly interpreted as the ability to perceive what someone else is thinking — a specialized form of ESP. A woman whom I met on a train was certain that I knew what she looked like after spending fifteen minutes with her over coffee in the club car.

Occasionally miscontrued as the sixth sense is the faculty of knowing when one approaches a large object such as a wall or a car. Known technically as obstacle perception, science has discovered that sound vibrations can be felt on the face. Its opposite, an awareness of space, can be detected by changes in air current as when walking by a vacant lot or into a large room. One totally blind boy had such acute obstacle perception that he could ride a bicycle along the sidewalk without bumping into trees, parking meters or pedestrians. Sighted people may also have this faculty, exercising it unknowingly when walking through an unlighted familiar room at night without banging into walls or tripping over furniture.

Overshadowing all misconceptions is the light-dark mystique. First, most legally blind people can perceive light. Not even totally blind people live under a shroud of blackness. One woman having no light perception describes the sensation as seeing gray or a pea soup fog. A totally blind man put it well by saying, "The sensation is that of seeing nothing. Your hand doesn't see anything — not blackness as the absence of light." Organizations and agencies serving the blind have perpetuated this dismal image of darkness by including such words as *lighthouse* or *beacon* in their names. A group of volunteers who assisted the blind called themselves the De-lighted Helpers!

Other qualities are attributed unjustly to the blind. They are musical, religiously devout, forever cheerful, or always despondent. Examined under scrutiny, these stereotypes have no substance and should not be attached to any cross section of the population.

Let's look back to your "then." You discovered your cause of blindness, since you're the best judge of how well you see or don't see. You have tried everything humanly possible (and perhaps spiritually possible) to restore that precious sense. As for your "now," you more clearly understand what legal blindness is, whom it affects, and what degrees of sight are within its limitations. No longer are you fuzzy about those seemingly miraculous or undesirable traits that possibly you yourself associated with the blind.

The rest of this book attacks the "what's." The person who has been sighted throughout his/her life and then loses some or all of this faculty is bound to be stymied about the unknowns that lie ahead. There are so many irritations — big and small — that no one else would think of, such as reading the mail, maintaining personal records, knowing what time it is, knowing the contents of spray cans. The list could be as comprehensive as living itself. Providing practical solutions to these and other difficulties is my intention.

Chapter 3

NOT ALL OF THE QUESTIONS,
NOT ALL OF THE ANSWERS

A t thirty-seven, Rosemary gave up her position as office manager because she couldn't see well enough to take shorthand or recognize clients who had appointments with her boss. Because her employer preferred shorthand to dictation, she couldn't transcribe his letters. "Can I find an office position where these tasks won't be required?" she asked, pressing for a definite answer. "I don't want to type all day. I would hate that much typing. How can I find a job where I can capitalize on my experience and previous skill, yet not be held back because I don't see well enough to perform all the paperwork chores?" For Rosemary, who longed for her life and especially her future to be wrapped into a neat package, there was no answer.

Sam is seventy-two, lives with his wife in a home for which he worked all his life. His vision is 20/200, the loss caused by glaucoma. His sight has been stable for the last several years. He and Martha, his wife of forty-eight years, live on their Social Security and his pension. A handyman and carpenter by inclination, Sam enjoys puttering — building a bookcase, replacing washers in the kitchen faucet for the widow next door, maintaining a small garden in the yard. No longer able to drive (Martha never learned), Sam wonders if they should give up their home to move into an apartment or senior-citizen complex closer to public transportation, shopping areas, church, and recreation. His rationale was that he and Martha are still healthy enough to withstand an uprooting. Yet they felt at home in the neighborhood they had known since they were first married.

At the other end of the spectrum is Sandy, a recent high school graduate. In a tragic auto accident the night of her senior prom, shattered glass cost Sandy all of her sight. Upon recovering from her physical injuries, Sandy thought she had to cancel college plans, that she could never achieve a career as an art teacher. Like any uncertain eighteen-year-old, she wanted absolute assurance that she could marry and raise children. She couldn't envision herself living with her parents until they were too old for the responsibility, then moving in with a younger sister. Exactly how would she survive on her own?

Forty-five-year-old Jerry underwent many medical treatments to arrest hemorrhages in his retinas caused by diabetes. With his rapidly decreasing vision, he could still walk without cane or dog guide. Obviously, his twenty-year job as a truck driver was out of the question. Besides his visual disability, would poor health prevent him from learning new vocational skills?

Leslie had poor vision all her life from retrolental fibroplasia— too much oxygen given to her as a premature infant. Despite legal blindness, she completed law school. A married career woman, she was working her way up the ladder of a prestigious law firm when her remaining vision faded. Would her employer expect her to continue the research that constituted a major portion of her job? Traveling to different courts meant brisk walks with frequent crossings of busy downtown streets. How would her law-student husband react to a wife who couldn't see at all? Could she run her home as before, or would he have to take over?

No book can guide you along the primrose path, the perfect way up that mountain. For some pitfalls there is no bridge. Blind folks vary as much among one another as does the seeing population. The only common element in many instances is lack of sight. Your needs and living situation can be totally different from those of someone else you know who is blind. For example, Braille can be invaluable to someone who cannot manage print. However, if your sense of touch is so poor that you can't discriminate letters, Braille will frustrate but not help you.

Your remaining vision (if any) is important. Bright sunny days may dazzle you to the extent that you can barely see the sidewalk, yet the abundant light is the difference between day and night for those not light sensitive. Age is a determining factor—a senior citizen's goals will not be the same as the aspirations of a high school junior. Have others in your household always depended upon you, have you relied upon them, or has it been a give-and-take compromise, or can it develop into one? Are you living alone and do you wish to continue living by yourself?

Unfortunately, there are no absolutes for coping with blindness. Some solutions can work for one person, yet be a dismal failure for another. Before accepting defeat, though, let me warn you—don't give up with the first or even second flop. Any newly acquired skill or modified old method takes time, trial, and error. After writing the section on pouring hot liquids, I rewarded myself with a cup of coffee. You guessed it—I spilled it as I poured. After filling hundreds of cups, I'm entitled to a mistake.

That brings me to a little lecture on self-forgiveness. You think that you have a task mastered, the kinks ironed out. Then you create a disaster. Harry, a sixty-three-year-old retired postal worker, was angry with himself. "I left the milk carton out on the counter yesterday morning," he grumbled. "Naturally it was spoiled by the time I got home."

"But Harry," I countered, "how long has it been since you made the same mistake?"

"About three months," he muttered, still annoyed. "There was almost a quart left."

"You wasted less than a dollar's worth of milk because you didn't see it as you walked out of the kitchen," I persisted. "You didn't want to miss your bus. Allow yourself a little room for weakness. The milk turned sour, but it shouldn't sour your whole day."

Harry was quiet for a few moments. "You're right," he begrudgingly admitted. "My memory has to take over where my sight left off. Just as I can't see everything I used to, I can't expect to remember everything, either."

Just as all answers are impossible to include, so, too, some questions may not be anticipated. "How do you know which side of the stamp has glue?" asked Sharon, a housewife who had been sealing and stamping envelopes for bills as her husband wrote checks.

"I must say I never gave it much thought," I replied. "I buy my stamps in a roll, always tearing them from the end that protrudes from the middle. It would seem that if you touch the surface of the stamp to the inside of your lower lip, you'll know if it has glue or not." (Incidentally, it works.)

For some activities there is no substitute for sight. Driving, accurate interpretations of studies made under a miscroscope, and performing surgery are straightforward examples. (A few legally blind people can drive with restrictions because of high-powered telescopic lenses.) Although unable to drive, many blind people are mobile. Visually impaired students pass college science courses, despite lab requirements. (There isn't much demand for blind surgeons, so I haven't bothered with that one.)

So that the how-to's and what-for's don't become too dry and uninteresting, I'll continue to inject anecdotes for illustration. Some are taken from personal experience, others from people blind all their lives, many from my best teachers, my students. At times you may think serious circumstances have been treated too lightly. I don't mean to dismiss blindness as an inconvenience, but that vein of humor can spell the difference between frustration and humiliation or that delightful release which is known only to human beings: laughter. Looking for a laugh (even though it's well hidden), can lead you off the well-beaten path of routine to a little excitement and variation that you will welcome and relish.

Enough philosophy and platitudes for the moment. Let's get on to the nitty-gritty, the real-life puzzlers that dot the scene for you as a blind person.

Chapter 4

PUTTING YOUR LIFE IN ORDER

W hat time is it?" I hear that question more often from people with poor vision than any other, so I'll tackle timepieces first.

If your remaining vision enables you to read a larger-than-average dial on a watch, check your local jeweler or discount store for watches that are within your visual range. You'll soon see that tiny, delicate ladies' watches or those with gold hands on gold dials are not for you. Some Timex watches can be seen by partially sighted people. A nurse's watch usually has an easy-to-read dial, although you might be wise to have the second hand removed to relieve the face of clutter. If you can't find a watch that is readable with your low vision, the American Foundation for the Blind and Independent Living Aids offer a variety of low vision watches. These have black dials, white numbers at 12, 3, 6, and 9, and prominent darts at remaining hours. (I shall list agencies and organizations to which I refer in Chapter 30.) Catalogs from these agencies show pictures of the watch in actual size; you can examine them and know immediately if you can read it. Low vision watches range in price from thirty-two dollars to sixty dollars. Other alternatives include a skin diver's watch, often found in a sporting goods store. Because skin divers check the time under water in poor light, numerals are large and contrast with the dial. The second hand is distinctive because its point is arrow shaped.

You may even be able to read the luminous dial at night. These watches are sold with a plastic wrist band that you'll probably want to exchange for an expansion band or leather wrist strap. If you are wont to jump into the shower or plunge into a pool while wearing a watch, a skin diver's watch naturally withstands the dousing.

Perhaps you have your eye on a digital timepiece. Watches with a liquid crystal display (LCD) are usually easier for a partially sighted user to read because numerals are bigger. Watches with a light-emitting diode (LED) dial are harder to see during daylight.

What if you prefer a watch to be read by touch, either because you can't see a print dial or choose not to hold a watch close to your face, being obvious about it? The term "Braille watch" can be misleading. You don't have to know Braille to read it. The crystal opens so that hands and dial can be felt lightly. Three vertical dots indicate 12, two appear at the quarter hours: 3, 6, and 9. Designating remaining hours are single dots. The hands are shaped just like those on an ordinary watch, the longer hand for minutes and the shorter hand (fitting more snugly to the face) for hours. By placing your index finger in the center of the dial where the hands are attached, you can follow them to the perimeter, using the double dots at quarter hours as landmarks. Hands on Braille watches don't move as easily as you would suppose, although they will not withstand rough treatment. Because the face of a Braille watch is more exposed to moisture and dust, your timepiece should be cleaned regularly each year, even though it is keeping accurate time.

At fifty-five, Mary Lou took an early retirement because her vision was declining quickly. As a retirement gift, her colleagues bought her a Braille watch. With chagrin and disappointment, Mary Lou told me, "I can't feel that watch. The hands and dots are too small."

When she showed me her prized but useless present, I agreed. Not having an acute sense of touch, she couldn't locate the hour hand, nor could she decide if the minute hand was pointing to 4 or 5, 7, or 8, etc. For Mary Lou and others who are buying a Braille watch for the first time, I recommend a man's watch. Women won't think of them as being dainty or glamorous, but if the final question is whether it is 10:05 or 11:10, even the most vain would rather be correct than fashionable.

Molly was twenty-one, but her severe diabetes had affected her sense of touch to the extent that she couldn't use a man's wristwatch. She could read the dial of a pocket watch that has large hands and oversized dots. Proudly wearing the watch on a chain around her neck, she felt as if she were setting a new trend.

Braille watches range in price from $32 to over $300. You can buy self-winding watches, electric quartz watches, and even a presentation watch with diamond chips instead of dots. They are listed in catalogs from the American Foundation for the Blind, Independent Living Aids, and Innovative Rehabilitation Technology, Inc. Sometimes local jewelers stock a few, but these tend to be from the more expensive lines. Local agencies for the blind may have an outlet for commonly used items for the blind. A call to one of these could save you the delay of waiting for a mail order.

If shopping for a clock to be read visually, again look for one with contrast between color of face and numerals and hands. Battery-powered kitchen clocks can be installed anywhere. Thus, you can be conscious of the time while you're in the bathroom, family room, kitchen or wherever you decide to hang the clock. Before deciding upon a clock, consider various lighting conditions, too. Sometimes a digital timepiece is tricky for a partially sighted person to read in bright light. You can also purchase low vision clocks from the American Foundation for the Blind or Independent Living Aids. The low vision digital clock listed has a display with two-inch numerals. Braille clocks have no protective crystal but bear double raised dots at 12, 3, 6, and 9. Single dots indicate remaining hours. Both mechanical and electric, they include travel alarm clocks, small desk models, and electric Big Ben clocks. They are also sold by the organizations mentioned previously.

Several enterprising students of mine have adapted their own Braille clocks. George, a sixty-six-year-old who never had an abundance of patience and lived by the philosophy that "you can make do when you have to," bought an inexpensive electric alarm clock from the dime store. He removed the plastic cover from the dial and asked his son to file notches around the rim to indicate numbers. Using double notches to indicate quarter hours, single notches at the rest, George can tell time from his "homemade

Braille clock." "Saved a lot of money to boot," he gloats. George insists that the hands of the ordinary clock, although never meant by the manufacturer to be touched, "hold up just fine."

"It's 2:45 PM." That synthesized voice certainly didn't come from any member of the library advisory committee in midmeeting. The source was Talking Time®, a clock slightly larger than a pack of cigarettes. Its owner, Ray, represented a state agency for the blind. Like many people swept up by the wave of technology, Ray had opted for a talking timepiece. Manufactured by Sharp, this battery-operated clock has an alarm that awakens a sleeper with a fifteen-second segment of classical music, then announces the time. The snooze feature announces time ten minutes later; the mechanical male voice urges, "Please hurry." Talking Time can also serve as a stop clock, can be set to announce time every thirty minutes, or can be used as a timer. It retails for about sixty dollars. If you can't find one through a dealer carrying Sharp products, you can also purchase Talking Time through the National Federation of the Blind. Because of its size, it may not be convenient to carry on your person—it's a little too big to fit into a man's shirt pocket. It can be your only alternative. A talking watch is close to production. It will simply announce the time but cannot be set as a timer or stopwatch. An even more sophisticated talking timepiece is a talking clock radio by Panasonic. It features a voice output, awakening you either to music or synthetically spoken time announcements. It costs about $120 from the American Foundation for the Blind.

You may argue that you can always turn on the radio or TV for current time or call local Time service. This is true, but not always convenient, especially in the middle of the night or when you're out for the evening and don't want to draw attention to your time check. Suppose you're at a neighbor's home and are trying to stifle yawns, wondering if it's late enough for leaving. Flicking on the local disc jockey or dialing Time are hardly acceptable alternatives.

Another timely matter is calendars. Wall calendars printed in larger-than-average type and having plenty of space for notations are best for partially sighted people. An appointment book, such as the kind used in a dentist's office, is another option. You'll need to convince the rest of the family to jot forthcoming errands and appointments in the designated large print calendar so that you, too, will know about the block party scheduled in three weeks or the kids' precamp physical next Monday. Their jottings should be more painstaking than they were when your sight was better. You will probably have to remind your family that you can't read hastily scribbled notes. They will either have to take time to write longhand large and legibly or, better still, to print.

"A wall calendar is fine because it hangs near the phone and is easy for me to follow," agrees Delores, thirty-five, partially sighted and mother of six-year-old twins. "But it isn't convenient to carry when I'm running errands and keeping appointments. What if I'm not sure of the time of the kids' dental appointment or want the address of the shoe store that is having a sale on children's tennis shoes?"

Delores has a good point. My suggestion was to copy the information she needs onto a 3 by 5 index card to tuck in her purse for the day. Because of the stiffness of the card, it's quicker to find than a slip of paper. The day's notation would read: "Judy and Penny go to dentist at four. Shoe Mart, 1023 St. Paul, open 9 to 6."

Braille calendars do not adapt themselves to notations. Some list only days of the week and dates on which they fall. The more elaborate list holidays. If you are a Braille user and need to maintain a list of upcoming events and appointments, several methods work. Write the day, date, place, time, and any other pertinent information on a 3 by 5 card that you attach to your Braille calendar with a rubber band. On that particular day, take the card with you. If you don't require it for future reference, discard the notation, or punch three holes into standard 9 by 11 Braille paper, writing name of the month at the top of each of twelve sheets. Bind the sheets in a small three-ring notebook. When you make an entry, write the day of the week (Th for Thursday, Sa for Saturday, Su for Sunday), the date, and whatever else you must know. Your note would look like this: Top of page — February; lefthand margin — M13; same line — clothes should be picked up from cleaner, which closes 5:30.

"But I don't see well enough to read my own handwriting," protests Charles, who, at sixty-five, had additional health problems besides loss of sight. "I don't have a lot to remember, but I can't miss a doctor's appointment." "It's up to you, Charles, to remind someone in your household to check the calendar for you. If another person writes down an appointment for you, it's your responsibility to ask that person to look every day for anything that affects you." I also advised Charles to ask the receptionist in the doctor's office to give him a call on the day prior to his appointment. She made a note in her own appointment book, fully understanding Charles' condition and concern, and was glad to comply with his request.

I have used this method myself to avoid reminders through the mail. My dentist's receptionist calls several days before my visit. The clerk in the insurance company calls to let me know that my homeowner's premium is due in a month. The vet's assistant gives me a buzz to alert me to bring my dog for his booster shots. If you make this request, office personnel are usually more than willing to oblige you, if they understand why you are asking for this consideration. In fact, it is less work for them to pick up the phone than it is to type out a notice to mail to you.

When Alexander Graham Bell invented the telephone, he probably didn't envision its inestimable value to people who are blind. If you are confined to your home or can't make as many social contacts face-to-face as you would like, you see it as a lifeline. It's also instant contact for a medical, fire, or police emergency. One of my first questions to a newly blind person is: "Can you dial a phone accurately?" Most reply that they can.

A few responses are similar to one from Gordie, a sixty-one-year-old former dock worker: "I never liked to talk on the phone. It's a waste of time. I guess I could dial a number if I had to." Not wanting to take his guess as a yes, I asked him to show me. "Just imagine that I'm from Missouri and seeing is believing," I gently urged.

Gordie made a few false starts before completing a number satisfactorily. Because he couldn't move from one digit to another quickly enough, the connection was broken, causing him to start over again.

"Not good enough," I prompted. "Gordie, if you were trying to reach your doctor or the police, time isn't on your side."

I showed Gordie how to dial quickly and correctly. I'll explain the technique to you, if you haven't already worked it out.

On a spin dial, the number 1 is about 1/2 inch to the left of the finger stop, a half circle of plastic. Moving to your left, numbers run in order—1 through 0, which also serves as O for Operator. When counting around the dial, don't insert your finger all the way into the finger hole—it takes too much time. Just slip your finger in far enough to know that it's a digit and move on.

Some blind phone users adopt the four-finger method. If right-handed, they put the little finger into 1, ring finger into 2, middle finger into 3, and index finger into 4, which also reaches to 5. For numbers 6 through 0, they start with little finger in 0, ring finger in 9, middle finger in 8, and index finger in 7, which also reaches to 6. Thus, a four-fingered dialer would dial 2 by slightly lifting all but the ring finger, or 8 by relying on the middle finger. (Sorry, but you lefties have to reverse this process, just as in everything else in this right-handed world.)

Push-button telephones are a different story. Numbers are arranged this way: first row from left to right—1, 2, 3; second row from left to right—4, 5, 6; third row from left to right—7, 8, 9. Zero is in the center of the bottom row. The two outer buttons have some mysterious connection with computer functions that I've never understood. You can either count, knowing that the three horizontal rows follow numerical order and that vertical rows are: 1, 4, 7; 2, 5, 8, 0; and 3, 6, 9. Some push-button owners push the three-finger approach. Again since majority rules, this technique applies to right-handed dialers and must be reversed for the left-handed few. Put your index finger on 4; it can reach up to 1 or down to 7. Your middle finger rests on 5 so that you can reach up to 2, down to 8 and 0. Your ring finger settles on 6, going up to 3 and down to 9. I have seen totally blind people dial as fast as anybody looking at the panel.

A few hints may save you from saying, "Sorry, wrong number." A piece of tape affixed to the outer rim of 5 on your spin dial phone serves as an additional landmark. To prevent pressing either of the outer buttons on the lowest row of the push-button phone, cover them with tape. You can buy a large print dial, which encircles your spin dial, providing half-inch high numbers. It is available from the American Foundation for the Blind. Your local telephone service center probably carries a panel of larger-than-average buttons that clamps over a standard push-button dial. Each button is about twice the size of those on the standard push-button panel and may be easier for some people to feel or see. To master dialing, practice with the receiver on the cradle. Start by locating and dialing each digit 1 through 0, then reverse by starting at 0 through 1. Next try even numbers, followed by odd. Give the number of a friend or relative a couple of trial runs, then pick up the receiver and make the call for real. Marsha, a totally blind fifty-three-year-old woman, lost confidence in dialing because she made so many wrong numbers. After we drilled on the technique, she called her daughter from my office. "I'm so excited," exclaimed Marsha. "That was the first time I had actually made a call myself since losing my sight six months ago."

"I have enough sight to read numbers," objected Paul, twenty-one, partially sighted all his life. "Why should I bother to learn by touch?" I reminded him that even his degree of vision wouldn't be enough if lighting were bad. Knowing that he would want to appear as unobtrusive as possible, I pointed out that putting his face an inch from the dial would attract attention.

He laughed when I told him of a recent incident when a fully sighted companion left our table in a restaurant to make a business call from a pay telephone. He returned soon, quite sheepish. "The light in the phone booth is burned out. I can't dial."

For once I had the upper hand and used it without too much ribbing to place the call for him.

A few people insist upon knowing where exchange letters are, although phone companies now issue seven-digit phone numbers instead of two letters and five numbers. If you're among the curious or just have to know in the remote event that you must convert letters to numbers, here goes. The letters Q and Z do not appear on the dial. Letters and numbers can be associated as follows: ABC in 2; DEF in 3; GHI in 4; JKL in 5; MNO in 6; PRS in 7; TUV in 8; WXY in 9. You'll notice that 1 and 0 contain no letters.

A few blind people, despite their best efforts, cannot learn to dial a phone. Age or an additional disability could account for their inability. Barbara, in her midthirties, is one of them. A drug overdose caused her total blindness. Her fingers had practically no sensation, nor could she control hand coordination. She relies upon Service 0—she can manage to dial zero for the Operator, saying that she requires "Service-0." With no further explanation, she gives the number she wants. The operator makes the call with no extra charge to Barbara's phone bill.

Speaking of additional charges, it is becoming more common for telephone companies to charge for Directory Assistance. Blind customers are exempt from this charge because for the most part they cannot consult the directory. Your telephone representative will be glad to send you a form to be filled out for this exemption. Since most Information operators repeat a number quickly, ask the operator to dictate it slowly because of your inability to write quickly. They are most willing to cooperate.

Assuming that you can dial yourself or use Service 0, you should have emergency numbers such as doctor, police, or fire close to your phone. Tape your Braille or print list to the wall by the phone. If you can't use either Braille or print, commit such numbers to memory, if possible. If you can't remember those few numbers, rely on the operator—time is not on your side when the matter is urgent.

Some telephone companies offer a service known as Speed Dialing. Instead of the usual seven digits to reach a local number, the customer dials only two. A woman told me that her elderly blind grandmother relied upon this service because she couldn't remember all the phone numbers she wanted to dial. First three on her list were police, fire, and doctor. Family, friends, and the nearby grocery store that delivered constituted the rest of the list. Forty numbers can be programmed. Like any other specialized service, Speed Dialing or its equivalent costs more money. It may be worth the extra charge to you in terms of time, convenience, and security.

Before hanging up on this business of dialing, expect to make a slip of the finger, misread a number, or memorize it with two digits reversed. Sighted people do that—considering the many calls I receive that are wrong numbers, I'd say plenty do. If your mistake is a local number, apologize and try again. If it's a far zone or long-distance call, notify the operator of your error, and you will not be charged for it. One of my students was calling a marina, 100 miles from his home. Misdialing the first digit of the area code, he reached San Diego, across the country. Because he immediately called the operator, the charges never appeared on his bill.

I'll deal with ways of noting phone numbers in Chapter 8. Be alert to ways of taking messages and, in turn, receiving them. Provided that you can write legibly enough for another to read, note the name and number of a caller on a scratch pad. Tear off that sheet so you won't inadvertently write over anything previously noted. You and others in your home should mutually decide upon a place for messages. If someone takes a message for you, the same system can be used. Again be sure that the message taker writes or prints legibly enough for you to read. If a felt-tip pen is necessary, lay down the law about others taking it from the telephone table. If you make it clear you can't read or write with another writing instrument, you're more likely to have their cooperation. Some people find that a child's blackboard, mounted on the wall by the phone, is handy. If you are a Braille reader, chances are that no one else in your home knows the system. You'll have to rely upon the message taker or another family member to read a handwritten note to you so that you can copy what you need in Braille. In turn, you can take messages in Braille to dictate to sighted family members — or, of course, type them. A phone rest attached to the receiver allows you to have both hands free to write.

An inexpensive cassette recorder is another device for all in the household to temporarily record messages. Agree on a signal that a message has been left — after dictating a message, rewind the tape and press the eject button — the open compartment door means, "Listen to the tape." To record directly from telephone to cassette, you can buy a telephone pick-up device, which fits like a collar around the earpiece. It sells for less than five dollars at Radio Shack. I have found an automatic answering machine to be most convenient. Sure, some people hang up without a word, resenting talking to a machine. But most friends and business associates do leave a message. I just have to remember to turn it on when I leave and to play back messages when I return.

Chapter 5

YOUR HOME IS YOUR CASTLE, NOT YOUR HASSLE

I t had been a frantic search—the frenzied tearing-the-house-apart hunt that only a woman who has misplaced her purse can understand. In the laundry basket, on the back of the stove, under the bed—even obvious places like the dining room table and the nightstand—I looked for more than an hour. When the doorbell rang and the washing machine repairman barely had time to identify himself, I burst out, "Do you see my purse? Can you help me find it?"

The startled man took a step backward onto the porch, almost dropping his toolbox. "Lady," he pleaded in self-defense and bewilderment, "No, I didn't take your purse, nor do I see it."

I caught my breath long enough to explain that I lived alone, had put my handbag down, and now couldn't find it. Would he please look around to see if he could spot it? Still in a state of semishock, he set down his tools, surveyed living and dining room, and calmly said, "Miss, your purse is on top of the china cabinet."

Mumbling something inaudible (no point in alarming the man again), I retrieved the cause of my anguish, made a not-to-be broken promise to myself, and turned to the task at hand: telling the repairman what was wrong with the washer.

I've forgotten (or never figured out) why or how my purse landed atop a six-foot-high china cabinet. What I do remember is that silent vow: to reserve three places in my house where I might leave my purse and any other frequently used belongings. Never would I stray from one of the three designated drop-offs, regardless of rush or distractions. My personal put-down places are stack cushions by the front door, family room table, and bedroom chair. If I stagger into the house with three bags of groceries, keys clamped between my teeth, bladder bursting, phone ringing, my tracks still lead first to one of these spots. The next time I want my handbag, there are only three possible places to look for it.

Whether your home is a one-room studio apartment or a thirty-room mansion, there are too many unlikely nooks and crannies in which your oft-used possessions won't be apparent to you. Take a quick inventory of those articles which you carry, put down, and retrieve most often. Your list may include glasses, wallet, cane, keys, briefcase, cigarettes. You want such belongings there, where you thought you left them. You don't need the irritation of losing and looking. Now take a mental tour of your home, selecting no more than three drop-off and pick-up points for yourself. One near the front door such as a hall table or end table can simplify matters when you come in with your arms full. The second could be in the rear of the house, apartment, or mobile home in the kitchen or den. If you live in a two-story dwelling, the third choice is logically upstairs, probably your bedroom.

After choosing your own drop-off spots, stick by that rule you made for yourself. Even if you are dashing to answer the phone or being met by exuberant kids or dog, hang together long enough to drop keys on hall table, not kitchen counter. Slipups turn into time-consuming, nerve-racking hunts that fray you and annoy others who may tire of heeding the plea, "Have you seen my keys, cane, . . . ?"

This idea might sound compulsive, even rigid to you. At least Mark, aged forty, thought so. He contended that since he had high partial sight, he wouldn't have to abide by that rule. "I changed my tune," he admitted. "When I went to grab my glasses to look at a piece of mail, I couldn't find them. I needed my glasses to look for my glasses. My wife and kids weren't home to help me find them, so I had to go over all the furniture—including sofa cushions with both hands—until I finally found them. They were on the back of the toilet. Now even if I have to get up, I put my glasses and other possessions where they belong."

I've mentioned the somebody elses in your home—although the number of live-aloners is growing, odds are that you won't be, at least until you adapt to your blindness. Hardest lesson of all for those significant others to learn is the "put 'em back" program. Linda, a sighted occupational therapist who is a friend and colleague, drums this point into the families of our clients. "If you move something six inches from where it was, then it doesn't exist for a blind person."

More discord and anxiety probably arise between blind people and their families over this conflict than anything else. If your wife, husband, children, or parent wants to borrow the screwdriver and returns it to another table, you'll look high and low for the screwdriver that can be seen at a glance.

George, a fifty-five-year-old computer analyst, recalled ruefully that his son moved the toothpaste from one shelf to the next in the medicine chest. George wasn't too happy when he started to brush his teeth with hair conditioner.

Dorothy, our friend the smoker, is set off when her husband pulls the ashtray toward him at the dinner table without telling her. Naturally, this policy can be carried to an extreme, as in the case of a totally blind man who wouldn't permit his wife to rear-range the furniture, ever! His rigidity calls for compromise—showing him the new arrangement sounds like fair play to me, so long as it doesn't present any blind-traps.

If you're employed, the "everything has its place" works at your job too. Your essentials might include felt-tip pen and paper, tools, coffee mug, and I.D. badge. Employees have personal space to use as their own, be it so humble as a locker. Not bound to you by marital or blood ties, colleagues will tire more quickly of being your "finders." At least folks at home love you!

Speaking of those hallowed walls called home, let's go back there for a few moments. Initiate for yourself and for other house-hold members the "closed door, open door" policy. Head off bumps to your head, hips, shins, and any other part of your body that can collide with a half-open room or cupboard door. Keep doors closed or flush against the wall. If a door is left ajar, crashing into it will do more than jar you. Cupboard doors such as kitchen cabinets and medicine chests are among the greatest offenders. The open door of a dishwasher or oven will make you wish you'd worn shin guards.

Another point in the open and shut case is drawers. Without thinking, you reach into the silverware drawer for a knife, not bothering to close it because you will be grabbing for a meat fork in fifteen seconds. Pivoting around from the counter to seize the fork, you crash into the sharp corner of the drawer. In early morning you rifle through dresser drawers, half awake and hardly able to find a pair of socks. You swing around in search of underwear and are painfully jolted into reality.

These precautions are other matters to bring before the family powwow. If you have tots who crawl into kitchen cupboards to empty them of pots and pans, latches will outwit the little ones. For children old enough to read and forgetful adults, post reminder signs at strategic points such as the bathroom mirror, closet doors, and front and back doors. The habit will become so ingrained that eventually you can take down your warnings.

Before slamming the door on the subject, doors that lead to potential danger should be shut unless, of course, someone is passing through. My basement steps drop abruptly from the kitchen. Although I'm thoroughly familiar with the layout of the house, I close it upon coming upstairs, even though I have to set down a brimming laundry basket to do it. I ask anyone going into the basement to pull the door shut. (I haven't heard protests of claustrophobia so far.)

An elderly blind person who tends to become disoriented could easily tumble down a flight of stairs. In fact, anyone with poor balance may suffer such an accident. Thirty-six-year-old Dennis, totally blind from diabetes, was in the midst of a reaction. He became disoriented and fell down the stairs, breaking a wrist. You can prevent that possibility by installing a gate at the top of stairs that opens when pulled away from the edge of steps. Such a gate should be waist high for an adult.

Another way to avoid *bbb's* (black and blue bruises) is to protect yourself when you lean over to pick up a dropped object. At forty-nine, Emil took a year off from his job as an auto company engineer for rehabilitation. Emil learned this lesson literally from the school of hard knocks. Without thought he swooped down to retrieve his comb that he brushed off the dresser. With poor depth perception, he didn't notice the corner of the dresser, although he clearly saw the comb on the carpet. Emil paid dearly for his impulsive move with a seven-stitch cut above his eye. As you bend over, shield your face with your arm; reach for the object with your free hand.

There's something in human nature that strives to save steps and time. So some self-educated efficiency expert came up with the scheme of leaving anything from hand soap to bed linen on the first stair to be carried up by the next person going that way. Since the plan conserved who knows how many steps and minutes, the same efficiency expert devised the formula to operate in reverse—a five-pound box of detergent, pair of roller skates, and a handsaw could be stashed on the basement steps for the next soul making a descent. The wizard who concocted this plot wasn't blind, or he/she would have made an unhappy landing, likely in the hospital.

Such pitfalls for a blind person are obvious. Whether you stumble up the first step over a sewing basket or down eight because someone left the drill, the consequences can be disastrous. In short, stairways must be absolutely free from obstructions. If climbing or descending steps is actually a pain as it is for an arthritis sufferer, you'll have to come up with a drop-off place near the stairway such as a table or shelf. An unwritten rule can be that whoever ascends or descends takes up or down whatever is there. By enforcing this agreement, everybody will need to watch what is put in the drop-off place—it could disappear unexpectedly. Otherwise, exercise from extra trips is good for you.

When you had good vision, arrangements of furniture were probably for convenience and appearance. Now look at it from another angle: Does your home contain blind-traps? I define *blind-traps* (an original term) as any furniture, fixture, or floor covering that can be bumped into, tripped over, or slipped upon in the course of the day's usual events.

Leading the parade in my book is the greatest pain-causer of them all: the coffee table. Whoever named it that didn't see piles of magazines, mail, burned-out bulbs, and even grass trimmers that turn it into a catchall depository. When I set up housekeeping, I didn't rummage through my parents' attic looking for one, nor do I have one now.

If you have a coffee table that creates more shattered shins than decoration, pawn it off on some receptive relative or donate it to charity—it'll do you more good as a tax deduction.

Other potential hazards can include a shelf that extends close to your head above a desk, table, or workbench. Unless you have military posture, you lean forward as you rise from a chair. Low-hanging lamps, plants, and chandeliers can make you see stars. A bookcase may jut dangerously into a room or can partially block a hallway. Of course you know it's there, but without the added safeguard of sight, you'll have to be vigilant 100 percent of the time or pay the price if you're not. Sharp corners on counters, especially bathroom vanities, can cause you to double over in agony. If possible, have them beveled so they are rounded. Scatter rugs can throw you, especially on polished floors. Get rid of them.

I shall smoke out the smokers among my readers without being judgmental. Large ashtrays, not the cute little dainty variety, are the only type you should consider. Dorothy, in her early sixties, couldn't break the cigarette habit, but she did give up small crystal ashtrays kept as wedding presents that she treasured for thirty-five years. With low vision she didn't notice that a lit ash dropped from her cigarette, smoldering in the carpet. Her husband saw it after it had burned a sizable hole. She now puts her six-inch diameter ashtray in her lap as she watches TV. Be selfish with your ashtray— sharing it with another smoker risks one of you getting burned while flicking ashes. Some blind smokers fill used ashtrays with water to be certain cigarettes have been extinguished.

To light a cigarette, touch its tip to the first knuckle of your right thumb, which holds a match or lighter. Move the tip along the thumb until it touches the flame. This is a surefire method of not igniting your cigarette in the middle or burning yourself as you move the flame in search of the cigarette. Lighters, by the way, are safer than matches.

No, your abode doesn't have to be as barren as a monk's cell— unless you're a monk, that is, nor does it have to be so free of furniture that you can shoot a cannon through it. (That's not such a popular pastime anyway.) Upon making your safety patrol and laying down a few ground rules for yourself and other householders, just remember that life and limb come first. Even if you think that your remaining vision enables you to see possible dangers, you'll realize that lighting conditions vary, your depth perception isn't what it once was, and you can't always be alert — not if you're human like the rest of us.

Before leaving the domestic domain, let me offer a few clues on the "seek and ye shall find" technique. If you drop an object such as a pen or fork on a bare floor, listen to where it fell. Then let your feet do the searching — tread lightly if it's breakable. If you locate the article with your foot, lean over or squat down to pick it up — don't forget to shield your face. If that trick fails, hands and knees are meant for more than scrubbing floors. Move those hands in gradually widening circles in front of you, then make ninety-degree turns, until you have made a full circle. Still can't find that blasted toothpaste cap? Ask someone else.

As for the keys to your kingdom, there's one way I've discovered to keep them straight. A key case works well because most people depend upon only two or three keys every day — perhaps your front and back door, garage, or car keys. (Even though you don't drive now, having a car key with you can save the day sometimes.) Allow only those frequently used keys to remain outside the case. Enclose the rest within by zipper or snap. Then you won't have to finger six or seven to locate the door key. Toting every key you own weighs down a pocket or purse. Finding your key quickly can prevent frozen fingers. If you insist on a key ring or chain, a piece of tape on your door key is instant identification.

Are maintenance chores a puzzle and pain for you? Personally, I fret and sweat over turning a screw. If you're among the mechanically inept and don't want to call a plumber to change a washer or a professional painter to give the back porch a new coat, try calling a nearby senior citizens' organization for names of people who do such work for older people. You may discover retirees having years of experience in such work who won't charge top dollar for it. Persons known to such groups are least likely to exploit you or walk off with anything from your home. If grass cutting or snow shoveling is beyond you, a call to the local high school will glean neighborhood youngsters who won't cost nearly so much as a landscape service.

Before launching into the chapter on lighting, there is a method you can use to insert a plug into an outlet without glowing yourself. Jo, forty-one, nearly totally blind, was almost in tears because she spent twenty minutes in the morning trying to plug in the coffeepot. Inadvertently slipping her finger between prongs and outlet, she was leary and frustrated because of the shock. First touch the receptacle to see whether prongs should be placed vertically or horizontally. You won't get a charge if you don't stick your finger into the slits. With index finger and thumb outlining the width of the rounded plate, insert prongs. It's not knowing where to aim the plug that causes trouble. If it's a three-pronged plug, decide whether the grounding prong belongs above or below. "It worked!" exclaimed Jo exuberantly. "To think that I used to install light switches. I'm not so afraid anymore of plugging in the coffeepot."

Chapter 6

LIGHT UP YOUR LIFE

G ary, a well-educated man in his midforties, fumbled uncertainly as he entered my office. Dropping a piece of paper, he crawled around the floor to find it. At first I thought I had forgotten to turn on the light. No, it was on. Gary's chart indicated his vision at 20/400. Puzzled, I inquired.

"Gary, has your vision become worse since you last saw your ophthalmologist? You act as if you don't see much at all."

"Oh, my eyes have been stable for the last several years," he quickly answered. "I just thought I'd be cheating if I used what I have."

"You are, Gary. You're cheating yourself...."

If you have some sight, be glad you do and don't try to limp along as if you were totally blind. Don't skimp on using your sight as much as you can. Your remaining vision won't be destroyed by overuse, even though there is an old husband's tale (sorry, couldn't resist) that insists sight will somehow wear out. Give yourself a break. Use the most appropriate lighting for you to see maximally. Proper illumination can be as good as magnification in most instances.

Partial sight and eye conditions vary among individuals. You will be the final judge as to which fixtures and lamps you rely upon in specific places for particular purposes. Those having retinitis pigmentosa or glaucoma are often light sensitive, needing to avoid dazzle and glare from strong light. Or perhaps you couldn't read or do woodworking without a concentrated powerful light source.

Let's trip the light fantastic through your home, stopping room by room to see if each is well-lighted for you.

Lee has been partially sighted all her life. Although the Snellen chart measures her sight at 20/400, she depends upon her low vision to its ultimate. As a part-time sales representative and full-time homemaker, Lee was ecstatic when her kitchen was redone. Shiny new appliances and fresh floor covering weren't the cause of her jubilation. At last, one of the chief centers of her operations was adequately illuminated.

Four fluorescent tubes, each forty inches long, offer good overhead illumination without shadows. Two fluorescent tubes have been installed above the sink, making rinsing, stacking and dishwashing a snap. Another fluorescent tube shines directly onto her work space—the counter—so that she can see well enough to chop, peel, and slice. A similar light is above the stove, enabling her to check foods as she is cooking.

Moving into the dining room and living room, you'll find overhead lighting, unlike lamps, casts no shadows. It should be sufficient for serving a meal, dining, and such cleaning chores as vacuuming or a card game at the dining room table. A fixture that you can raise and lower over the table is handy. Don't fret about buying a crystal chandelier—you can purchase simple pull-down lamps inexpensively. A dimmer switch or rheostat adjusts lighting as needed, such as a bright light for serving a meal or softer illumination while eating or relaxing.

Your living room or family room is a good place for directional lamps. You can adjust goose-necked lamps in any direction. Suppose you enjoy an easy chair for reading, crocheting, or mending: The light should fall over your shoulder so that it doesn't glare at you. When buying incandescent bulbs, don't think that bigger is always better. I heard of a woman who invested in a goose-necked lamp, which she placed beside her favorite recliner. She installed a 200-watt bulb. As she tried to scan newspaper headlines, heat-triggered perspiration trickled into her eyes. As she held the paper, her arms felt as if they were at a barbeque. So hot under the collar that she couldn't focus on the paper, she maintained that she couldn't read at all. An understanding rehabilitation teacher replaced the bulb with one of 75 watts. Our friend now reads headlines with comfort and without eyestrain.

Three-way bulbs allow room for adjustment, depending upon what you're doing. For people who are light sensitive, General Electric soft white bulbs (frosted incandescents) reduce dazzle.

The bathroom is another area for good lighting, especially when you rely upon your sight to shave, take medication, or apply makeup. Some people prefer a fluorescent tube on each side of the medicine cabinet. Others use a globe of three or four incandescent bulbs above. Since fluorescent often casts a bluish tinge, this may be a consideration of yours if you must be exacting about colors. While we're in the bathroom, don't overlook a night light. It can be your target for those middle-of-the-night visits.

Your bedroom should have good overhead lighting for dressing and undressing. But alas and alack—it's the closet that usually falls dismally short in this department. People with normal vision can turn on the ceiling light or bedside lamp to pick out the right skirt or shirt. You may have to drag out half the clothes you own before finding that tweed jacket or brown plaid blouse. A wall-mounted light will shine directly on the clothes rod to your best advantage. Again a fluorescent tube is a good choice. A trip switch turns off the light as you close the door. If wiring the closet is likely to send you to the poorhouse, hold out for a battery-powered lamp such as those used by campers. Just remember to turn it off or the cost of batteries will turn you off.

As you go upstairs and downstairs on your mental tour, don't overlook those stairways. A switch at top and bottom is a must. What good is a light if you have to climb the stairs to flick it on?

Despite well-lit basement steps, one of my students still wasn't sure when she reached the bottom step. Her son painted the last step black to contrast with light linoleum. It wouldn't win an award from Better Homes and Gardens, but she won't make a misstep either.

Wandering down to the basement, keep an eye out for special work areas. The laundry room should have good overhead lighting for sorting, loading washer and dryer, and for ironing. (That's a good place for the 200-watt bulb that fried the headline reader.)

The next time you buy a dryer, demand one with a light inside. You won't have to crawl halfway into it looking for the kids' socks. A freezer with a light saves frostbitten hands when you're hunting for those pork chops. If you can't find a freezer with such a luxury or are stuck with the one you own, put a light directly above.

If you have a workbench and want to illuminate large projects, fluorescent light doesn't cast shadows. If you are painting, staining, or refinishing, try putting your work on a surface of contrasting color. An old white sheet under a dark piece of wood can make light-years' difference. When painting in a light shade or cutting out pastel fabrics, place dark material such as a discarded table-cloth beneath your work.

At twenty-six, Pat lost much of his vision from diabetes. As a former tool maker, he was eager to continue his hobbies of wood working and tinkering with cars, so he designed himself a versatile light. He attached one end of a twelve-inch length of flexible rod to a magnet three inches in diameter. To the other end of the rod he secured a twelve-volt light. When using a circular saw or band saw, he places the magnet atop the tool; as the saw moves, so does the light, enabling him clearly to see the line without shadow. The magnet base is heavy enough to support the fixture on flat surfaces. While working on his car engine, he hooks up the light to the auto battery. The flexible rod will bend in any direction. As he works, he can adjust the light with a flick of his finger. He fashioned a similar contraption with a clamp instead of a magnet to mount on tools made from hard plastic.

Storage areas in the basement should be lighted, too. You don't want to trek across the basement with a jar from the fruit cellar to stand under the light, checking to see if it's Aunt Millie's peach preserves. Nor should you wonder if that gallon of paint is white exterior or violet enamel unless you trundle it into bright light.

Since the attic serves as the primary catchall for those who have one, don't forget to put a light up there either. If you're smart, you'll avoid it like a teenager's bedroom. But when you have to stir up the dust to locate your wedding album or probe the depths of a long-forgotten trunk, don't wait for a sunny day to do it. It's OK to be in the dark about what's up there, but when you brush away those cobwebs, let there be light.

As you step outside, is the vestibule (if you have one) well lit? An overhead fixture simplifies kicking off boots and decoating lots.

Once out the door and on the porch, is your porch light high enough to illuminate the steps? One of my partially sighted friends clued me into this shortcoming at my home.

Perhaps you enjoy the backyard for barbecuing or basking in the soft summer breezes. A floodlight at both corners of the house will give you as much light as possible. Although a gaslight is decorative for the front, it doesn't provide enough illumination for most people. A light that comes on at dusk and turns off automatically at dawn will enable you to get out of a car at night. It is not powerful enough for a backyard light.

Home owners who have a garage often slip up on adequate lighting for this building. Some people muddle by with a bare bulb hanging from the ceiling. If you tinker with cars or are an amateur furniture refinisher, invest in several more electrical outlets to brighten your hobby times. A switch at the side or back door ensures your never walking into the garage's dark interior, possibly tripping over a tool.

Michael, a partially sighted man of twenty-seven, sets aside a particular place for reading print. Because he suffers from nystagmus (uncontrolled eye movements), plopping on the couch isn't a good choice. It's virtually impossible to hold reading material still. He can't stop unwanted, jerky eye movements, but can stabilize his book or mail on a desk. Because his vision is low, he uses a high-intensity lamp. His model has two settings, low and high, which he adjusts according to print size. A high-intensity lamp directs strong light onto a restricted area one foot in diameter. It's also handy for scanning a page in the typewriter, sewing, soldering, drilling, and cleaning contact lenses.

Some lamps have a clamp so that they can be attached to a desk or workbench. A one-tube fluorescent is convenient because it is inexpensive and easy to mount. The entire fixture can be discarded. Called a Bright Stick®, these serve best for projects that require broader illumination such as painting, sanding, or sorting laundry. You can find them at a well-stocked hardware store. They are about twenty-five inches long and cost from $11.00 to $13.00.

When lighted makeup mirrors hit the market, Lee thought they were invented and intended just for her. She recommends those that are magnified.

When power fails, or you need to look somewhere not near an outlet, act as if you're a Boy Scout and be prepared. A battery-powered camping lantern should see you through a blackout. While browsing among camping and marine supplies, you can find a six-volt flashlight with a beam as powerful as four flashlights combined. Battery-operated fluorescent tubes are also available. When you have to check a file cabinet, look inside the fusebox or furnace, or examine the thermostat, a flashlight with a magnifying lens may be helpful. You can buy them at an optical company, stamp store, or low vision clinic.

Innovative Rehabilitation Technology, Inc., has listed a battery-powered flashlight with an extra wide-angle beam. It is purported to be especially helpful for people with retinitis pigmentosa who must travel at night.

Sometimes light can work against you, as in the case of light sensitivity. A television screen that reflects daylight or artificial light has reduced visibility. All you have to do is turn the set to a different angle.

Most partially sighted folks prefer to sit with their back to a window or lamp. They can better see others with whom they are talking. This trick could have significance to you in arranging office furniture or choosing a seat in a restaurant.

Even people without light perception should be conscious of a well-lit home. Just because you can flit around your home without crashing into the couch, or grab for the bath towel without missing, don't assume that sighted people can do the same. I have timers on living room and family room lamps just in case I slip up on being the evening lamp lighter. I check lamps periodically to be sure that bulbs haven't burned out. (Shake a dead bulb and you'll hear a tinny sound from the wires inside.) Of course, a well-lit home is a safety factor. Besides endangering other householders or visitors, failure to have enough illumination adds to the image of gloom and darkness cast upon blind people. Even dogs need light, since their night vision is worse than a human's. I usually ask guests to turn off any lights they have switched on, which often happens without my knowledge. Wall switches are usually up for on. I just remember, "Down and out." If the reverse occurs, and you can't remember, put a bit of tape at the off position. Science For the Blind sells a light probe that changes pitch when held near a light source.

Perhaps you're still in a fog about what lighting to use where, and for what purpose. One partially sighted woman sought help from a lighting and fixture store. She openly discussed her eye condition with the salesman, telling him about her trouble spots at home and what activities she wanted to perform.

A man with partial sight was more of the do-it-yourself sort. He went to a home and builders' show to see what was new in the home-lighting front. Large hardware stores are another source. Some electric companies still have consumer relations departments; you might try calling your local company to find out if one of their staff would help you to assess your needs and make specific suggestions.

For more professional assistance, personnel from a low-vision clinic or an agency for the blind are experts in lighting as well as magnifiers and lenses.

Sure, you're conscious of conserving energy. Lights expend very little power—at this time, it costs six cents to burn a 100-watt bulb ten hours. You could reduce costs by turning off lights when not in use, since it doesn't take more energy to turn a light on again a few minutes later. Let's end that argument forever.

Although you can't make all the adjustments immediately, start checking them off your list as soon as you can make modifications. Your expenses for additional fixtures and lighting are considered medical costs and can be deducted from your income taxes. The power is in your hands.

Chapter 7

STRETCHING YOUR SIGHT
WITH LOW-VISION AIDS

E ighty-year-old Joseph sat disconsolately in the nursing home recreation room as football players charged across the TV screen twelve feet away.

"How's the game going?" inquired Dr. H., Joseph's ophthalmologist, who stopped for a quick visit.

"Dunno," was Joseph's terse reply. "Can't see a damn thing."

Dr. H. resolved that problem with one quick move. He pulled the table model TV within two feet of his friend, watching with satisfaction as his patient's lifelong enthusiasm for the sport revived.

Perhaps nursing home personnel, like so many people, suffer with the misconception that sitting too close to a color television will expose the viewer to radiation. Maybe it was so in the early days of color television, but not now. You can plant yourself as near as you need to be.

Other myths shroud use of the eyes, sometimes cutting people off from taking advantage of what's left. Although said before, repetition may shatter this fallacy once and for all: Using your remaining sight will not cause eye damage. Your eyes won't burn out or wear out. Holding your face close to an object or wearing strong glasses will not result in harm. Both methods achieve magnification that compensates for decreased sight.

People having retinitis pigmentosa were formerly cautioned

against exposing their eyes to sunlight, the reason being that ultraviolet rays increase retinal deterioration. Consequently, one eye would be bandaged. Now darkly tinted glasses solve the dilemma. However, retinitis pigmentosa victims were not risking their vision by seeing — ultraviolet rays were the villains in that case.

Another wrong to make right is that you shouldn't use glasses or magnifiers unless they are prescribed by an ophthalmologist or optometrist. Not true. Aids that you beg, borrow, or buy may serve you just as well as any prescription. That's not to discount the expertise of a professional. Because of his years of training and experience, he or she is your best bet in finding low-vision aids. Just don't dismiss any find that you make on your own.

"My eyes get tired after reading more than a half hour," complained Verona, a partially sighted English instructor in a community college. "Sometimes images get fuzzy and my head swims."

Verona is a victim of eyestrain, or fatigue. It happens to people with normal sight, but takes longer. When correcting papers or preparing for class, Verona should work in shorter spurts. A student assistant should relieve some of the tedium for her, too. She should review lighting conditions to be certain they are optimal. But she won't become totally blind from those reading sprees.

Eye conditions that dictate restricted use of vision are rare. If you still quaver with qualms about overextending yourself, talk with your ophthalmologist or optometrist to set your mind at rest.

Since television watching is so much a part of our lives, inability to see the screen can leave a void for many folks. Two gadgets may help. Beamscope® is a magnifying lens that fits over the screen. It comes in two sizes to accommodate large and small sets, and must be installed. Because magnification is low, it's best for people with high partial sight. Moving it away from the screen increases magnification. You must sit directly in front of the TV, looking through the center of the Beamscope, or images will be distorted. For this reason, others won't bless your device. You might have to hole up in your room with your own TV to keep peace in the family. You can find them in discount appliance stores and department stores for about $100.

Another device which came onto the market recently is the Fresnel® lens. Advertised as a low-cost alternative to a TV projector, it is approximately three feet long and two feet high. Place the stand in front of the screen for magnification. It costs less than fifty dollars and can be ordered by mail. It magnifies one to two times. Again it is most helpful to folks with good partial vision.

Without being too technical, let's define a few terms. There are three types of lenses. Telescopic aids will magnify and increase your distance vision. Microscopic lenses magnify an image at close range. (When referring to a magnifier the × means power of magnification. For example, a 3× magnifier enlarges an image to three times its size.) Prismatic lenses correct the divergence of light rays and sometimes increase narrow visual fields. These half-glasses are mounted on a Mr. Whipple-type frame and are almost always worn over prescription eyeglasses.

You can buy some telescopic, microscopic, and prismatic lenses without a prescription, but many are especially ground for a patient. Contact lenses are always prescribed.

"Nothing will help my eyes. They're just plain bad and nothing will improve them."

Many folks having a little sight, especially older people, take that staunch stance. They turn off mind and motivation to try to stretch what they have. You won't find a substitute for the real thing: normal vision. Learning to use the simplest device takes time, perhaps training, and plenty of patience. Maybe low-vision aids won't boost your vision very measurably according to acuity, but the boost to your morale is beyond measurement.

Expensive, sophisticated low-vision aids often land in dresser drawers, put there by people who expected too much or didn't have needs that justified the effort of becoming accustomed to them. Before you or an agency spends hundreds or even thousands of dollars for precision lenses, try your luck with the inexpensive, easy-to-use aids.

Your eye condition, what you want to see, your physical health, and even your moods will affect your vision. Folks who never go out alone shouldn't concern themselves with reading street signs or house numbers. People who can't handle prolonged print reading because it is too taxing needn't worry about stand magnifiers or closed circuit TV magnifiers. If your astigmatism cannot be corrected satisfactorily, prismatic lenses aren't for you.

Before beginning the search for low-vision aids, sort out your life. What is reasonable for you to expect to see? Do you need to consult the phone book, bus schedule, or stock quotations? Would watching a baseball game or opera mean heaven on earth? Would you feel more independent if you could thread a needle visually or have a lens that hangs around your neck so your hands are free to work on crafts? Can you get by with reading spurts such as a menu, identifying mail, or checking a price tag?

Don't be discouraged if you try an optical aid and it doesn't do you an ounce of good. Return to it later to experiment with different intents—reading a newspaper, street sign, bingo card. These aids aren't useful for all activities. When it fails on every count, chalk it off as useless for you and try something else.

Only you can pass judgment on the effectiveness of low vision aids; it's usually not a matter for someone else to choose what looks promising for you. You may end up leaving family and friends with long faces when they think they brought you the ideal gift, yet, you wouldn't buy a pair of dentures for another person, either. When buying from a store or optical company, inquire about refund or exchange policy. Fiddling with an aid while under the salesman's scrutiny isn't a fair run. The real test is at home, on the street, or in buildings. When purchasing by mail, you ought to know specifically what you need. It might be a replacement for an aid you once had or have used before. When mail order is your only choice, insist upon a possible refund, unless the item is only a few dollars.

Hang onto your lens though you later discover one that does the job better. Instances may crop up that you never thought of trying, such as extracting a sliver from your youngster's finger. Or you might come across someone who could benefit from your castoff. One woman dug up her grandfather's magnifying glass that he bought at the dime store twenty years ago. It was first in her collection, which now numbers over thirty devices.

Low-vision clinics are the logical beginning of your quest. They specialize in expanding partial vision to its utmost. Usually staffed by optometrists and sometimes by ophthalmologists, these clinics boast an array of both nonprescription and prescription aids, often having at least one model of a closed-circuit TV magnifier to demonstrate. Their philosophy is that when an ophthal-mologist tells a patient that sight loss is serious and permanent, it isn't time to throw in the sponge of despair. Their intent is to thoroughly assess a person's residual vision, to give advice about realistic expectations of its use, and to work with a patient painstakingly so that he can derive the most from the aids suggested.

Doctor Donald H. Lakin is director of Low-Vision Services at Detroit's Optometric Institute and Clinic. He maintains, "We're not a quick-fix solution, nor are we miracle workers. A person who can barely distinguish day from night can't hope to leave with 20/20 acuity."

These experts take each patient's complete physical and eye history, with emphasis on the eye disorder. They pose direct questions to the patient about his adaptation to partial vision.

You can simplify this evaluation by making a list of your goals before your visit. Let it be a brainstorming session — the optome-trist will counsel you by sorting out the impossibles from the reasonables. Again, samples of what you want to see are most helpful, such as textbooks, computer printouts, and needlework.

The more vision you have, the longer will be the examination and the greater will be the benefits from aids. Assessment could consume three visits, from two to three hours each. You will have a chance to work with various aids, some mentioned later in this chapter. It's better than a do-it-yourself, trial-and-error run, be-cause the optometrist will show you precisely when and how to use aids — and will advise you that sometimes light, or getting yourself closer to an object, will work just as well.

Among low-vision aids are precision lenses ground exactly to your specifications. Feinbloom® lenses are among the most sophis-ticated and are of fine quality. People who can use them usually have to work their way up to this point. Other lenses include reading glasses, telescopes that clip onto or are mounted on spectacles, reading adapters that attach to telescopes, contact lenses worn with or without glasses, and prismatic lenses. Although telescopic lenses cannot be affixed to ski or skin diving goggles, other prescriptions can be ground into this equipment for visually impaired enthusiasts of these sports. The science is now so exact-ing that lenses can be made for use a specific distance from work, as for an office worker who would like to keep printed matter thirteen inches away from his eyes. Of course that requirement can only be met under certain conditions and does have some disadvantages in the bargain—your optometrist will explain them if you're interested.

After your aids are in hand, return visits are ideal. Best results will require training. For example, a woman who fixated on the "black spot" caused by macular degeneration had to go back several times over a three-month period until she could concentrate on the rest of her visual fields and not her "blind spot." Only then did the simple magnifier do her any good. Telescopic lenses that you wear distort distance. You reach for a doorknob that isn't there, or back away at an intersection from a car that isn't close. The procedure is far more complicated than buying a pair of shoes and walking away in them.

Cost of initial exams ranges from 50 to 125 dollars. It increases with the thoroughness of the assessment. Some clinics offer sliding fee scales. Although many clinics are nonprofit, some are not. For people who meet eligibility requirements, the state agency for the blind might assume payment. Medicare does not cover these exams, but Medicaid may partially pay, although often its pay scales are unacceptably low. If you have optical coverage from insurance, it may cover part of the fee. Some insurance policies allocate money for health care; if you haven't shot your wad for something else, you can apply those dollars to your examination. Fees for youngsters may come from state or private agencies for children.

When costs for low-vision examinations come from your pocket, it's like any other expense: time for a priority review. It's common sense to discuss fees and methods of payment before your first appointment. A retired minister opted to buy a prescribed aid instead of a new television because he wanted desperately to read with ease. A fifteen-year-old boy begged not to be fitted with special lenses that would enable him to begin driver's training—he just didn't feel ready for the responsibility.

You can locate low-vision clinics through agencies for the blind, your ophthalmologist, or optometrist. If distance and time work against you, go to a local optometrist. Should he tell you that he can't accommodate you, ask him who will. A teaching low-vision clinic is often more economical because the examination, counseling, and training are so time-consuming. An optometrist in private practice doesn't ordinarily have that much time. Should your search net you zero, write to the American Optometric Association.

Although low-vision clinics are a starting point, don't stop there. None can expect to stock everything. Be vigilant at such places as optical companies, pharmacies, hobby shops (that sell needlecrafts), stamp and coin dealers, camera stores, and jewelers. Again, take with you samples of what you need to see, such as print of varying size, a needle to thread, or a crossword puzzle to work. When trying out a telescopic aid, ask permission to take it outside.

One enthusiastic user of low-vision aids derives all that is possible from her 20/400 acuity. She believes that a monocular is a good starter for folks who see poorly because they can rely upon the better eye. When both eyes are the same, people have a preference, just as with the dominant hand. Because this device is handheld, it can be maneuvered to the best advantage. A monocular is for short-term use such as identifying a bus or looking for an address.

"Loupe" is a generic term for a type of monocular. It can be handheld or clipped onto prescription glasses. It varies in strengths and styles, and ranges in price from fifteen to fifty dollars.

Walters makes a line of monoculars, one of the most popular being $7 \times 25 - 25$ refers to the breadth of the field in millimeters. This lightweight device can be slipped into a pocket or purse. Its focus is adjustable so you can read a sign overhead or a book title across the room. It goes from a few inches to infinity. It is so convenient to handle that you can watch television or a sports event by propping your arm on the arm of a chair. The 7×50 model is much heavier, but users report that it is good for people having tunnel vision because it increases the field so well. A partially sighted man is so adept with his monocular that he can whip it out of his pocket to check a sign without breaking stride. Walters' monoculars cost from seventy-five dollars to one-hundred dollars.

Selsi manufactures a less expensive line of monoculars, some as low as fifty dollars. Although designed mostly for distance, some can be equipped with reading adapters.

When looking for a magnifier, remember that focusing is less critical with the weaker strengths. In this case, more isn't necessarily better. If you have high partial vision, that is, can read quarter-inch print with reasonable comfort with the naked eye, you'll probably find 5× or less adequate. But if your residual vision is so low you can't see large print with comparative ease, you should look for magnification of 5× or more. Hold your head as close as you need in order for the image to be sharply defined. When reading with a magnifier, three factors come into play: head, lens, and printed material. The secret is in adjusting lens and page— keep your head as still as possible.

A handheld magnifier is best for quickies such as reading a tag or setting a dial. Steady now—focus the lens between yourself and the object to be scrutinized. Bausch and Lomb makes a 2× lens that folds into a leather pouch. For people with less vision, a double lens, one 3×, the other 7×, is made by Donnegan Optical Company. Depending upon user's sight and circumstances, the lenses can be employed singly or as a pair. Either aid costs less than ten dollars.

If you have experimented with handheld magnifiers, you realized that, despite the steadiest hand, it's hard to keep everything from moving just a little. Those mounted on a stand are meant for prolonged reading. A bar magnifier by Bausch and Lomb, either six inches or twelve inches long, magnifies the height of letters, but not their width. You slide it down the page as you read. The shorter lens costs $3.50, the longer five dollars. Donnegan markets a stand magnifier of 3× power for thirty dollars that does not require focusing. A 4× magnifier comes with a light. Sloan manufactures more powerful stand magnifiers of 7×, 11×, and 13×. These devices should be available from a well-stocked optical company.

When buying a stand magnifier, a critical feature to look for is a plastic base that doesn't obscure light. Be careful not to block light with your hand as you move the apparatus.

The only fair way to experiment with a magnifier is when lighting is optimal for your eye condition. Otherwise, it's like running a race with your shoes tied together. Refresh your memory with Chapter 6.

Some folks favor illuminated magnifiers because light itself magnifies and the power of the lens needn't be so great. A few complain that batteries wear out quickly. Some models operate off electricity. The following devices are available from the American Foundation for the Blind, but can be ordered for you locally. One example is a $3\times$ device placed directly on the page. Its maximum field is two and a half inches when your eye is near the lens. It costs about seventeen dollars. The Mini-battery Lite® has an extension arm with reflector that directs light where needed. It costs $14.50.

Another lighted magnifier, made by the Dazor Lamp Company, is a $3\times$ lens about six inches in diameter. The fluorescent tube which encircles the lens comes in bright white, soft pink, or blue. The device operates in three positions, one of which rests almost on top of your work. It is of most benefit to people with high partial vision. Besides reading, users find it helpful when shining on a page in the typewriter, or for sewing, knitting, crocheting, or other precision activities. The table model costs about ninety dollars. Because it was originally designed for reading blueprints, you might find one through an engineering company, or write directly to Dazor for the dealer nearest you.

American Foundation for the Blind also markets several magnifiers for specialized use. Coil offers one that can snap on many types of insulin syringes for reading calibrations for $4.50. Another Coil magnifier attaches to sewing machines, enabling a user with enough vision to thread the needle. It costs $2.75. For those who want their hands free to work on crafts, a neck-suspended magnifier rests on the wearer's chest. Also made by Coil, its powers are $1.5\times$ or $3\times$, both for $9.50.

Prismatic lenses are least requested among nonprescription aids. By directing divergent light rays, they can help correct blurred or double vision and sometimes increase narrow fields. If you think that such lenses might improve your sight, take your glasses or prescription for them to the optical company.

Although specific low-vision aids have been mentioned here, we are barely scratching the surface. These descriptions are just a glimmer of what is out there. Their prices change, usually upward just like everything else—don't blame me for inflation. Agencies and companies that market them will be listed in Chapter 30, "Where to Go for the Answers You Couldn't Find in This Book." Just constantly be on the lookout—if it works for you, it's good.

Whether you pay three dollars in a dime store or thousands of dollars at a low-vision clinic, your optical aids deserve optimal care. You can clean glass lenses with a tissue. Plastic lenses scratch easily so there's no room for elbow grease. Rinse dust from them under the faucet or wipe with a soft cloth. You can buy plastic lens cleaner with polish for $1.50.

Technology for the partially sighted takes its most sophisticated step forward in the closed-circuit TV magnifier. The two leading manufacturers are Visualtek and Apollo Laser. The device consists of a TV screen, a camera with zoom lens, and a board to support printed material. Powers range from $3\times$ to $60\times$. Letters appear on the screen in light green on a dark green background, or its reverse. The more traditional black on a white background and its reverse are also available. (Green is more restful to the eyes.) Besides reading, a user can quickly learn to write by watching the screen instead of pen and paper.

Visualtek models come in two sizes: twelve-inch screen and nineteen-inch screen. You can opt for such features as a typewriter attachment to enable you to correct errors, fill out forms, or type checks. A camera system can project letters onto a standard television screen, although images are not so bright or distinct. A line marker adjustment projects only one or two lines at a time, reducing eyestrain. There is also an adapter for reading microfiche film.

Understandably, many people hedge about closed-circuit TV magnifiers. The price can be prohibitive to underwrite yourself, since it ranges from $1895 to $2595. The device does not replace prescription reading glasses because it is not particularly portable—the lightest model weighs thirty pounds.

Advantages of these machines lie in less fatigue and eyestrain and speed and ease in reading and writing, especially for prolonged periods. Holding a heavy book is tiring. When you hunch over printed material, muscles become stiff and cramped. (If you're vain, it doesn't look good either.) You can sit normally erect before this instrument. You move the board on which the reading material rests by nudging it with your finger. Some persons who could not otherwise manage print are able to read.

If you are reluctant to make this investment because you suspect that your vision will eventually fail, some consolation lies in knowing that there is always a good market for used equipment. The cost is a legitimate medical deduction.

When considering a closed-circuit TV magnifier, try as many varieties of print as possible. Start with the worst samples—small type, hard-to-decipher handwriting, bad contrast, or blurred print. Work your way toward better material. The company representative will be anxious to show you how to use the device to your best advantage. You can write to the company for the name of the representative closest to you for a hands-on demonstration. If you're a curious window shopper, you might find one in an agency or school for the blind, some public libraries, or special needs offices for disabled students on college campuses.

Closed circuit TV magnifiers have opened employment for many partially sighted people. They include typists, computer programmers, teachers, and representatives for Internal Revenue and Social Security. A sculptor does some of his most intricate work while using this aid. When the need for such a device directly relates to employment, state agencies for the blind will sometimes underwrite its purchase. Even older people who have been avid, lifelong readers can adapt to this machine, although they must understand that reading will never be as fast or facile as it was with normal vision.

Don't exaggerate your high hopes for low-vision aids into false hopes. All the king's horses and all the king's men won't totally restore your vision again. Returns on your investment depend upon motivation, accommodation (one doesn't work for everything), patience, and sometimes financial resources. The capital with which you make that investment is the sight which remains. Even if your vision is likely to deteriorate or fluctuate, it's up to you to make the most of it while it lasts.

Chapter 8

MINDING YOUR OWN BUSINESS

READING MAIL AND
KEEPING PERSONAL RECORDS

W e consider the mailbox a treasure chest. It's the first stop we make upon returning home. When at home we listen for the familiar clunk of the lid dropping, wait till the mail carrier reaches the neighbor's, and rush out to check. Just like a fisherman who lands a carp instead of a perch, we often end up with a fistful of bills and ads. Letters, postcards, and dividend checks are least likely pickin's.

Before discussing how to sift wheat from the chaff, let me make one point sharper than that of a letter opener: It's *your* mail when the address bears your name. That's a matter of law. No one has the right to open it, although sometimes that happens in a well-intended gesture of helpfulness. If you can't read that material yourself, it's your decision as to whom the reader is. Sure, you lose privacy by having someone else look at your bills, letters, bank statements, or federal income tax check. But remain in control by choosing your reader and what mail he is to peruse. You probably don't care if the neighborhood gossip plows through political campaign propaganda for you while her nine-year-old listens. You may *not* want the same bigmouth to tell you the amount of your credit-card billing, or to announce to the world the contents of a love letter. Base your decision by asking that the name and address be read to you. It's perfectly OK to say, "I'll check that later."

When reading, don't feel obligated to explain that the $700 bill from the department store is the furniture you just bought, or how Mortimer Snodgrass fits into the family tree. That's your business. Your reader is simply there to get the job done.

Your out-of-town friends and relatives should remember that someone else will be exposed to the letters they send to you. Most well-intentioned people who promise to learn Braille never do — nobody in my family ever did. Besides, not all blind people know Braille. A completely confidential way of maintaining privacy for you and your correspondents is to exchange cassette tapes. Most people have or can gain access to a commercial cassette recorder. You can buy reusable mailing containers with reversible address cards. Your address is on one side, the receiver's on the reverse. Those suffering mike jitters shouldn't give up on recording a letter. Don't attempt it in one sitting — turn off the machine and go back when you have more news.

Braille, large print (14–point type and larger), and recorded material can be mailed postage free. Write or type in the upper right corner: FREE MATTER FOR THE BLIND. It will go first class, but cannot be sealed. You can buy a FREE MATTER FOR THE BLIND stamp from *Dialogue* Publications. Those sending Braille, large print, or recorded material to you can also use this franking privilege. This privilege does not apply to ordinary mail. You may land in the clink by trying to pay your phone bill that way!

Let's sort the day's harvest. Ads are easy to detect because they are either without an envelope, such as a flier or circular, or they are in the form of a tabloid-size newspaper. Coupons often come in a fat five by seven manila envelope. You may learn to recognize regular monthly bills by date of arrival, cards with perforations, or distinctive marks such as an open window. If you write regularly and want your friends' replies immediately identifiable to you, ask them to do something unusual to the envelope, such as a bit of cellophane tape in the lower left corner.

These sorting techniques are usually safe, but not always foolproof. If you cannot decide between two possibles — Visa charge or an ad for magazine subscriptions—separate them and wait for someone to solve the mystery. In short, don't toss before you're absolutely certain what's in hand. You may be sorry. When you are certain, a small wastebasket inconspicuously placed near the front door ensures that the don't-wants go no farther.

Folks with enough vision to peruse their own mail will do it the same way they always did. Some people prefer to check their own bills, bank statements, and business and personal letters themselves. They save lengthier pieces, such as catalogs or school tax proposals, to be read aloud. Because your limited sight means you read more slowly, reserve a particular place for going over your mail. It should have adequate lighting and, ideally speaking, be close to filing space. A desk with a reading lamp or high-intensity lamp (see Chapter 6) would be a natural for you.

"I feel that it's asking too much of my kids to look through anything that isn't absolutely necessary," said Joan, forty-five, divorced mother of two teenagers. "I can read some of the mail, but I give out when it comes to fliers for the supermarket and hardware store. I want to know what the specials are, but am reluctant to tie them up for too long."

I suggest to Joan, and anyone else dependent upon another for reading aloud such materials, that you don't hold out the expectation that every word will be covered. In the case of the supermarket ad, Joan's youngster could quickly read the sales by name of item only: raisins, coffee, peanut butter, soap, pork, tissues. When the list triggers interest, she could ask for the price and size of product. She can cut the hardware flier reading time by saying, "Skip auto supplies, paint, and tools. We need new lawn furniture, and I'll stock up on window cleaner if it's a bargain. . . ."

You can reduce aloud reading time for other materials by asking your helper to cover only headlines, topic headings, or the first sentence of each paragraph. Then request further reading when necessary.

Again, stay in control. It's your mail, and you should decide what is important for you to know and what should be omitted.

Chances are that you live with other people who are sighted. When mail is addressed to you, you should have a designated place for it to be left by whoever empties the mailbox. Remind others that anything sent to you should be put there — a drawer in the hall table, under a paperweight on the desk, or atop the refrigerator if you think toddlers or the dog will get at it. One student uses a conventional mail basket found in offices with In and Out compartments. Just be sure the personal mail drop-off is near the front door. No one will fancy a trek upstairs to leave your daily haul on your bedroom dresser.

Once the mail is gathered and sorted, you might think about that which requires action: bills, checks to cash, invitations and letters that need an answer. I'll cover bill paying and check cashing in the next chapter, "It's Your Money: Can You Count on It?" You need a mail run-down at least once a week, per-haps more often depending on how much you get. If working with a reader, chit-chat and refreshments come after the session so that the business at hand won't get out of control and the stack still stands. Matters for immediate or near-future attention such as utility bills, announcement of the next PTA meeting, or a note from Aunt Mabel regarding her intended visit in a month can go into a Manila envelope labeled in Braille or large print: IMMEDIATE ATTENTION. You can mark the out-side of a bill envelope in Braille or large print with minimal information:

Electric due 12-15 $22.74

You'll have some idea of contents of letters and invitations by a few key words, again in Braille or large print on the envelope:

Betty Ryan's baby shower 1-22, RSVP by 1-15

Notes on a personal letter envelope could read:

John's son starting college

Sue thinking of moving to N.Y.

Jordans expecting daughter to announce engagement

If these reminders aren't enough, you can read the letter again later, being certain of the identity of the sender and thus choosing an appropriate reader, if necessary. Brief notations can be enough clues to answer a letter in a month or more.

Most people toss most of the mail they get. To save yourself or your assistant from sorting through junk mail, you can eliminate much of it by writing the Direct Mail Association. Your name will be taken off the mailing lists of many direct mail order firms. For those pieces that fall through the cracks, call your post office to ask your mail carrier to drop off Form 2150 so you can fill it out and send it to those companies not covered. If you receive unwanted mail from a local concern, just call to ask that your name be removed from the mailing list. An explanation about your difficulty in handling printed material will expedite that matter.

Now that the mail has been tended to by sorting, pitching, answering, or paying, what do you do with the residue and other records that pile up? Some of these papers aren't coming to you via the postal service. We're close to being buried under a mountain of paper. It is foisted upon us with the purchase of almost every item, thrust into our unexpecting hands at street corners.

Recently I worked with a woman who claimed that she couldn't find her kitchen table.

"You aren't disoriented in your home?" I questioned, frankly bewildered.

"No," she laughed sheepishly. "I haven't canceled the newspaper yet. I hold onto it, although I can just make out the big headlines. Because it's hard for me, I don't get through the pile as I intend to do. There are professional journals, travel folders—the stack is working its way to the ceiling."

I can give only five words of advice: Whenever possible, cancel and pitch. Collar or corner a family member or friend who doesn't mind reading aloud for a reasonable read-and-throw session. If you have a huge accumulation, the kitchen or dining room table is spacious enough for spreading. Several trash bags on the floor await filling. One hint about your helper—he cannot be of the pack-rat variety—the more ruthless, the better. Depending upon the amount you have amassed and the patience of you and your assistant, you may require more than one session. After the grand clearance, you need to resolve never to allow unnecessary papers to jam your file cabinet or desk or to heap on your kitchen table.

What's prime pitching material? Everything that isn't absolutely necessary for your survival. Keep the essentials such as receipts for utility bills, charge accounts, medical and dental care, major purchases of appliances, and home improvements for at least a year. Hang onto income tax returns because the IRS can audit for the last three years. Warranties protect you from paying service charges for usually a year; but when the TV passes its first birthday, send the guarantee and those of other guaranteed purchases that have expired to the great beyond, the garbage can.

Perhaps parting with some mementos would drive you into a two-month depression. Reserve one drawer, chest, or box and call it your Memory Box. Into it you could stash the owners' manual from the car you had to sell, the first paycheck stub from your first job twenty years ago, your high school prom program, the baby pictures, and a matchbook from the restaurant where you and your husband had your first date. When a wave of nostalgia sweeps over you, rifle through your memory box. Just don't store any other necessary documents in that place.

Whether you're a sentimentalist or a born saver, you have to reckon with the fact that you can't read comfortably (if at all) through all those papers. This concentrated effort will probably uncover papers that you long ago forgot that you had. You may find receipts for paint that has since peeled from the garage, expired give-away offers, and never-used coupons. One student couldn't believe that, during her clean-out campaign, her son found a receipt for a $1.98 can of putty that her husband (now divorced) bought twelve years ago.

The object of your pitch-and-sort project is to whittle down what records you keep and organize them so well that you (or somebody else) can lay hands on a desired piece of paper within minutes, if not seconds. Several students have objected, "I don't handle the paperwork anymore. I leave it up to my wife. She sees better than I do. If she wants to find something and can't, that's her worry."

Then I tell them about Mary Lou, a woman who read large letters printed with a felt pen. Her husband is a long-distance truck driver, spending much of the time on the road. One afternoon he called long distance frantically asking Mary Lou to find an insurance policy. He needed the number immediately. With magnifier in hand, Mary Lou went unsuccessfully to locate the policy as her husband waited impatiently on the line. Finally, she suggested that he call back. She had to resort to calling a neighbor for help. Both felt uneasy about plowing through personal documents. The neighbor finally found the policy at the bottom of the dresser drawer. You can't bully or coerce your partner into organizing, but you can use the fact that he won't always be around and may unwittingly surrender privacy to prod him in this direction.

What do you do with the remains of the pile, the must-hang-onto stuff? Your keep-and-find system might be as simple as a shoebox holding business envelopes, or as elaborate as a four-drawer file cabinet replete with Manila folders. It depends upon the number of people in your household, the complexity of your life-style, whether you are in business for yourself, and many other factors. I'm a file-by-year organizer. A relentless nonsaver, I keep my records in business envelopes stored in a metal cashbox. It holds these number tens perfectly. At the beginning of the new year, I braille envelopes with the date, such as Jan. 1983, and respective categories: utilities, paycheck stubs, home insurance, health insurance, money order receipts and canceled checks, income taxes, house payments. Then I clean out papers from the preceding year, pitch those I don't need, put a rubber band around the remaining envelopes and stack them in a basement storage cabinet. When delving in the cabinet, I toss out unnecessaries from the last year.

Progressing through the year, I put each paper into the envelope so that it is nearest the front, thus keeping chronological order. When deciding to keep a money-order receipt, or to readily identify it, I write the receiver name, date, and amount in Braille on it. Because this paper is so flimsy, it would be hard for a new Braille user to read the dots. Depending on your vision and Braille skills, use large print or at least categorize so that someone else can look up a particular receipt quickly. You can mark envelopes in large print. If Braille dots don't stand up well enough for you on an envelope, write your category on a three by five index card and staple to the envelope.

Income tax time is an unbearable reckoning for everybody. If you file every document bearing on taxes such as medical and dental receipts, charitable contributions, and statements of interests in your envelope marked "Income Tax," you'll avoid the mad scramble, because you've been gathering all year.

When establishing your personal filing system, it's safer to be too general than overly specialized. For instance, if the phone company questions your payment of a bill three months ago, you or somebody else can sift through the contents of the "Utilities" envelope—there's no need to separate telephone, gas, electricity, and water. Your categories might include: Social Security, Medicare, school records, family health records, credit card accounts. Most important is to bring order out of chaos and stay with it. As soon as the canceled checks are in hand, put them away.

I remember a student who was enthusiastic about registering for college classes. I asked him how pre-registration had gone. He answered dismally, "I didn't have some papers that were required and couldn't complete the procedure." It took him three days to find the papers in the hodgepodge of his shoebox at home. Being responsible for his own record keeping was a grand awakening.

Some records are permanent and not renewed each year, such as birth certificates, marriage licenses, house deeds, and instruction manuals for appliances. Several copies of a statement proving onset of your legal blindness to prove eligibility for Social Security, disability insurance, or other entitlements should also be included. I label this envelope "Permanent Records" and keep it with the annual filings, just in case I require such information immediately.

I read about an executive who insisted that he never allowed a piece of paper to pass through his hands more than once. A high standard to set, but an excellent ideal for which to aim.

A few blind people, including myself, have had trouble initially when applying for a safe deposit box. The bank employee who served me insisted that my companion could remove the contents of the box without my realizing it. I countered with the obvious—I wouldn't ask any friend to go through the box with me if there were the least suspicion of his integrity. If you meet the same objection, stick by your guns. Denial is based upon an individual's edginess, not on the law. Before calling the bank president in a rage, talk with the branch manager. I know of no law or institutional regulation that prohibits rental of a safe deposit box on the basis of blindness. Any holder of a safe deposit box is wise to have a cosigner; however, if the cosigner dies, the box legally must be opened by an official from probate court.

Your own list of phone numbers and addresses also falls into record keeping. People who still read print tend to rely upon the ordinary small address book or personal phone directory with a sliding lever to open at a specific letter. You probably will have to write larger than before, causing notations to become cramped on a page. Consequently, your writing becomes less legible. Consider parting with your address book and use 3 by 5 or 4 by 6 index cards. You can note name, address, phone number, and other pertinent information on the same card, writing or printing as large as you like. By filing these cards alphabetically in a box with clearly marked dividers, you can add and delete as necessary. Occasionally sort through your file box, pitching out the card for the dentist who moved out of town or the auto mechanic who gave you a raw deal. Some people like a Rolodex, which is a semicircular wire track onto which cards can slip easily. In some cases, the cards aren't big enough for large writing.

A man can carry a few file cards in his pocket or briefcase along with a felt tip pen. I know a woman who stashes hers in a small cosmetic bag in her purse. You can always pull out the necessary card to take with you for an errand or appointment.

If you can read Braille, file cards are more desirable than large sheets of Braille paper. People who have learned Braille recently are slow in reading and writing. Your object in noting is to make it as brief and simple as possible while retaining a consistent format. Again, 3 by 5 or 4 by 6 cards usually allow enough space, one name per card. Those bought in an office supply or stationery store are better quality, bearing dots that last through years of handling. Lighter weight cards from dime stores or discount stores do not retain Braille as well.

If you file your directory in a box, write the card this way: On the bottom line, last name only—skip first name or initial unless you're afraid you won't remember it. Moving up, write the phone number and nothing else on the next line. Don't bother with an address if you won't need it. If a street number is important, it goes on the third line. Reserve the fourth line for city and state if you won't remember them. Eliminate them if you can, copying only the zip code. Place the card with the Braille away from you. When you look through your box, you'll find the name of a friend first on the card. As your finger finds the right card, you can pull it out to check further. It is awkward to hold your hand to read brailled file cards that face you in the conventional manner of filing.

Perhaps you want to braille file cards so that they lie flat. Put the person's name on the top line, phone number next, address on third, and city, state, and zip on fourth line. Punch holes in the bottom of the card and place in a small three-ring binder. This binder directory works when you don't have a lot of numbers to record. If there are too many, it becomes thick and unwieldy.

Unfortunately, there is no convenient way of making a personal directory by people who cannot read print or Braille. By being in this predicament, you realize that your memory for commonly dialed numbers expands. Other than asking someone to look them up for you, recording on a cassette tape is a make-do solution. While dictating names and other notes, allow enough silent time so that you don't have to listen to half the list before locating the desired information. You could separate letters (for instance, A's from the B's) by blowing softly across the mouth of an empty bottle. The sound is like a distorted foghorn and is audible in the fast forward or reverse modes of your cassette recorder. Allow enough unrecorded tape for each letter designation so that you can make additions later. Though not a fully satisfactory method, it's better than nothing at all.

You will probably be calling Directory Assistance for new numbers. By explaining that you do not see well, you are tipping off the operator to dictate the number slowly if necessary.

Yes, it's hard to plan and execute a system of sorting and reading mail, filing personal records, and maintaining phone numbers and addresses. Stay on top of that paper mountain. Don't let yourself become engulfed in a landslide.

Chapter 9

IT'S YOUR MONEY

CAN YOU COUNT ON IT?

I sn't it amazing! That man is able to tell the difference between a one and a ten."

I was standing next to that remarkable blind man, struggling hard to keep a straight face as the cashier handed him change for the restaurant check. Once outside, I turned in mock bewilderment: "Tell me, what's your secret?"

The mystery is that there is no secret. I've heard tales of this feat being accomplished, but never have encountered anyone who can identify bills by touch. If these rare individuals exist, we'll pass over them to reach the majority—those who cannot see well enough to distinguish denominations.

Before you move on by thinking that your partial vision is sufficient to recognize paper money, consider poor lighting conditions such as a dimly lit restaurant or a taxi at night. You may be able to spot a ten from a twenty by holding it three inches from your face, but do you want to extract every bill from your wallet? You're not exactly waving a bankroll around, but prudence dictates that anybody should handle cash with caution.

Now that we've established the fact that you can't feel fives from tens, let's work out a way for you to know what's what. I call my system the tightwad principle. It's quite logical: the larger the bill, the smaller I fold it, because I don't want to part with it. Singles are unfolded; fives are folded in half to form a square. One more fold identifies a ten—it is folded in quarters. Although I don't ordinarily carry anything higher, I wouldn't toss a twenty—just fold the ten again so that it is in eighths. For those few who favor two-dollar bills, I would treat it as a single folded lengthwise. You're flirting with danger if you carry more than twenties, despite what it does for your sense of well-being or for the plain wish to minimize bulk.

Coins are a cinch compared with paper money. Dimes, quarters, and fifty-cent pieces are minted with milled or rough edges. On the other hand, pennies and nickels are smooth edged. I know an old lady who is a poker addict. She found nickels and quarters hard to separate before dropping her bet into the pot until she realized that quarters are larger—she never misses now. Susan B. Anthony dollar pieces reared their confusing heads for a short time, but I haven't seen any in ages. They are slightly larger than quarters.

You have several options for toting your cache of cash. Some people don't like to fish through pockets, wallets, or coin purses for loose silver. If you are among the compulsively organized, a coin keeper is for you. It has slots for quarters, dimes, nickels, and pennies. Coin keepers also feature hooks for keys, snapping or zipping closed. A small inside pocket provides room for a few bills.

A wallet with a divider separating two compartments offers space for singles and another for higher bills. If you carry more than one folded bill, don't fold them together. It can happen that when pulling out a ten, you accidentally drop another folded with it. If I have five or more bills of the same denomination, I leave them flat so I can remove one without dislodging the rest.

A sighted man I know uses a money clip. It seems a natural for a blind person, because it fits inconspicuously in pocket or purse and will keep bills folded until released. It has a small pocket convenient for credit cards. Loose change jingles in his pocket.

One student is a devotee of a coupon caddy for carrying paper money. The size of a commercial checkbook, its plastic sheets with tabs divide various denominations for her. Beginning at the front, she starts with ones; fives go next, then tens. Extra compartments are left for a couple of checks or credit cards. The case snaps shut. You can find a coupon caddy in a stationery or card shop, or the novelty department in a dime store or K–Mart. It is flat enough not to bulge pocket or purse.

A small money holster is a pouch with shoulder strap. It must be worn under a jacket or sweater to achieve its intent of a secret place for carrying money. They are available in luggage and billfold departments. Senior citizens and travelers especially like them because there is no money in purse or wallet in pocket.

Having a handle on sorting and organizing bills once you know what they are, you can eliminate guesswork by being sure that you don't have many different denominations to worry about. When cashing a check, ask for all tens. You won't have to puzzle over more than a possible five and a few ones. You could ask the teller to put your tens into a money envelope, and the rest into your hand. Ask that the five be identified first, then the ones.

Some tellers or clerks will say, "The five's on top," or, "Your five's on the bottom." You take it from there. You've narrowed the identification process to three denominations. A plastic folder that is meant for travelers checks will fit paper bills perfectly. If you hide cash at home, you could store only tens in it. A bank teller would probably give you one without fuss or charge.

Before putting your cash on the line, let the salesperson know that you're aware of what's in your hand. If a clerk in a drugstore tells you that the bill is $7.92, casually say as you hand it over, "Out of ten."

Newly blind people are suspicious of being cheated. Just because it's never happened to me doesn't mean that it won't or hasn't befallen someone else. When you receive more than singles, ask the salesperson to identify bills, even if ten people are bearing down upon you in the checkout line with grocery carts. Put them away in your prescribed order before moving on so that you'll be in control during the next transaction.

As I have said before, nobody can be vigilant 100 percent of the time. Occasionally a bill is out of order. I've passed off a five or a ten as a one. A clerk or waitress, who is a total stranger, has corrected my mistake, perhaps prompted by the watchful eye of other customers or people who feel their integrity is on the line. Maybe

I'm naive enough to think that an innate goodness has burst forth.

Jim is totally blind and had operated a vending stand for fifteen years, selling candy, cigars, magazines, and sundries to those frequenting the downtown police station. A man approached him to ask for a one dollar lottery ticket and claimed that he had a twenty dollar bill. When the customer received his change, he moved around the display, picking up several items. He bought first with a ten dollar bill, then with a five dollar bill. Because no one was around to verify the customer's paper money, Jim had to take his word for it. Using individual drawers for each denomination, Jim was able to confirm his suspicion later. The top bill in the twenties was a one. The unknown buyer had swindled him out of thirty-five dollars in money and merchandise.

"Lots of people are mad at the world when they come to the police station," Jim recalls philosophically. "That guy took out his anger on me."

You can learn from Jim's costly misfortune. Whenever in doubt, wait until your money can be verified.

Of course money isn't everything, but having a little on your person adds to your sense of dignity. Unless you're flat broke, don't go anywhere without a little cash — at least change to make a phone call in case you must. Upon losing sight, some people surrender cash transactions to others. Even if you start slowly by paying the paperboy or settling with the waiter, it can add immeasurably to your confidence. Folks who are shut-ins, never going out to shop or dine, should have a little cash of their own. Insignificant as it seems, those few dollars signify security.

Bill paying is a drain and a pain for everybody. This won't be a lecture on budgeting or how to get the creditors off your back — definitely not my bag. Credit counselors are the experts if you corner yourself into overextending your buying power. You can get their advice free from a community service agency, or by asking at your bank. My advice adds up to how to pay your bills on time.

Let's start with the regulars, such as utility bills. Many banks, savings and loan associations, credit unions, supermarkets, drugstores, and neighborhood offices accept on-time cash payment for gas, electricity, telephone, and water. You might have a few cents tacked on for the service, but it's cheaper than postage and check costs. It saves time in addressing envelopes. As utility bills arrive, I put them into an envelope that is attached to my passbook with a rubber band. When I cash my paycheck at the savings and loan where I do most of my business, I pay utilities at the same time. The teller stamps "paid" on the stub of each, giving me a permanent record. Should the gas company call to challenge my payment for last January, it can be retrieved from the file envelope marked "Utilities."

As for the monthly house payment, the savings and loan was one jump ahead. The manager informed me of the service of deducting it automatically from my savings account, saving me from remembering to send a money order on the first of the month. Provided that your mortgage is with the same bank or savings and loan with which you have a checking or savings account, that method will work for you, too.

As for irregular bills, such as department store charges, taxes, club dues and insurance, recipients get their fair share via money orders. I tuck stamped, addressed envelopes into the passbook for the biweekly bank visit. The teller fills out the money order, puts it into the corresponding envelope, and is cooperative enough to slip it into the outgoing mail. I file money order receipts immediately upon returning home (see Chapter 8).

If you visit a bank, savings and loan, or credit union regularly, it helps to patronize the same branch. Tellers and managers come to know you and your special needs. They are more than willing to fill out deposit and withdrawal slips for checking and savings accounts and to provide other personalized services. Although staff members of financial institutions know the ins and outs of their business, don't expect them to anticipate difficulties imposed by visual impairment. It's usually a case of ask and ye shall receive. I have heard of a bank security guard who reads mail two or three times a week to a blind man who lives alone in the neighborhood. You can't get any more personal than that.

Kay, our friend the social worker whom we met at the beginning of this book, found that her friends became a little edgy when balancing her checkbook. The problem was not that they mistrusted their arithmetic. They felt that reading her bank statement and check register was an invasion of her privacy. She followed my suggestion of bringing her statement to the bank for a teller to reconcile. Being completely disinterested, the teller doesn't care how Kay spends her money. Besides, tellers constantly handle money and probably immediately forget individual expenditures. As a matter of courtesy, Kay asked the manager first about the feasibility of this service. He gladly agreed. Bank statements are usually in light blue ink, a challenge for those with some reading vision. Some banks may charge for reconciling checking accounts, but chances are they won't if you explain your circumstances.

Another way to skirt the problem of bill paying is to find out what other transactions a financial institution provides. You may opt to pay auto, health, or home insurance in monthly installments. It is possible that these can be drawn from your checking or savings account. You will receive a monthly statement as a record of payment. Some banks and savings and loan associations don't charge for money orders that are withdrawn from a savings account.

Checking accounts aren't for everyone, but you may find them most convenient. Because the variety is bewildering — no service charge for minimum balance, monthly service charge, etc. — you have a right to fully understand before applying. A handful of explanatory pamphlets may not help, so ask a teller or manager to run through different accounts before you choose. While such an expert is on the line, inquire about the electronic transference of funds for other possibilities of paying regular bills.

Some partially sighted and totally blind check users find Guideline checks helpful. The size of a commercial check ($8\frac{3}{8}$ by $3\frac{3}{8}$), they bear raised lines to be followed by the totally blind and bold print for those who can read it. You can fill them out by hand, or type out a check. Tellers may not be aware of their existence because they are listed in the commercial check catalog. Registers are the same size, providing plenty of room for your larger-than-usual writing or printing.

A check template is still another option. It can be cut out of cardboard, heavy plastic, or made from metal by the American Foundation for the Blind. You've learned the format of your check, so filling in the appropriate slots shouldn't be too hard.

"But I just ordered 200 checks with a pretty sunset scene, and my name and address imprinted on them," objected Ben. "I can manage to write the check. It's keeping the register that gets me. There's not enough room in my checkbook."

If you face the space crunch, there is no rule that says you have to follow the register in your checkbook. Use a notebook that allows as much paper as you need. Braille users can operate in the same way.

Truncated checking accounts are becoming more popular. Maybe you emptied several shoeboxes of canceled checks during the pitch-out. This system does not return canceled checks—just a monthly statement. If you need a canceled check to prove a disputed payment, take the statement for that month to the financial institution. By tracing through the number of the desired check on your statement, a teller can give you a copy within minutes. Usually the first twenty-five duplicated canceled checks are free; a small charge can be made for additional copies. I.R.S. audits call for unlimited duplications without charge. Just think—less paper shuffling, fewer records to file.

Automatic teller machines are sweeping the banking scene, somewhat depersonalizing financial transactions. Unless you can read directions on the screen or have someone do it for you, you're running a risk by memorizing the layout of buttons. Machines vary according to manufacturer and can be different for each branch. After two or three miscues, the monster swallows your card as protection against an unauthorized user. Arguing with a computer is to be avoided at all cost.

However, if you can't bear the thought of a financial emergency, or like to be daring, you can memorize the buttons of a particular automatic teller. One totally blind woman relies upon it in cases of dire emergency. Otherwise, she collars someone in her office to help her with the transaction.

Getting to the bank might be inconvenient or impossible. In some cases, you're afraid your check might be stolen from the mailbox. You can fill out a form to authorize sending any government check to your checking or savings account. These include Social Security Disability Insurance, Supplemental Security Income, General Assistance, pension, and occasionally paychecks. You could ask your employer if this benefit is possible if you don't want to make the weekly or biweekly trip.

People who are housebound or for some other reason can't handle banking can opt to appoint someone with power of attorney. This procedure is standardized so that you can apply at a bank or savings and loan, or the forms can be brought to you for your signature. If signed at home, a witness is required. You can be specific about the powers given to your trusted one: cashing checks only, making deposits but no withdrawals, or any combination. Again you are calling the shots.

When handling your own banking business, you may want to take home a supply of deposit and withdrawal slips to be filled out before the actual transaction. Then you won't be poring over them while twenty people stand behind you in line. Otherwise, a teller is always glad to do it if you aren't able.

Perhaps you're of the plastic money persuasion. When alone and not able to read the charge slip, you're wisest to have someone else besides the cashier verify it for you. A sighted visitor to Japan used a credit card during a night on the town. American Express received charges for $8,000, even though he spent only several hundred. American Express had to reimburse to the tune of $8,000, and the responsibility fell back on the cardholder who didn't stop to examine his charge slips.

You know your buying habits better than anyone else. Carrying credit cards can spare you from toting cash or the nuisance of writing checks. The buy now, sweat it later types may find their convenience not worth the temptation. When you obtain a credit card through a bank at which you have a checking or savings account, you can use a debit card for your purchase with any enterprise that accepts that credit card. Payment for your bill will be automatically withdrawn from your account. Don't pull out that debit card unless you intend to pay up in full.

Asking a total stranger to fill out a personal check is a risky business, a not-unless-you're-against-the-wall ordeal. When it's a matter of must, request a manager or supervisor to fill it out. A busy cashier most likely has good intentions, but can slip up because the ranks are getting restless behind you.

"What if I wanted to go on a clothes-buying spree and didn't think cash too safe?" wondered Redgie, a thirty-year-old medical transcriptionist blind since birth. "I can't write a check either."

Redgie can rely upon travelers' checks, which come in varying denominations and are nonnegotiable until signed by her. Some credit unions and AAA issue them free to patrons. The rest of us have to pay 1 percent.

Before changing the subject: I adopted a trick that saves me from scrambling for change at home. I used to be caught changeless when I asked a friend to pick up a half gallon of milk, or clothes from the cleaner's. To save myself from the owing end or overpaying (who can remember a debt of $1.39?), I stash several dollars' worth of loose change in an old cup in my dresser drawer. I can come close to the right amount. To ward off financial disasters, I keep a fifty dollar traveler's check hidden—just in case the well runs absolutely dry.

Many churches don't take the chance of members' remembering to make regular donations. Reminders take the form of weekly envelopes imprinted with the member's name, address, and date. Sorting out the right envelope for each week is more bother than I want. I opt for the once-a-month contribution, typing my name, address, month and year, and amount. Even church collections have gone the way of computers. For the sake of money in hand, the keeper of the moneys is willing to undergo a little more work to chalk up my donations in a way that meets my income tax purposes.

Managing your money or entrusting it to others is one of the most sensitive areas in your life. Regardless of your everyday vigilance and long-term precautions, expect slip-ups—yours and other people's—to happen occasionally. It occurs in big business, so why think that your personal business should be free from it?

This one happened to me: The call from Recordings for the Blind in New York was startling. I had just sent this organization, which records books, a money order for a few dollars with a request for their newest catalog of selections. Were they so responsible, I wondered, as to follow through with a long-distance call about such a routine matter? The kicker came when I discovered the money orders had been shuffled in my purse. Instead of five dollars, I had posted $119 intended for an insurance company. Naturally, the insurance company thought I had invented a ruse for paying in five dollar installments. The next time the phone rang, it was the insurance representative, asking the whereabouts of the full payment for the policy.

Errors in handling money can be costly and embarrassing. If you overlook a bill and receive a late charge as a penalty, call the firm to explain what happened. Most personnel will be sympathetic to your limitation of reading and storing printed material, and will probably waive the penalty. If you just don't have the money, it's only fair to let your creditor know that you realize the debt is due. Tell him why you can't pay it and give a reasonable expectation of when you can put something toward the balance owed. Companies don't want to repossess your furniture, car, or appliances. The bank, savings and loan, or mortgage company isn't itching for your home. Their patience is more long lasting than you think, but these people aren't mind readers. They need to be aware of your circumstances first. Laying low and leaving them in the dark isn't fair play.

Should you have cash on hand that you can't identify, don't panic, and don't try spending it, either. Maybe you forgot to ask for all tens, or the teller didn't hear you. Or you were in a rush and didn't fold your money after a purchase. Ask someone you can trust to sort it out with you.

By knowing how to handle money and to pay bills, you are moving toward self-esteem. Whether you manage it yourself or direct someone else in its handling, you are making another stride toward taking charge of your life.

Chapter 10

IF YOU'RE ABLE, LABEL

T alk with most blind people and you're bound to come up with a few laughs and even some horror stories about misusing substances meant for entirely different purposes. One student sprayed her bedroom with Ban to freshen the air from smoke. Another dumped a small can of Dole pineapple into a tuna fish salad he was making. Someone else started brushing her teeth with a tube of hand cream. Even a sighted friend began squirting a can of oven cleaner (instead of Endust®) on the dining room table. (That was a costly mistake because she had to pay for its refinishing.)

"I can see what I'm pouring, setting, spraying or taking," you insist. (So could the woman of the oven cleaner saga.) All well and good. Large print, Braille, and other markings are a nuisance, no doubt. But if there is any doubt, the extra trouble to save your neck and lower your blood pressure and frustration can even be cost-effective.

Not only does degree of sight dictate the extent of labeling, your responsibilities within the household and the assistance from family members also have a bearing. If you never set foot in the kitchen except as a passageway to the family room, forget about marking the oven dial. Washer and dryer may be off your limits, so scratch them off your list. Consider only what is within your realm; there's no use creating unnecessary work for items you never touch.

But would you be likely to run appliances or work with tools if you had some way of monitoring their settings or contents? Without realizing it, you might be boxing yourself in or just plain copping out. Suppose no one's at home and you want to turn up the furnace thermostat. These dials generally bear small numbers, often faded. Or your wife is visiting her mother and won't be back for three days. In the meantime, you've run out of clean socks and underwear. Three days is a long time for such a plight. Perhaps the chicken pot pie she left in the freezer burned to a cinder because you set the toaster oven to broil instead of bake.

Before pinning down objects for the labeling project, let's run through some of the methods for marking. Available from the American Foundation for the Blind are some specialty aids: Dymo® tape labelers for Braille and large print. Trim the tape to the desired length. By spinning a dial and squeezing handles, you can imprint Braille or inch-high letters, peel the backing, and adhere the label to a hard surface. (Sighted people can also use a Dymo labeler for Braille because letters are also designated in print.) Writing Braille or large print onto Dymo tape is cheaper but more time-consuming. Label-on® tape comes in a dispenser, like cellophane tape, and holds dots well. You can also write on it with a felt tip pen. You could be lucky and find it in a local office supply, or purchase it from the American Foundation for the Blind. This organization also offers Braille plastic labeling sheets with peel-off backing. Less expensive than tape, they require cutting for the proper size. Hi Marks® glue won't mend the broken handle of a fine china cup, but it does provide a dot you can feel and see — it's bright orange. It resists heat, cold, and scrubbing but may not withstand the persistent nails of your seven-year-old.

Common items that turn up in everybody's buffet junk drawer (we're all entitled to one disaster area) will also work in many cases. These include rubber bands, electrical or masking tape, gummed paper such as mailing labels or stickers, 3 by 5 index cards, and even bright red nail polish.

Again, organization is the answer. Sorry, but it's another instance of memory-stretching. Even the most retentive memory lags. You can't predict distractions either, such as the sink overflowing when you're hunting for the bottle of vitamins. The rule of thumb is: If you don't immediately know an article by its placement, size, shape, color, or printing on the container, then you'd better do something about making things clearer. If the only spray under the sink is Lysol® for the trash can, you're not likely to use it as furniture polish that is stored somewhere else. The tall, slender plastic bottle in the bathtub organizer is your favorite shampoo. You won't mistake it as hair conditioner if it always returns to that resting place and, of course, you don't change brands of either.

"I buy shampoo and hair conditioner made by the same company," said twenty-five-year-old Diane. "I like them both. Do I have to look for a different brand of one so bottles won't feel alike? I don't want to risk rubbing conditioner into my hair when I'm ready to shampoo."

"I'm in sympathy," I answered with a laugh. "Once you find hair preparations you like, hang onto them. Just put a rubber band around the neck of one bottle. For tubes of lipstick that feel the same but are different shades, slap a bit of tape on one."

When you're in the bathroom, the medicine cabinet is the last place you want to play guessing games. Prescription bottles can be labeled in Braille or large print with Dymo or Label-on tape. The name of medication and dosage, plus expiration date, should be enough information. You can print big letters on gummed white paper to stick to the bottle. In fact, your pharmacist would probably comply with that request if you made it. Should the bottle not be big enough to accommodate the label, ask for a larger size. While you have that pharmacist collared, you might ask for the conventional pill bottle rather than the child-proof variety—that is, if little hands aren't likely to invade those shelves. I overheard an old lady telling a druggist that she had to stop a stranger on the street to open a child-proof bottle for her, and she wasn't blind either. When these conventional containers are empty, you might want to save them for patent medicines. Some aspirin bottles would challenge Houdini, because you have to align the cap marking with a red arrow.

Ingenuity comes into play when you can't read large print or Braille. Strips of tape or rubber bands help. Rely upon as many markers as number of pills taken each day—two tablets, two markers.

I met a woman in poor health who couldn't read print and

didn't know Braille. As an additional precaution, she put medications for her stomach disorder on one shelf, those for a heart condition on another. Knowing which is which can mean her life and health.

To save yourself from relabeling renewed prescriptions, save the container.

To avoid mix-ups with spray cans in the bathroom, you could decide to mark with tape or rubber bands those which are used on your body, such as hair spray or deodorant. Anything not so identified is not part of your personal hygiene, such as room deodorizer or tile cleaner. A piece of tape around the toothpaste tube assures you, in the groggy early morning, that you're not using your teenager's acne preparation.

Strolling into the kitchen, you could well be dazed by the array of gadgets and foodstuffs that need to be staked out. Since appliances are the most mystifying, let's start with the biggy: the oven and its dial. Our local gas company drilled tiny jewelers' screws into my dial at every 50° interval. Thus, 25° and 75° settings are a cinch to hit by lining up the pointer between screws. I just have to be a careful counter so I don't end up baking a cake at 450° instead of 350°. Taking a cue from the gas company, the manufacturer of the microwave oven I bought indicated time and temperature with the same screws.

Perhaps you don't want to be so elaborate, or your utility company's customer service department isn't so obliging, or you live a hundred miles from this resource. Try a dot of Hi Marks at the 350 degree setting, the most frequently set temperature. If you can see it, a dot of bright red nail polish will accomplish the same. With a little practice, you can set the oven heat lower by moving left of the mark or higher by going right.

"I can see well enough to set the oven," objected Bessie, who thought that her career as a homemaker was in jeopardy if she made special adaptations for tasks she had performed hundreds of times.

"How do you know you're on target?" I wondered.

"I always use my magnifying glass," she persisted.

Bessie and many others like her are adding one more chore to cooking—hunting for the magnifier while putting on the roast or slipping in a cookie sheet. When she accepted my advice, she discovered one less step in the kitchen.

Other appliances will be easier to operate with a mark-up. Blenders, electric frypans, toaster ovens, food processors, and the temperature control on your refrigerator and freezer with easy-feel or easy-see indicators tailored to the settings you use more often will take the guesswork out of their operation.

Some appliances have built-in indicators not meant for blind users, but finding and memorizing them saves you some bother. Dials that click, pointers that set specific temperatures by alignments with dents or grooves in plastic or metal, or push buttons help. Turning a pointer according to times on a clock may also be feasible. Push-button gadgetry usually costs considerably more than a rotating dial, and may be more elaborate than you really require.

Fishing around a shelf of canned goods or frozen foods can be a grab-and-guess game. It's more than an unpleasant surprise when you're making a cherry pie to open whole kernel corn instead of cherry pie filling. A little sight goes a long way in identifying foods by pictures on cans or packages. Your vision may be so low that you have to turn the label toward you to be sure you recognize peas from lima beans. Storing food packages and cans so that the visible identification is facing you as you open the cupboard door saves you from pulling down boxes or cans.

Arranging your cans and boxes systematically also helps, regardless of vision. Once you get the hang of it, you know without thinking that the left end of the second shelf is canned fruit. To the right you line up canned vegetables. Another shelf can hold canned juices or soups. It's only a little more effort when you're putting away groceries. Incidentally, don't leave that task as a matter of trust to someone else, especially if you are the chief cook and bottle washer. Some well-meaning soul could tuck the chili powder among the crackers and you won't find it until spring cleaning rolls around again.

Back to the vagaries of tin cans, whose contents you can't determine by size or placement. Again, 3 by 5 index cards come to the rescue. Just write the name of the food, such as green beans, corn, peaches, or orange juice on the card. If someone else is likely to help you in grocery shopping, such as a neighbor or stock clerk, note the same information in print. Then you or your helper can fasten the card to the can with a rubber band. When opening the can, put the card in a kitchen drawer. The accumulation serves to keep your shopping list updated. Although there are more elaborate marking kits for sale, I have recycled cards through this route for more than ten years.

A woman in Maryland had people who don't read Braille in mind when she invented Lobels®. They are small, magnetized replicas of common fruits and vegetables that adhere to can lids. You can buy similar identifiers that are decorations for refrigerator doors. They are sold in kitchenware departments.

You can work out a method of separating food categories by cardboard dividers that protrude slightly beyond cans. You would alphabetically arrange vegetables to the right of the divider, fruits to the left. As you remove them, be careful not to fill the empty space. Knowing that the gap has been left by the green beans you had for dinner yesterday, you won't be startled by opening peas instead of corn today.

Frozen food packages, particularly fish, can be a puzzle for people with 20/20 vision if not clearly marked. Whip out the Magic Marker®, or whatever you can read, and clearly print name of food on freezer tape. Index cards don't stand up well in the freezer because of moisture. I cut up disposable Talking Book magazine discs and Braille them, making permanent markers, again attaching them with rubber bands. Organizing packages so that fish, vegetables, and different kinds of meat each have their own assigned spot is another great help. Providing everything else fails, or you can't be bothered marking, try a rubber band code. One could indicate fowl, two for pork, and three for beef. It's easy to confuse a pork roast as a beef roast, or pork chops as steak. Shapes aren't easy to discern when they are the consistency of granite. You can always sneak a peak at frozen vegetables by opening the bag; close it if the broccoli you sought feels like asparagus.

If a freezer is in your near future, opt for the upright. Shelving offers organizing opportunities. You may never be heard from again by half crawling into the chest type to dig out fish filets for supper.

Even grandmothers now rely upon some prepared foods such as cake and brownie mixes, instant potatoes, frozen or ready-to-mix piecrusts, and hundreds of quickly prepared dishes. Most directions are in fairly large print; if beyond your vision, take note in your own way, with Braille or large print. Get down to essentials such as what and how much to add, temperature, and cooking time. Fasten to a box with rubber bands and save for recycling, unless you have sworn off a certain brand of brownie mix forever. When print and Braille are not for you, an alternative is having a friend record the preparation on cassette tape.

So you spice up your life with a lot of herbs and spices. You can always play smell and tell. Perhaps you wouldn't be wild about a sniff of cinnamon followed by a waft of red pepper. Besides, the nose goes on strike after a challenging sniff test. Everything smells alike. Spices and herbs hang around the shelf or rack for a while. Mark them with three-letter abbreviations such as cin for cinnamon, pep for pepper, ros for rosemary. White gummed paper will do for print, and Dymo or Label-on for Braille. Some spice cans bear generously large print and will save you the bother if you can see it.

What's under the sink besides pipes? Anything dangerous such as insecticide, disinfectant, or liquid drain cleaner should be instantly recognizable to you. A piece of tape acts like a red flag to warn you to be certain of contents before pouring or spraying. Put a strip of masking tape on can or bottle top and you'll just have to switch lids when you buy a replacement.

Since you've used Hi Marks glue for kitchen appliances, keep it in hand and head for the thermostat. Relying upon yourself as a thermometer isn't an accurate way of gauging the temperature in the house. (Some students tell me they turn it until they are comfortable.) Possibly you have jacked it up to eighty-five degrees. When you get your heating bill, your blood pressure will zoom over 200. Select two readings reasonable for you—sixty-eight and seventy-four degrees, for example. For the dial that is set with a lever that slides left for cooler, right for warmer, put a dot of glue or bit of tape at the desired points on the dial. Line up the lever and you're all set. For the circular dial that revolves clockwise for warmer and counterclockwise for cooler, two tactile points can be put on its face. A third tactile mark serves as the line up on the outer rim, which is stationary. One student had to dash for a flashlight and magnifier every time he suspected that the kids had turned up the furnace to full blast. A quick check with his finger now tells all.

I met a blind woman who played roulette with the washing machine dial. She'd spin it until water started rushing and the motor chugging, those signs of life being enough for her. That gal quit tempting fate when several pairs of delicate curtains disintegrated from the normal cycle and hot water. She marked the washer and now programs the machine as a matter of choice, not chance. Most people rely upon three cycles for all of the laundry: normal, permanent press, and delicate. Throw in the rinse-and-spin setting and you've covered the waterfront. Brief Braille labels or glue dots will do it. If you stick to glue or tape, try one mark for delicate, two for permanent press, and three for normal. With this logic, the number of markers increases with the intensity of the cycle. A diagonal strip of tape or diagonal dots is the clue for rinse-and-spin. Gauges for filling the washer and water temperature usually click. Manufacturers tend to be reasonable—filling for a small load is left, for a full load is right. Cold water is to the left, medium in the middle, and hot to the right. Those machines that offer a variety of choices may require markings for those most often used.

The same technique applies to the dryer. Your concerns are time and temperature. One mark can represent ten minutes, two for twenty minutes, and three for thirty minutes. Small strips of tape can identify such temperature controls as gentle heat, regular, and air only.

While we are down in the basement, I'll give lip service to an area into which I never venture: the workshop or workbench. A former colleague who is a real whiz with gizmos passed along this tip: Folks who dabble in such things usually sort screws, nuts, bolts, washers, and nails according to size. Store them in small containers such as jars or tool organizers. To the outside of each container glue a sample of what is inside. When hunting for a quarter-inch screw or a fistful of roofing nails, you won't have to look farther than the indicator you have posted.

Let's take a random jaunt around the house to put to rest some hit and miss messes you may encounter. Record collectors will find it handy to write a key word or two in large print or Braille to affix to album cover and corresponding record. Aim always for the same place on the cover, such as the top left corner, and label Side One only of the record. People with a little sight might not have to label all recordings, just those having print that blends with a decorative background. Vertical racks with dividers can allow for arrangement according to artist or type of music.

Still on the recording track, a clue to the identity of cassettes saves you from popping them into the machine to hear what's there. Cassette organizers, vertical files, or those that open like a book with pockets for storage, are convenient. Some people keep cassettes for music, to record information, or correspond on tape.

Print books and magazines can still be part of your world, although your vision doesn't extend to reading the body of the text. Large print or Braille can enable you to pull a title quickly from the shelf. Paperbacks or magazines have covers thick enough to bear Braille dots written directly upon them. That measure saves tape and time.

I heard about a partially sighted insurance salesman who relies on certain references frequently. She marks the sections of books with different colors of tape so that locating a specific reference can be done more quickly. Her file drawers are also easy to spot, being labeled in large print.

A student who is legally blind thumbs through a dictionary often. He uses sturdy alphabet tabs of varying colors for immediately finding a desired letter. Sighted people don't find such modifications offensive. In fact, they come to depend upon these aids, too.

Picking out the correct color of thread can save you stitches in time, with br for brown, wh for white, and bk for black being enough for a label. People having a little sight can become confused by some pastel or dark colors. They should mark enough to guard themselves from error. An option for people who don't use print or Braille is lining spools on spindles.

Shoe polish is another substance that doesn't allow much margin for error. Once, I energetically swabbed brown wax onto black shoes. They never looked the same, despite persistent scrubbing. Moral of the shoe polish fiasco: Buy different colors in varying shaped containers, slapping on some tape. Do something to be sure, not sorry. Sure, you can fall back on neutral, but that doesn't cover the scuffs. Not always certain of where you're putting your feet down, you are bound to have plenty of such scrapes.

Typing teachers will groan and glower at this one. A dot of Hi Marks on the letters f and j will keep your fingers resting on the home keys. Also mark the numbers 4 and 7. (Secretaries I have surveyed all 'fess up to looking at numbers.) As you will discover in Chapter 18, typists don't look at the keys. But those seconds saved in checking to be sure your hands haven't wandered from the home row add up. People with low vision find this trick especially helpful, because their eyes can remain on the copy.

You certainly don't want to shuffle through cards in your wallet when looking for the Visa or Blue Cross card. Again, if you can't see them, you can either alphabetically arrange them or mark them with a Braille or large print label. Your indicator should be placed on the opposite side of the embossing so that it can go through a machine.

Your labeling requirements obviously will vary according to personal possessions, life style, work habits, amount of vision, and help available to you. The object of this project is to make what you need to identify within your perception as easy as possible. Naturally, the less sight you have, the more adaptations you may devise. But usable sight doesn't automatically mean instant recognition. You can, in many cases, conserve time and energy by not scrambling for the magnifier, glasses, or flashlight. Once the identifying mark is there, it will remain in place for a long time.

Before buying new appliances, check to see if any are manufactured with premarked dials. Sears and G.E. are starting to offer this option. Because local dealers may not know of it, ask them to find out. The American Foundation for the Blind markets a variety of kitchen appliances such as electric frypans, blenders, and crockpots with tactile settings. However, this bonus touches up the price—it costs virtually pennies to make your own.

The broadest method of labeling is, of course, organization.

Snoop around anything that resembles a clutter control shop—there is one by that name in our area. You will discover organizers for the kitchen, bathroom, and bedroom. They include shelves for storing cans or spices, revolving trivets, toolboxes, racks, and storage chests. Prices at such stores may run high, so don't overlook finding the same idea less expensively marketed in a hardware or dime store. Office supply, stationery stores, and artist supply shops offer a wide range of colored tapes, stick-on labels, tags, tabs, and decals. If you can see it, feel it, and remember what it stands for, you're on the path to less confusion and fewer mistakes. There is no failsafe method that guarantees you won't slip up again. Trying a few techniques cuts down on frustration, although you should never let yourself become a slave to labeling. There are too many other incidents in life about which you can laugh, cry, or scream.

Chapter 11

HOW ODD

ONE SHOE'S BROWN, THE OTHER'S BLACK

G us is a totally blind programmer who works for a large company. Like other businessmen, suit and tie are his daily garb for work. It was one of those mornings when Gus, then a bachelor, was having a race with the clock. The tick-tock had the upper hand because he had forgotten to pull out the alarm. Upon reaching work, he found out first from his secretary that he was wearing one brown shoe and one black shoe. Many colleagues at different intervals throughout the day thought they were breaking the news.

Gus gave them a stock reply: "I have a pair just like them at home."

If you add vinegar instead of cooking oil to cake mix batter, or brush your teeth with shaving cream, nobody but you knows. Unless you decide to remain forever in blue jeans and T-shirts, a slip-up in what you wear will be noticed by the world. Like it or not, a blind person and what he wears attracts more attention than a sighted counterpart. So that you won't feel like hiding your feet under the desk or perhaps your entire self because you blew it with a mix-up instead of a mix-and-match, here are a few hints.

If you have enough vision to distinguish colors, scratch this problem off your list of concerns. Some legally blind people, although having good usable sight, are color blind—the trait seems mostly characteristic of men but is transmitted by women. Provided that your color discrimination is good, add extra assurance with a well-lit bedroom and closet. When some families of shades leave you bewildered, zero in on them for separating or color coding.

I have met a totally blind professional man whose wife faithfully lays out his clothes for the next day, right down to tie and socks. Since both are happy with this arrangement, I'd be inclined to leave well enough alone. But if his helpmate should be away from the house for a few days, or he is out of town on his own, his possible color combos could end up as trend setters or clock stoppers.

The rule of thumb for labeling household items, whenever necessary, also applies to clothing and shoes. That with which you cover your body, however, becomes a part of you, more so than items used infrequently. You associate color of garments with their cut, fabric, length of sleeve, buttons, stitching, cuffs, lapel widths, and hundreds of variations worked into differing styles. Such subtleties become give-aways regarding color identification. For instance, your gray slacks are gaberdine while the corduroys are brown. The blue print blouse has ruffles on the front, but the solid kelly green is tailored.

Quandaries come when the feel-alikes don't look alike. An ounce of prevention can be worth a pound of puzzling. The next time you're tempted to buy two garments made exactly the same but in different colors, you are headed for possible disastrous consequences. But you may be a risk taker or not want to send the undistinguishable brown and green slacks to the charity drive. You can save face and clothes.

Let's start from the bottom up. Trying not to be chauvinistic, I must admit that women tend to ride the color and shade range more than men, so their wardrobe can be more of a challenge. If you have two pairs of shoes that look alike but are different colors, separate them in a shoebag or shoe rack so they aren't near each other. As an extra precaution, put a piece of tape on the inner sole, just beyond the heel. Its placement won't irritate your foot. The other pair remains unmarked. Naturally, you should check before shoeing yourself for the day. If you're likely to buy particular shoes to wear with a special outfit, you may accumulate a large shoe wardrobe you don't wear often. You'd better label boxes with Braille or large print or you'll be somewhere in red shoes and a purple dress.

Vertical shoebags that hang from closet rods, aligning shoes in paired pockets, allow quick discrimination of footwear by touch. These arrangements permit you to work your way from top to bottom, knowing that each set of pockets holds only one pair. Horizontal shoebags with four or more compartments don't check out as quickly by touch.

"I don't have enough room in my closet for shoebags," complained Louise, a homemaker who shared coveted closet space with her husband. "I store them in boxes and stack them on the shelf above."

"How would you find the silver sandals you want to wear to a cocktail party?" I asked.

Louise had to chuckle about the corner into which she boxed herself. She reported that she pulled over a chair and painstakingly examined the contents of every shoebox until she struck gold—or silver in this case. Louise resolved the space crunch by investing in a couple of shoe racks placed on the closet floor. (She saw them as more convenient than labeling boxes.) To avoid the remote chance that she would put on two odd shoes, she arranged them so that least-alikes were next to each other, with tennis shoes next to dress shoes and bedroom slippers next to everyday shoes.

Line up your footgear under the bed and you're asking for chaos, even if you see to tell them apart. They're likely to be kicked awry in the first place, and you will end up sorting them out on your belly among the lint balls. Someday someone (maybe even you) will be cleaning under there. The cleaner will be kicking as the shoes scatter like feathers in a wind storm.

Socks and hosiery can create more mix-ups if you're not on guard. Men frequently find it expedient to buy socks all the same in a neutral color such as charcoal gray or black. Fashion-conscious gents probably wish to coordinate socks with suit and slacks. A box with compartments can keep your color scheme straight, especially if somebody else does the laundry. The first row on the left could be for green (either solid or predominant), the second for brown, and the third for blue. Even if you remember the system, don't expect your launderer to know the code. Mark your divisions in print. If you launder for yourself, buy one color of a certain texture, another with a different feel. Pin them together when you drop them into the hamper. You can buy Sock Locks from some supermarkets or K–Mart. They are small rings through which you pull socks to keep them from separating.

You can color code with small brass safety pins that won't rust in the laundry. One horizontal pin could indicate blue, vertical shows brown, diagonal black. Leave the pin in the sock and attach its mate before dropping into the hamper. The American Foundation for the Blind offers aluminum tags with colors stamped in Braille, but these kits consist of ten colors, two tags each. Besides, not many men I know wear pink. French knots or other stitching can represent colors, which is great if you happen to be handy with needle and thread. The pin method works for other garments just as well.

Women have an easier route in that pantyhose are an almost universal type of hosiery. Those in neutral shades are the best bet. Those colored hose worn with particular outfits can be separated into bags that are labeled or hung on the same hanger with the corresponding garment. Compartments in hosiery chests also work. A sighted friend warned me of her mismatch. She was in the habit of picking up knee-high nylons worn under slacks. She bought them at occasional dime store sales. She collected an array of shades. While at work one day, she looked down and wondered if anyone else had noticed that one ankle was rosy pink and the other taupe. Moral: When you buy a bunch of knee-highs, get 'em alike. Being so persnickity about that minute detail of your costume isn't worth the effort of sorting when those with good sight can't readily distinguish shade with hose in hand.

Before I finish socking it to you, some ladies like to save pantyhose with runs to wear under slacks. Again, good vision isn't always a guarantee of run detection. Put one pin on the waistband. As soon as you discover the run, designate the pair this way and store them in a for-slacks-only bag.

Moving up, we don't encounter many indecisions with men's

underwear. It can be flamboyant with bright colors and inscriptions. For the male, out of sight, out of mind. (Fellows do like to be cautious about white undershorts beneath white slacks.)

Lingerie isn't such an easy question for ladies. Slips and bras, camisoles, or chemises should match in light or dark the outfit to be worn, if it is at all see-through. You can separate darks from lights in different drawers or put them in hanging baskets in the closet. Tailored lingerie for darks and lacy for lights is another differentiation. Or use pins on one set but not on the other.

Outer wear, which the eyes of the world fall upon first, is the biggest question. When it comes to classifying which shirts to wear with a man's suit, you can allow the hanging suit to be a marker. All shirts to the left can be worn with that suit. Matching or contrasting ties for that suit can hang on a tie bar to the right. If you have shirts that complement more than one suit, pin color coding can help. Always put the marker pin in the same place, such as inside the right seam near the hem. You will automatically reach for that area when making a color check. To show that a shirt will go with blue suit and brown, put another pin inside the left seam.

Whether you're marking blouse, skirt, slacks, sweater, or T-shirts, keep the number and position of pins consistent. If horizontal means blue for you, then your blue indicators on all garments should be horizontal. Inside the fly on the right is a good place for slacks. On the underside of the tie, an inch or so from the end, is a good spot for a marker.

Suppose you think tactile markings too much bother. Hanging go-togethers—one hooked through the hanger of the other—is another alternative, although somewhat restrictive. I fell into a rut that way. I didn't vary outfits because I didn't mix and match a coordinated salmon print blouse with skirt and vest. A friend suggested that blouse and vest would look good with a brown skirt and beige slacks. Familiarity can bring a restricted wardrobe if you don't seek a color-conscious helper once in a while. But before expanding your fashion frontier, consult with somebody prior to being daring. Even if you think you're safe with a solid neutral shade such as gray or beige with another color, your ingenuity may pass by just looking OK, but might not be the combination you would choose if you could see it clearly.

Accessories such as handbags and scarves can be tricky. Wrong choices can upset, not offset your outfit. Again, sorting and storage can save your appearance. One partially sighted woman can't tell dark shades of green, blue, and brown. So that she won't burst her memory bank, she tucks an index card with the color's name into each purse. Wise lady—why worry about remembering that the purse is navy blue when she puts it away at the end of the summer?

Outdoor wear isn't hard to identify because we use those few winter jackets and coats repeatedly. Hats, scarves, mittens, and gloves can vary enough by texture so that they need no label attention. Because my hands turn to ice with the first frost, I buy two pairs of identical mittens in the fall. If I lose or abuse one, I have an immediate replacement. To keep mittens and gloves together on the closet shelf, rubber band them together. They could be tucked inside coat pockets, too. When in doubt about matching scarves, put them on the same hanger.

Jewelry isn't an accessory you want to mix: One gold earring and its double in silver isn't exactly fashionable. My solution isn't particularly decorative, nor is my jewelry on display. A sighted friend suggested a small fisherman's tackle chest, about a foot square. Drawers that measure two inches by three inches are handy for storing go-togethers such as a necklace and matching bracelet. A large drawer at the bottom catches odd pieces. I have an earring tree for primarily gold and silver, keeping each color on a separate section. To prevent necklaces and chains from tangling, I put them on a device made for that purpose. It looks like a clothes hanger with knobs for suspending necklaces—one side for gold, the other for silver. Having jewelry of a variety of colors is interesting, but more than my ingenuity and time can tolerate. If you're more venturous, store it in containers with compartments that you can memorize or label. Then you won't have mix-ups when you're striving for match-ups.

Lest you be caught with your pants down or dress ballooning, let me belt you with this thought. The male gender lucks out again (or leads a dull life, however you look at it) by wearing brown or black belts, sometimes white. It's easy to buy two basic belts with identifiers such as buckles, texture, or width that aren't alike. Women's dresses, suits, and skirts often include a belt to be worn with the garment, mostly for the sake of accent. This is all well and good unless the belt and garment part company on the way to the laundry or cleaner, or your garment falls on the floor and it becomes a mystery as to which belt belongs to it. If you don't want to play match-the-belt games, buy a metallic gold and/or silver belt. Either will complement an outfit and will eliminate the guess work of which goes with what.

Most mismatchings are coincidental and accidental. Curious to see how many colleagues at work would mention a hideous (and intentional) combination, I let my warped sense of humor run rampant one April Fool's Day. Atop a blue and green plaid skirt I wore a purple tweed jacket—truly enough to turn a thousand ships the other way. Our secretary nabbed me as soon as I took off my coat. But hers was the only voice of disapproval. The woman pouring coffee for me in the cafeteria nearly spilled it at the sight of that startling ensemble. Gasps from others were sure signs of their notice, but no one else dared bridge that delicate gap. Unable to stand myself too long, I changed into a matching jacket later that morning. I had my laughs, but also proved my point. It may be that not even your closest co-workers or friends will tell you that something is strikingly amiss. Not wanting to be caught with something flagrantly awry in your dress, you might ask those close to you to discreetly let you know about any miscues. It might be so glaring that you wouldn't wish to appear before the boss or stand in front of the P.T.A. without correcting your mistake first. Not able to remedy the situation right away, you could at least try to stay out of view as much as possible. It could be as simple as removing earrings that don't go together or sending somebody to the dime store for a pair of socks.

Again, specialty shops provide ideas for organizing closets and drawers. There are racks that stand on the floor with dowels for hanging pants, baskets for underwear and stockings, and boxes for sweaters. Dime store notions counters or sewing shops offer an array of sew-on or iron-on tape, alternatives to marking pins. (Different shapes could represent different colors.) However you manage your wardrobe and accessories, the well-dressed man or woman announces to the world awareness that eyes are upon him or her.

Chapter 12

YOU NEEDN'T SHIP OUT
WHEN YOU HAVE TO SHOP

Y our name isn't Mother Hubbard, but like the rest of us, your cupboards become bare, clothes tacky and outdated, furniture succumbs to the ravages of time. We've covered handling money and identifying what possessions you have. What if you are out of milk and nobody's home, or you yen for a new coat or are in the market for a couch?

Let's hit groceries first. You can survive without additional clothes and furniture, but starving is the pits. Just as among sighted people, there are several types of shoppers: nevers, occasionals, and do-it-for-the-households. If you can't physically get to the store, or wouldn't be able to carry back more than a package of yeast if you could, you'll obviously depend upon others to go to the store. As a back-up, you might make an agreement with a neighbor who would come through in a pinch if your regular shoppers aren't available. Despite the number of large, impersonal supermarkets that operate on a buy-and-carry principle, a few small neighborhood stores are holdouts, still practicing home delivery. Even though your favorite neighborhood store doesn't offer this service generally, you could approach the owner to learn whether an exception would be made in your case. You may not get your order until one of the employees is on his way home, but at least the goods will be coming.

Burt and Bessie are a couple in their midsixties. He is totally blind and has a heart condition; she is severely diabetic and unable to read well enough to check labels for his low-sodium diet or her diabetic diet. This couple is physically unable to go regularly to the market and neither can risk ingesting the wrong kinds of food. Both receive a hot meal at lunchtime from Meals at Home, a federally subsidized program through which volunteers deliver wholesome meals that follow dietary restrictions. The program is also known as Meals on Wheels. Because proper nutrition is so essential to health, and because many individuals would otherwise be unable to live at home when they cannot shop or cook, they are eligible for the program. You can locate such a program through a community service agency, public health department, or major church in your area. Your doctor must fill out a form stating your need for such a service.

Many senior citizen residences and organizations bus their members to a supermarket and/or shopping center once a week. Although you are not a member of such a group, they may be willing to let you come aboard. So what if you are committed to shop only on Wednesday afternoons; a trip there and back is better than walking or taking the city bus.

Perhaps your jaunts to the store are a once-in-a-while event for a few items. If you walk, you can't lug home vittles for a family of ten for a week. Even a half gallon of milk and a dozen oranges can give you an arm ache, especially if one hand holds a cane or dog guide's harness. Try a canvas shopping bag or back pack—the kind with straps that fasten around your waist equalizes weight. A four-wheel folding cart is easier to pull or push than the two-wheel model.

Unless you consider shopping an outing or social occasion, you want to get into and out of a supermarket as quickly as possible. If you have enough sight and know the layout of displays and departments, you will carry on as does anyone else. When it takes you twice as long to locate a box of frozen peas and your fingers become frostbitten in the freezer compartment, you're wasting your time and not proving anything except that you can withstand pain. When you can't find an item readily, follow the example of Winny, the seventy-five-year-old with poor sight. She explains to a nearby customer that she can't always see well enough to read prices and labels. Zap—she has in hand that package of sharp cheddar cheese and is on her way. If she overlooks jelly in an aisle, she stops a stock clerk with the same explanation.

Maybe your vision is so poor you couldn't find a fifty-pound bag of potatoes unless you tripped over it. What do you do if your grocery trip is solo? Sharon, a housewife with three teens and a husband to shop for every week, didn't inform her hubby that her rapidly failing vision was not sufficient for this task. As he, an avowed supermarket avoider, waited in the car, she painstakingly maneuvered a cart up and down the aisles, poring over cans and cartons with the strongest magnifier she could find. She started bringing home tomato paste instead of tomato sauce, and never knew about bargains she missed. She always looked for familiar packaging.

"Sharon," I urged, "if your husband isn't inclined to grocery shop, why don't you ask the manager to assign stock clerks to accompany you? They know merchandise because they're refilling shelves constantly. Besides, those kids are happier helping a customer than stamping sixty-nine cents on cans of kidney beans."

Never having thought of this avenue, Sharon approached the manager. She told him that finding specific items was now beyond her and that assistance of a stock clerk could make a world of difference to her. With the problem openly stated and a solution offered, the manager immediately acquiesced.

"I'd be glad to have a stock clerk go around with you," he said. "When you come into the store, stand by the cashiers. As soon as they see you, they can call a clerk."

Sharon's first jaunt with a stock clerk in tow was a real test for them both. Having run out of practically everything, her purchases totaled nearly $200. They went up and down each aisle, the clerk pulling the cart as Sharon held onto the push bar. Although he had her handwritten list, he reminded her of general displays that they passed, just in case she forgot to note something. Her helper found it a diversion as I predicted.

As she left, he quipped, "Before you come in to stock up for the summer camp next time, call me. I'll just take one of everything off the shelf for you."

I felt confident that this suggestion would work for Sharon

because I tried it when moving into a new neighborhood. Pleased with the cooperation of the supermarket staff, I wrote to the store's main headquarters, sending a copy to the local office. As I knew it would, that letter reached the supermarket I patronize. Added to the personal thanks was praise from above. Now if I stop to shop with a friend, stock clerks still ask if I need a hand.

A stock clerk's familiarity with sales and in-store coupons can save you money, so don't hesitate to inquire about specials or generic items. Your assistant will gladly tear out coupons from the flier on weekly specials if you ask about particulars while you're shopping.

Another service you can take advantage of is the bell to summon the butcher. He is most able to find desirable cuts of meat, and would be willing to slice or cut meat for you. When I buy steak, I request that the steaks be cut into individual servings. He will also cut up a whole chicken for you, or give advice on types of roasts.

Produce managers can select fresh fruit and vegetables; the person behind the delicatessen counter will be happy to fill you in on varieties of prepared salads, special cold cuts, and pastry. Just ask and you will know.

When picking up dairy products, ask for the expiration date. One student bought bargain containers of yogurt, only to bring them home and find them spoiled. Your helper may not remember to look for the expiration date.

Regardless of soaring food costs, you still have to eat. Food co-ops may cut your expenses somewhat. Such groups buy in quantity, passing savings to members. They vary widely in merchandise, with some offering prepackaged bags of fresh fruit or vegetables and others letting you choose for yourself. Some sell dairy products and meat, while others do not. They are sponsored by churches and local community groups. You can pay off a percentage of your food bill by working at the co-op. A totally blind man defrayed his grocery bill by bagging several hours a month. You can get more information about food co-ops and other forms of cooperative buying by calling toll-free: *1-800-424-2481.*

Other blind people have found different approaches to the grocery shopping dilemma. One totally blind couple phones in a list to the local supermarket. After a stock clerk gathers the items, a friend picks up the purchases for them. A partially sighted university professor tells me she calls a small store that delivers. Prices are higher, but she'd rather pay a little more for the convenience. Another blind woman goes with her neighbors, who are faithful Sunday morning shoppers. I used to pay neighbors to shop for me when they did their own marketing.

The system of stopping by the check-out cashier works at the dime store and hardware store, too. I'd be as much at a loss tracking down pliers or rubber bands as I would be digging up a can of crabmeat.

Trial and error shopping ventures, mine and others, taught me a few lessons never learned in the classroom. When possible, shop at the same stores. As employees come to know you, they are more likely to step forward with a hand. A person's name is music to his ears. When an employee is helping you, ask his name. Use it a time or two during the encounter. Try not to stop during the busiest times such as Saturday afternoon. When the staff has been particularly accommodating, a note to the manager adds even more pride to the service provided. Everyone appreciates recognition.

Shopping for clothes isn't necessarily a whole new game. Many sighted people, especially women, feel more comfortable with somebody else—it can even be entertaining. If you're lucky enough to have one or more clothes hounds among your friends, invite that friend to accompany you on a spree. These folks usually enjoy spending money, even someone else's. They have a quick eye for sizing up a rack of garments and selecting those appropriate for you, from which you can choose. Of course you should discuss with your companion price ranges, color preferences, and occasions for the clothes, such as work, evening wear, and sports. Leave yourself open for checking out new styles, colors, or fabrics that you may not have considered. But when it comes to making the actual decision, don't let anyone con or bully you. When it just doesn't feel right, remember: You're the one paying for and putting on that garment.

Some partially sighted folks are able to shop quite capably by themselves. Their pitfalls might be in reading price tags, sizes, or determining exact colors. When in doubt, ask another customer or sales clerk. What a shock and embarrassment to bring a jacket to the cashier thinking it was marked $39.95, only to discover that it is $89.95. Another disappointment is to think you have picked out a pair of navy slacks; taking them home, you find the pants are black.

A certain camaraderie exists among shoppers. They are usually more than willing to come forth with information upon hearing, "I have poor vision and can't see this tag," or "I'm not sure of this color. Could you help me out?"

Some stores, especially discount, are scarcer on salespeople than the proverbial snowball in July. If you frequent these stores, take a companion to back up your choices—it's a safer bet. You save yourself the confusion of locating merchandise scattered in an expansive area or tucked into obscure corners. Some sales are final, with no turning back after a buy, giving you yet another reason to go with someone else.

Your heart may be set on matching or complementing a garment already in your wardrobe. Take that item with you. It's a gamble to depend on your memory, or that of your companion, to team up a matching skirt for your lavender sweater or a shirt for your plaid sports jacket. Colors can take on a different hue under fluorescent lights as opposed to sunlight.

A salesperson who waits on you regularly and who is honest in appraising clothing for you is a precious find. Such relationships grow out of visiting a store often enough for this employee to know your tastes, budget, and needs. I discovered several such gems in my travels. I trust their judgment enough to allow me to shop confidently alone. One of these saleswomen has so much integrity that she will advise me against buying a dress that she says doesn't do anything for me. She may give the go-ahead on a less expensive suit. After making a decision, I ask her advice about jewelry and accessories to wear with the outfit. She reads to me laundry and dry cleaning instructions. Occasionally she calls to tip me off about a shipment of change-of-season clothes or a shouldn't-miss sale. Salespeople probably won't think of these extras, but are glad to comply when you ask for them.

Clothing dollars often go further at a thrift or resale shop. When your budget requires a tight rein, quality of goods is often better than at a discount store. Selections are not as good, though. They are frequently under the auspices of churches or other charitable organizations, although some are commercial enterprises. Goodwill Industries and the Salvation Army also have outlets. Because these shops usually are not open every day, you should call ahead. The pace is not as harried as at discount stores, and you're likely to get assistance from the staff if you need it.

Do you stand among the ranks of Christmas shopping procrastinators? Jostling throngs are no place for a blind person, even one who braves the masses alone. Remember that friends are busy taking care of their own last-minute errands. By setting and sticking to Thanksgiving as your deadline, you can sit back in smug satisfaction and security and let the others fight it out.

When shopping for the biggies such as appliances, carpeting, draperies, etc., the phone is the first step for ferreting out best buys. When making initial inquiries, note the salesperson's name with that of the store. By planning ahead (not always possible when the washer emits its last gasp) you can ask if your intended purchase will be on sale in the near future. Alert others to check print media for you. In some locales you can call a service to ask if stores in your area will be having specials on what you need. Call the Chamber of Commerce to see if such a service is available.

Don't hesitate to insist upon a fair hands-on demonstration when buying an appliance. You should be looking for ease of operation, dealer's awareness of possible adaptation by the manufacturer for tactile markings, and the possibility of your own raised markings if necessary. For example, dials that turn a pointer under glass, or a porcelain stove top with no feelable delineation of burners, are not for some blind people. Run through the settings once on the showroom floor—you can memorize them later. Pull out the refrigerator and oven shelves to be sure you can put them back. You're going to live with that appliance for the next ten years or more. You ought to feel comfortable with it. By explaining to the salesman that you will need a little more time, he won't be standing on one foot, wondering why you don't come to a conclusion.

Be sure you understand warranty, payment terms, and local places for repair. Before signing any contract or agreement, have someone read it to you if you can't read it.

A Sears salesman went out of his way when I bought a washing machine. My inclination headed me toward a push-button model with eight cycles. He frankly informed me that most people used only three or four cycles and that the less costly model worked just as well. Being relieved that he was attuned to my needs by his advice about marking the dial, I sent a note to Sears's main offices commending his thoughtfulness. A copy landed in his personnel file and probably helped in a promotion he received six months later.

When furniture or draperies are in your foreseeable future, it's not a good move to go it alone when shopping. Naturally, your tastes and price range are guidelines, but color and accent of existing decor are key factors that almost demand good vision. Often other family members will chime in on the choice. Otherwise, choose a friend who can take a good look at the room to which you are adding. You need to have an intuitive sense that this companion has an eye and some experience in home decoration.

Another source of ideas is an interior decorator. He will provide free service if you plan to buy from the store he represents. Trained to assess color schemes, fabrics, and furniture designs and arrangements, these people can offer invaluable advice by suggesting ideas you wouldn't have considered previously. You may not be aware of all the possibles on the market. Not only can he point out specific eye-appealing features, he also can tell you about such practical matters as what furniture will bear up best under kids or what colors of carpeting are least likely to show dog hair.

I went this route recently when I bought woven wooden window shades. I explained to the decorator on the phone that I was blind, and would be relying on her to help choose window coverings that would complement the rustic decor of the room. I figured forewarning was fair. She wouldn't be floored when I greeted her at the door. Besides, she had more time to think about the samples she would bring. Because I expected this costly investment to last many years, I invited a friend to lend her expertise on color and pattern, decisions I felt unable to make alone. Although comfort and convenience rank highest, I cannot forget esthetic appeal for people who live with or visit us.

My great adventure into this realm came when I thought a painting would set off the stark white wall behind the sofa. In mind was a basic concept of the sun setting over a lake, sailboat in the horizon, and rocks on the shore. I called a local artist to see if she could execute this imaginary painting. When I told her I was blind, she paused, and then wondered,

"Why do you want a picture? You said you couldn't see at all."

I told her I had a little sight at one time, and a vivid memory of color. She visited my home, sized up the living room and exact place for the proposed painting. She agreed to have it framed and hung.

Several weeks later she reported that she had two paintings done. I could choose either one or opt to buy neither. Again I called upon trusted friends. They unanimously picked one after holding both against the wall.

It must have been a good choice. The artist, happy with my friends' commendations, hung the painting herself. I've had compliments on it ever since, and a good story to boot.

Mail order shopping is another route you might like to sample. You may be able to peruse catalogs yourself or find someone who is both descriptive and patient. Naturally, you'll follow the same common-sense advice issued to all mail order customers. One word of warning: Once you order from some companies, your name is on their mailing list forever. If you don't want it there, make this clear when you write for a specific item.

A few firms still sell directly to customers in their homes. These include Amway, Stanley, Tupperware, and Fuller Brush. Products tend to cost somewhat more, a price you pay for not stepping out the door. Some food plans claim they have satisfied blind customers by making periodic deliveries of large quantities of food. I know no one who has tried this service.

Even if shopping isn't your bag, it's a necessary evil in the life of most of us. My final words of wisdom: Get to know merchants and salespersons if possible, and look for friends who have good taste and like to shop. When alone, don't let false pride in the guise of independence lead you to wrong judgments. Remember, too, by not depending on family members or the same friends to always help, you allow them freedom to go about their own business. Your solo forays may add to your self-esteem.

Chapter 13

CLEANLINESS IS NEXT TO
GODLINESS—OR IS IT?

I never realized housekeeping was so much work," mused Tom. At fifty-nine, he took an early retirement because his low vision couldn't meet the demands of his mechanical engineering job without many accommodations. He and his wife chose to reverse roles because she was anxious to resume her nursing career.

Many students have become homemakers so their partners could enter the work force. They pitch in as chief cook and bottle washer, as well as home tidier. For some this is the first time ever. For those who have lost their sight, it is the first time to manage such tasks with decreased or no vision. Like Tom, they find keeping house occasionally an eye opener, but almost always manageable.

Starting in the kitchen seems most natural. It's the area where everything gets messy and out of order regularly, and it is the last place you want to let go. Busing those dishes from table to sink is easiest with a tray. As you clear the table, keep your hands low, with fingers curved. This way, you'll be less likely to overturn a glass or send coffee cups skittering. As you organize to wash by hand, put glasses and cups toward the back of the counter. (It's a good idea to instill this habit into other family members who leave glasses on the counter's edge or in the sink.) It's hard to see a clear glass; when you don't see one, there's the risk of sending it to a shattering end. Separate sharp knives and kitchen shears from the rest of the silverware—it's too easy to cut yourself when reaching for a handful to drop into the dishpan.

As you begin, wash, rinse, and dry breakables such as glasses, fine china, and stemware first. Potential hazards that are sharp are next to get out of the way. You can go at the rest of the task in relative peace. Even if you let dishes dry in a drainer, it's wise to dry and put away the fragiles and sharp implements. When reaching into the rack later to put dishes away, you won't break precious dishes or cut yourself.

To ensure that the last dregs of spaghetti sauce or stew have been scoured from pots and pans, rinse under hot water and examine the bottom and sides with your fingers. You'll know by touch if you didn't get it all. Vegetable oil sprays such as Pam®, applied before cooking, make this job of scrubbing simpler. Consult with the cook so you won't spend half the evening scrubbing utensils.

Then there are those fortunates who have a dishwasher. You probably won't run it after every meal. Systematic filling from back to front saves hunting for empty space as it nears its capacity. Placing covers beside dishes and lids next to their matching container speeds up the putting-away process. As you fill the silverware holder, aim fork tines, points of knives, and kitchen shears down to avoid reaching for a nick instead of a knife. By unloading clean dishes first onto your trusty tray, you can assemble and return to cupboards and drawers the dishes and silverware that belong in each. It saves time by putting cups back all together into one cupboard, bowls in another, and plates onto a different shelf, rather than randomly reaching back and forth. Remember the open door of the dishwasher—it's a blind-trap that is one of the most shin-shattering blows you can inflict upon yourself.

Garbage disposals have a propensity for chewing up silverware and anything else that bypasses the rubber guard. Check inside before turning it on. (A handful of baking soda eliminates foul odors.) Trash cans are also responsible for the disappearance of silverware. Check plates before scraping them into the trash. Also examine before pitching newspapers in which vegetable peelings are wrapped. Your silverware collection will last longer if you take these precautions.

Stains, especially those in the sink, escape detection by touch or the watchful eye of the partially sighted. Ask someone if you're removing them completely. If the answer is negative and kitchen cleanser doesn't seem enough, try a paste of baking soda and water for stainless steel. My sink is porcelain and porous. I make a solution of a quarter-cup laundry bleach and water, allowing it to soak in the sink for an hour. The neighbor with whom I checked gave it a clean bill.

If you wrap a piece of dry paper towel around the faucet, take a firm grip and move it back and forth, it will cut down on soap residue. By dipping an old toothbrush into soapy water, you can reach those hard-to-get crevices and grooves on faucets and appliance dials. Rubbing alcohol will make chrome gleam.

Cups also collect unfeelable, unsightly stains from coffee or tea. Baking-soda paste or toothpaste removes such stains safely, even from fine china. Commercial cleaners can be too harsh.

Your coffeemaker will produce a better brew if thoroughly cleaned periodically. Running drip makers through their cycle with white vinegar removes residue of coffee oils. Commercial cleaners such as Dip-it® or a solution of a tablespoon of baking soda in the water are ideal for percolators. Although you may not see the buildup, you'll taste the difference after cleaning.

Cleaning the refrigerator is one of those prices we pay for the convenience. It helps to allow the supply of food to exhaust itself to the lowest possible degree. Refrigerators that don't automatically defrost require this procedure three or four times a year; otherwise they work twice as hard because of ice buildup. Pans of hot water or an electric defroster speed up thawing. Several layers of newspaper on the floor around the appliance absorb dripping water and catch crumbs, but count on a mess whatever you do. As I empty shelf by shelf, I put the contents into small cartons so that returning the items will be a more organized process. Although some people use baking soda and water for wiping the interior, I rely upon dish detergent and water, rinsing with the baking soda solution. Detergent gives an extra wallop to the sticky spots. An open bowl of baking soda inside the refrigerator will keep it smelling fresh for months.

Before undertaking this project, be sure that you know how to turn off the appliance and return the dial to its original setting.

You should also be able to remove and return shelves. Mechanically inept, I wrestled with shelves until I called a neighbor's son—I was totally tired and frustrated at the end of the ordeal. Oh, and vacuum the grill at the back once or twice a year, since the coils collect dust and the dirt cuts down on cooling.

Cleaning ovens is another challenge. Before using chemicals, you should understand their directions. You'll need to open windows wide, so it's not a project for the dead of winter. I usually hire someone to do this chore for me, but I do know of totally blind people who do it themselves. Soaking racks in a solution of ammonia and water in the bathtub is a good start. Since you won't be able to feel encrusted food or grease as well while wearing rubber gloves, it's a good idea to have somebody check your job before you call it quits.

Such preventive measures as wiping up oven spills as soon as possible save a lot of work later. When you know that grease spattered or the pie ran over, a handful of salt on the bottom metal plate cuts smoke and helps absorb the spill. Wipe the oven out with a damp cloth when it is cool.

If you abide by the spring and fall cupboard clean-out regimen, the same grouping, shelf-by-shelf, facilitates putting back. Attack one cupboard at a time if you haven't enough cartons or counter space to accommodate foodstuffs, pots, and pans. It's also an opportunity to discover long-forgotten spices, old boxes of cake mix, and other commodities that have outlived their shelf life.

As for the kitchen floor, I'm a hands-and-kneeser myself. Before getting down to scrubbing, you have to remove excess dirt. Many folks have an electric broom, received as a Christmas present five years ago, stowed unused in the basement. One student, the housewife with three teenagers, fell into this category. She was complaining that the kids tracked in gravel from the driveway. She had considered this appliance more of a nuisance than it was worth. Sharon is now a strong supporter of electric brooms. It picks up gravel, mud, dog hair, cookie crumbs, and even the cup of sugar one of the kids dropped. Her husband installed a hook inside the pantry so she can grab it almost instantly.

If you don't have an electric broom and can afford one, look for the type with a container to be emptied after each use. You won't have to bother replacing disposable bags. Regina and Eureka make such machines. A heavy-duty electric broom will also be convenient for touch-ups on carpeting between vacuuming.

"I can't afford an electric broom," maintained Mary. "How can I sweep the floor and be sure I get all the dirt?"

It's down to the basics of broom and dustpan for Mary and many like her. I told her to sweep systematically. If the room is large, sweep up two piles instead of one — you'll lose part of the pile trekking from one end of the room to the other. Rely upon appliances, doorways, and windows as dividers for the sections if necessary. Gather your sweepings next to a wall so you're not trying to pick them up in an area without boundaries. Provided you can get onto your knees, a short-handled dustpan is more maneuverable. A whiskbroom allows you to be closer to the pile. By walking around the floor (if so inclined) in your bare feet, you'll discover any spots you missed.

Back to the nitty gritty of washing the floor. By approaching the task on your hands and knees, you'll be getting into corners and along edges. If this feat is beyond you and you must remain on your feet, a sponge mop with a squeezing device works well. Again, sectioning the floor with landmarks gives you orientation as you work. When you think the floor is particularly soiled, going over it again with fresh cleaning solution is a wise precaution.

Waxing the kitchen floor went out with hula hoops and yo-yos. But if you can't be convinced, go easy with floor wax. Apply liquid sparingly to your sponge or rag, making long, even strokes. To avoid streaking, buff with a dry rag in a few minutes. Never mind what the can says.

Accidents happen. When picking up pieces of broken glass or china falls to you, a broom and dustpan are safest, or you can loosely wrap a dish towel around your hand or wear rubber gloves. After retrieving larger shards, the electric broom is great for sucking up splinters. If you can, ask somebody to check the kitchen and surrounding area. Broken glass can fly surprisingly far.

When it comes to a choice among kitchen floorings — carpeting, inlaid linoleum or tile — cast your vote for linoleum or tile. Sure, it's a cinch to vacuum crumbs from tightly woven carpeting, but not so simple to be certain that you sopped up all the gravy or broken egg.

Dusting is another chore that could fall under your responsibility (or rag). It's one of those cases in which you can't be sure whether the furniture needs it this week or might slide by for another few days without attention. Resign yourself to the assumption that it is necessary. If family members are habitual junk collectors, leaving old newspapers, crayons, apple cores, and half-full ashtrays on top of tables, take a paper bag on your rounds so you won't make repeated trips to the trash can. Before applying the duster with vigor, check surfaces to see what unknowns lurk there. Some people bring a TV table along on the dusting tour on which they place objects before wiping surfaces. I just remove knickknacks to a place on nearby furniture. Some furniture polishes eventually leave a film. For those who feel compelled to apply something to wood, a lemon oil or tung oil occasionally applied will be enough treatment. Since you can't feel or may not see white rings or other discolorations left by glasses, this is another check point for a sighted person.

Cobwebs can accumulate in the least expected places. Corners attract them like magnets. They also gather high above hot air registers in the winter. Take a swipe with a rag on a broomstick every once in a while at the obvious places and con somebody into getting those you missed.

Before vacuuming, it's prudent to check for objects on the floor that could jam the machine. Crayons, coins, matchbooks, and bobby pins can do more damage than breaking a belt. If you can't see such hazards, make a patrol in slippered feet or better still, get someone else to pick up such offenders. Vacuuming boils down to dividing the room into small sections delineated by furniture, windows, or archways, just as you may have done in the kitchen. You may want to hold the extra vacuum cord in your free hand so you won't tangle it in the machine. (Some vacuum cleaners come with a retractable cord.) As you approach lamps, the TV, or other electric appliances, be wary of cords on the floor. Short, slow strokes of the vacuum are most effective. Overlap as you move to hit places you might miss. Heavily trafficked areas deserve an extra lick, and going over them vertically and horizontally will do it. Spots such as the one in front of the TV where the kids snack, or the area by the couch where the dog naps also need attention. Attachments are handy for giving furniture, carpet edges, and corners a once-over occasionally.

Stains on carpeting and furniture are difficult to remove completely if you don't see well enough to know when they're completely gone. It's another of those questions without an answer. When you know something has spilled, a mild commercial carpet cleaner won't hurt. Spray or rub it in gently, then blot with a towel. Fresh club soda works well for red wine and pet stains. When you can't see what you're doing, your best bet is to immediately wipe up what you can and issue an SOS.

Shampooing carpeting and furniture is another task I consider beyond the realm of possibility if your vision isn't adequate. If you can't afford professional cleaning of rugs and furniture, entice or hire a sighted person to do it with rented equipment. I've had the same man cleaning my carpets and furniture for years. I trust him so implicitly that I leave key and money with a neighbor. He comes while I am at work, does a thorough job, and leaves. I don't have the bother of dodging out-of-place furniture or rumpling up paper runners.

Making a bed is a task you don't forget after you lose your sight. By standing at the foot, you can determine the evenness of sheets, blankets, and bedspread without bouncing from one side to the other. Your spread might be one with a design that should be centered exactly. To hit your target, put a safety pin on the underside near the hem. Align it in the middle at the foot of the bed. When you turn the mattress, resign yourself to knocking everything off the dresser and nightstand unless you take a few precautions. You will get farther ahead by calmly removing lamp, clock radio, and whatever else may go sailing before you start flipping.

The bathroom is a place where you want to put forth more effort at cleanliness. A partially sighted woman I know scrubs the toilet with kitchen cleanser to be certain it is spotless. She uses tear-off plastic gloves to protect her hands. I'm a long brush and bleach user, paying special attention to porcelain around the drain and under the rim. You can feel scum in the sink and detect the bathtub ring by touch. I find liquid cleaners such as Fantastic®

or Formula 409® rinse more readily than cleansers. Don't forget to toss the shower curtain and bathroom rug into the laundry occasionally. Mildew accumulates around the shower because of poor ventillation. Keeping the curtain pulled aside and opening the window when the bathroom becomes steamy will eliminate that problem. Mirrors need wiping and treatment with window cleaner once in a while. They develop a soapy scum which you may not see and certainly can't feel.

Provided you have time, ambition, and are physically able, washing walls isn't beyond you, even if you are totally blind. Start with your tried-and-true cleaning solution, plenty of clean rags, and a sturdy stepladder. Work from the bottom up, wringing your rag well before washing. This method is less likely to cause streaking because dirty water won't be dripping down a soiled wall. Again, windows and doors can stand as landmarks. As you move along the wall, allow the width of your shoulders to serve as a measuring stick. Overlap your strokes to avoid missing spots. Change your water often and use a fresh rag. This will cut down the possibility of streaking.

I met a partially sighted woman who told me that a friend offered to clean one room a week during Lent as her form of penance. This well-intentioned friend was trying her best to say that the visually impaired lady's walls were dirty. With newly acquired visual aids, the partially sighted woman saw exactly what her penitential companion was talking about. She attacked the walls with gusto and suggested that the other woman seek some other form of penance.

You need not be the neighborhood streaker when it comes to washing windows. Your choice of a cleaner might be ammonia or vinegar and water, a wetting agent such as Basic H®, or a spray cleaner. My method is to wash each window horizontally and then vertically, running my rag-wrapped finger along edges and into corners. Again, frequent changes of water and rags seem to eliminate streaking. Drying with newspapers is another streak preventative. Three-track aluminum windows are tricky to replace. If you can't do it yourself, lean panes and screens beneath their corresponding windows. Someone else can put them back in seconds.

Curtain washing often coincides with window cleaning. If yours are almost dry when they come from the washer, fold them immediately and hang them up right away. They will finish drying on the rods and won't wrinkle. As I take down curtains, I return rods to their corresponding brackets so I won't have to sort them out while holding curtains ready to hang. Some curtains have a double hem. When you insert the rod, be sure it is wending its way through the second hem from the top. I wash curtains by the room, which is another organizing technique. Since I want to get them up quickly, there isn't much time to sort.

After undertaking such major projects as washing walls, windows, and curtains, you are fully entitled to seek someone with good vision to inspect your job. So what if you missed a patch on the dining room wall, streaked a pane, or left a couple of panels of curtains unevenly arranged? Expectations of your cleaning can't be those of a person with full vision. It takes your helper only a few minutes to rectify your error. What's important is that you accomplished a big task and it's a darned sight better than it was before you started. You ought to be proud of what you did, and for heaven's sakes don't apologize or mumble excuses for little mistakes.

It all comes out in the wash—or you hope it does. You might be doing your own laundry, or that for the entire household. If washer and dryer were unknown entities before now, have someone show you specifically how to operate them. Label dials if necessary. When you are doing family washing, you can't be expected to know everyone's clothes. If you can't distinguish light clothes from dark, plant a hamper or basket for each beside the washer. They should be clearly marked for other family members to use. When you suspect that garments have spots, presoaking in Clorox 2®, Biz®, or other such agents is the safest approach. You're not so likely to hit the soiled area with spray if you can't see where it is.

A sighted friend rubs a dampened bar of Fels Naptha® soap over obviously soiled areas such as collars, elbows, and wrists of shirts and blouses. Just as with carpet stains, there is no foolproof way of knowing you have it all out—it may be a question for better eyes than yours. If you live alone and are certain that you have a spot that will be hard to remove, you might as well pass the garment along to a friend to be included in his laundry, or send it off to the dry cleaner.

When dark clothes look like they have sprouted white freckles, it's a sign that all the soap isn't being rinsed. Pour a gallon of cheap, white vinegar into the washer and run through a full cycle. The vinegar solution will thoroughly dissolve soap residue in pipes and hoses.

Mesh bags that can be made or bought in a dime store notions department keep baby clothes, kids' socks, and other tiny articles from being swallowed by the washing machine. Having everyone pin socks together before tossing into the laundry eliminates the mating game for you. A cure for those who won't cooperate is to hand out a basket of socks to pair off while relaxing in front of the TV. When deciding what belongs to whom—kids' clothes can be confusing, as well as teenagers' with adults'—assign the distribution project to another family member. After all, you did the laundry. Somebody else divvying up to rightful owners sounds like a fair rule to the game.

Sheets, towels, and pillowcases also can be hard to match up. I have all white sheets and pillowcases for this reason. A sighted friend gave me that idea because she maintains they can be bleached occasionally without fear of destroying patterns. Don't rip up your linens if you already have matching sets. Either mark them with pins or put them into the sort pile with clothes for your helper to work out. Your sorter can fold a top sheet so it encloses the bottom sheet and pillowcases. You'll find such sets easily in the linen closet. The same system works for towels and washcloths that go together. When buying new linens, or even pajamas, you might consider the same pattern to eliminate this step on wash Monday.

As you empty washer and dryer, you may not notice clothes that cling to the sides or bottom. Make a complete circle with both hands moving in opposite directions to locate any strays. Move your foot gingerly around the floor near these appliances to detect any dropped laundry, since you can't hear a sock falling. By not filling your laundry basket to overflowing, none of the clean wash will leave the fold.

Although washers have lint filters, they don't catch it all. By tying an old nylon stocking to the end of the hose that empties into the laundry tub, you'll save wear and tear on the drain. And while we're filtering, don't forget to empty the lint filter on the dryer—otherwise it becomes a fire trap. A wastebasket next to these appliances is handy for lint and emptying pockets before clothes go into the wash.

The top of the dryer is convenient for blocking hand washed sweaters. You won't be taking up valuable counter space in the kitchen, nor are you likely to forget that the delicate garment is there and plop something on top of it.

I know a sighted woman who is so fanatical about ironing that she presses dust rags. Apparently these days of permanent press left no impression upon her. Admittedly, some wrinkle-resistant fabrics still require touching up. Steam irons seem to do the job most effectively. Set up your ironing board so that you have plenty of room to move around it. Sheets of brown wrapping paper on the floor will allow dropped garments a safe landing without soiling, while newspapers might leave an ink spot. A funnel permits spill-free filling. You are less likely to scorch or press in wrinkles if clothes are damp to start. If you can't iron immediately after taking them out of the dryer, sprinkle, put into plastic bags, and store in the refrigerator. Most irons are set with a lever that is off when at the far left, becoming hotter as you slide it to the right. It's another appliance with which you must be familiar before starting to work. Smooth a section of the garment on the board before you apply the iron. Apply the hot iron with even strokes, keeping your free hand well clear. By moving the garment systematically across the board, you will press uniformly. Gently touching it when you are through, you may notice some areas that are cooler than the rest. It is probable that you have missed them with the iron and they should be reironed. A sprinkling bottle close by can be your rescue should you inadvertently press in a wrinkle. Moisten the area, exert a little more pressure, and it should disappear.

Many blind people are apprehensive about handling an iron, and I suggest they practice with a cold iron first. People who iron without sight are naturally afraid of being burned. To prevent self-branding, your conscious effort must be to keep your free hand far out of the range of the iron as you move the appliance over material. Also be aware of the hole from which steam is spewing. Returning the iron to the same place on the broad end of the board with the cord hanging over the edge toward you enables you to locate the handle without fear. Several hangers on a rack or hook near your ironing spot permit you to hang garments immediately, without taking many steps. The less moving you do in these quarters, the less likely you are to singe yourself or knock over the iron. When interrupted, turn off the appliance.

So it's your turn to entertain. Visually handicapped people who live alone and plan to invite guests are smart to ask a visitor or two to come early, before the rest of the gang arrives. Who knows— you could have left a duster on the buffet, or the puppy could have dragged your underwear into the dining room. Despite your pains-taking efforts to present a spotless home, these little things can happen. You can greet your guests more confidently with the assurance that all in your domain is well.

While you are about your chores, interruptions are bound to occur: the phone rings, the kids come in, the dog wants out. No matter how immediate or urgent the interruption, stop long enough to move your cleaning equipment out of the way so you don't inadvertently create a blind-trap. While scrubbing the kitchen floor, Ben left the bucket by the open basement door. Upon returning after the phone call, he knocked the pail down the basement steps. I never asked him what he said, but I'm sure he spent a long time sopping up sudsy water. Other blind-traps you can avoid come when crawling under furniture to clean: Be care-ful of your head when you rise.

Housecleaning is a routine job. To maintain the upper hand, you must establish some regularity. By being as thorough and consistent as reasonably possible, you're not setting standards that are out of reach. One student, who had been a meticulous house-keeper when fully sighted, admitted she had to give up those lofty ideals when her sight failed.

"I stick with it and leave the overlooks and missed messes to my husband and kids," she says. "In fact, it's more comfortable for all of us now that I don't strive for utter spotlessness."

Some people take housekeeping seriously, working it down to a domestic science. You can become an efficiency expert on keeping your domicile clean by reading such experts as Peg Bracken in *I Hate to Housekeep* and Heloise's *Household Hints*. These books, as well as several others, have been recorded as Talking Books.

Mark Twain sagely said that fighting dirt was a losing battle because the earth is a ball of mud. You probably have done some or all of the chores mentioned in this chapter. Adapting techniques and building confidence are mainly what you require for keeping that ball of mud, for the most part, at bay.

Chapter 14

NO ONE'S IN THE
KITCHEN WITH DINAH

And that's the way it oughta be! By observing basic safety rules, relying on that all-encompassing organization again, and adapting or learning a few techniques, you won't burn down the house and will save yourself from starvation. Nor will you poison yourself or anyone else. You may resume your role as chief cook or assume the position of first chef. In some instances, you may be allowing other family members to go about their own business, not fretting because they have to be home to serve you lunch at high noon or put dinner on the table at six.

The mere mention of a blind person in the kitchen can conjure images of potential danger. You'll need to be even more on guard for the danger of fire. It isn't inevitable, and with care, it's not even likely. There is a dress code for cooking, or, more clearly stated, for clothes not to wear. Flowing garments such as bathrobes, filmy nightgowns, or even a tie can catch fire near a lit stove. A stove beside a window can set curtains into flame. Handles of pots should be turned to the side to avoid tipping accidentally. Take off such jewelry as necklaces or bracelets because they can become hot or catch on a utensil. People with long hair should tie it back, not only for sanitation's sake, but because it can be another hazard.

Bessie had been a homemaker for thirty years. When her vision failed, she prided herself on being able to prepare full meals for her family. She reached into the oven with a dish towel to remove a casserole, and then tucked the towel into the refrigerator handle, just as she had done thousands of times before. What Bessie didn't see was the cloth beginning to smolder. Fortunately, her son came into the kitchen at that moment. Seizing the towel, he doused it in the sink. Moral of this tale: Oven mitts are a must. The longer the better, too, because they can protect your arms up to the elbow. Barbecue mitts will do. You can buy them in the kitchenware department of large supermarkets. My mitts hang on a magnetic hook on the refrigerator near the stove.

When placing a pot or pan on a burner, center it by putting your hands around the bottom. Then turn on the burner. Should you be turning meat or stirring a full pot, turn off the burner before you begin. There won't be the danger of spattering grease that can catch fire.

The war still wages between gas and electric stove owners. Those on the gas stove side insist that when the power is off, heat doesn't linger. If you're fearful of an open flame, try a flame tamer, which diffuses heat so that cooking isn't too rapid. Provided that your sense of smell is intact, you'll know when the pilot light goes out. Automatic pilots for ovens can be expensive to repair. You can purchase a camp stove lighter from a camping or sporting goods department—Sears and Penney's market them. They emit a spark so you don't have to use a match. Electric stoves have the disadvantage of controls on the rear. Be conscious of steam or hot utensils as you reach across to the dials. To prevent burns from an element that is still cooling, put a full kettle of water on it.

On the shelf above my stove is a coffee can filled with baking soda. The plastic lid slips off easily so I can grab it immediately in case of a grease fire. Salt also works. Never use water on a grease fire because it spreads the flames. Naturally, a kitchen fire extinguisher is most effective.

The heat's not off the precautionary measures. You are probably concerned (and rightfully so) about pouring hot liquids. You'd be smart to cool it first by practicing with room temperature water from the kettle or coffee pot. Even partially sighted people suffer their share of puddles or scalds because their depth perception isn't accurate. Line up the spout over the center of the cup with your finger. From here on, it's a matter of personal preference. You may want to listen as increased depth changes pitch. You might prefer picking up the cup to judge by its weight. One partially sighted instructor insists on pouring a polite cup: about half full. I'm a finger pourer myself. With index finger over the rim of the cup, I stop when liquid touches the fingertip. If that beverage is meant for somebody else, that somebody can just as well pour his own. If you use cream or milk in coffee or tea, add it first. Again, weight, or your finger, is the best gauge. You'll soon learn whether you want to just cover the bottom or need a quarter of an inch. To add sugar without dumping half of it on counter or table, encircle the rim of the cup with the thumb and index finger of your free hand. You'll know exactly where your target is. American Foundation for the Blind sells a sugar dispenser that pours only a half teaspoonful each time the container is tipped. Sugar cubes are another alternative.

So you've mastered the pouring method. Even folks with 20/20 vision make mistakes. There's no use crying over or sopping up spilt milk from the floor. A plastic tray on the counter (the kind used in a cafeteria, not the fancy type) will collect any spills. You can pour your mistake into the sink, rinse the tray under the faucet, dry it, and start all over again.

To drain water from cooked vegetables or pasta, a Locklid® saucepan from the American Foundation for the Blind is helpful. This three-quart aluminum pan features a lid that locks into place. By turning the pan upside down over the sink, you allow liquid, not food, to escape through perforations around the rim. Otherwise, a collander will do. Empty the pan into a collander, and then remove the drained food to a serving dish. A wire basket used for deep frying will also work. You put vegetables or pasta in the basket, set it within the pan of water, and lift it out when cooking is complete. If you're ambitious enough to feed a large group, hefting a big pot of just-boiled potatoes isn't going to prove you're a weight-lifting champion—ask someone else to drain them.

Removing hot grease can get you into trouble if you're not alert. A baster is ideal for draining grease from meat loaf and other forms of ground beef. Just be sure the empty container into which you discard the grease is perfectly dry, or it will foam and run over. An empty soup can will do. Keep the baster vertical so it won't drip. A sleeve used to keep beer cans cold will prevent your container from getting too hot as you fill it. Those who are fussy about skimming grease from gravy can use an ice cube held in tongs. Excess grease clings to the cube. Real fussbudgets can cool gravy in the refrigerator, since grease forms a film on top that is easy to skim off.

"I'm afraid of cutting myself," bemoaned a lady who hadn't ventured back into the kitchen for more than a year after losing some of her sight. "How can I be sure of not chopping my fingers instead of a green pepper?"

First of all, sharp knives are safer than dull ones. You won't have to hack with a keen blade. Put your index finger atop the blade as you grasp the handle. Always be aware of the proximity of the hand holding the food. You might want to pinion the food with a fork as you cut. Absurd as it sounds, pay attention to what you're doing. The world's fastest food chopper can't carry on a conversation while wielding a knife—that's when accidents happen. Nor is slicing or chopping a mid-air stunt—you're inviting a chunk out of yourself. Placing food on a chopping board gives you stability and additional awareness of exactly where food and knife are. Food choppers and vegetable slicers eliminate the need much of the time for pulling out the paring knife. Kitchen shears make quick work of cutting up poultry, celery, rhubarb stalks, stewing beef, and carrots. The Magna Wonder Knife®, from the American Foundation for the Blind, has a serrated blade and a guide that can be adjusted for varying thicknesses. Some foods require extra-thin slicing, such as scalloped potatoes or cucumbers, for which this gadget is ideal. Potato peelers instead of paring knives are safer and more effective for spuds, apples, carrots, and cucumbers.

In some cases you might want to ask yourself if it is really worth the time and effort to grate and chop some foods, especially if you use them infrequently. Some foods come frozen in this form, such as green pepper and onions. Grated cheese is a big seller in the dairy department.

When deep frying gives you the heebie jeebies, whip out the wire basket again. You can pull out chicken, doughnuts, and mushrooms in one fell swoop. Frozen french fries are more cost-effective than beginning from scratch, and can be baked in the oven in twenty minutes.

"How do I know when something is done?"

That question crops up more often when we're on the cooking subject than almost anything else. Your best gauge is your nose, especially when cooking meat. It doesn't take too many tries when frying hamburger or broiling steaks to sniff when they're ready. Browned meat also has a different texture because it is drier and rougher. You can check with the tines of a fork held lightly in your hand, or feel the meat with a paper towel wrapped loosely around your finger. Being conservative means that you can always pop the meat back into the pan for a few minutes. When meat is too well done, it's almost a lost cause.

Timers help, too. You can buy a timer with raised dots at every two and one-half minutes from the American Foundation for the Blind. Or you can purchase one from the dime or hardware store and dot it with Hi Marks glue. An ingenious student found a timer at K–Mart that clicks when the dial is revolved for each minute. Many people set their talking clocks as timers. Some folks who lose their sight give up on timing foods when they can no longer read the stove timer. Timing food may not always be accurate because of variation in quantity and exact temperature, but it serves as a dependable guide.

Turning meat is another perplexer. Start by turning off the burner. Impale meat such as a pork chop or chicken on a fork, easing it over gently. If it doesn't slip from the fork, pry it loose with a table knife. Holding the frying pan handle in your other hand offers more security. To be sure that every piece has had its fair turn, arrange them in a clock formation to provide you with orientation. Don't overcrowd your pan or you'll lose count.

Frying eggs need not be a nightmare, but it was for a totally blind man who recounts an egg-frying fiasco from his bachelor days. He insists that the egg slipped from the spatula and he never found it. Had he used a tuna fish can from which top and bottom had been removed, he probably wouldn't have lost his meal. Crack the egg into the middle of the can. One friend starts the egg and pushes the toaster down at the same time. As the toast pops up, the egg is done. You can buy an egg pan from a hardware or kitchen wares store that is especially made for this chore. Eggs slip out easily when fried in a bit of butter or oleo. You can't use that utensil for anything else, though, and clean it by wiping with a paper towel and a little salt. You can also follow the poaching route—the less fat, the better. Using a small Silverstone® frying pan, add a dab of butter and pinch of salt. When the egg is done, fish it out with a small spatula or slotted spoon.

Along with eggs goes bacon. Knowing which strips have been turned and which have not can be more irritating than a jigsaw puzzle. Frying them in a small baking pan in the oven eliminates that guessing game. Otherwise, a glass bacon press placed upon bacon in a frying pan will radiate heat, making turning unnecessary. The same method applies to sausage. You can find bacon presses in a good kitchenware department.

A partially sighted housewife named Mary was proud she had given up frying food altogether. Broiling and baking meat, poultry, and fish all began when she lost her sight and didn't know for sure when pork chops or fish filets became brown. She even makes hamburgers for her hungry five-member family by arranging them in a shallow pan and baking them for twenty-five minutes at 325 degrees. She doesn't have to turn the burgers.

A man with low vision lives alone and doesn't finish a box of cornflakes in a hurry. He crumbles stale flakes and uses them as a coating for oven-baked fish and chicken. His is another example of feeling more comfortable baking or broiling foods. Not only is this method easier for people with impaired vision, it is more nutritious for everyone.

Dig around your utensil drawers for those seldom-used items that may bail you out of uncertainties. (Incidentally, sharp knives and kitchen shears shouldn't be in there. Hanging them on a rack will save a nick in time.) A nest of measuring cups and individual measuring spoons may top your list of handies. You used to add wet and dry ingredients by instinct, but your depth perception (if you have any) isn't what it used to be. You can dip out exactly a half cup of sugar or a full cup of flour, leveling it with a table knife. Liquid seasonings and flavorings such as vanilla or lemon extract don't allow much room for error. By storing them in tightly covered containers such as large medicine bottles or baby food jars, you can dip out whatever you need. I ruined banana bread by pouring vanilla by the glub—it turned out to be more like ¼ cup. By putting cooking oil into a large wide-mouthed jar, you can spoon it out. Why pour an inch into the bottom of a frying pan when you only wanted to lightly coat?

I'm one of those who can't separate an egg by pouring the white from the shell. A funnel works just fine. As the white runs out, the yolk stays in. You can also buy an egg separator at the dime store. Hang onto that funnel for filling salt and pepper shakers. A wire whisk will whip those whites to their frothiest best, saving you from whipping out the electric beater.

Wooden spoons don't conduct heat, so you could leave one in a pot for occasional stirring.

It's hard to fish ears of corn from a boiling pan. Try a pair of tongs. Some people like tongs for turning meat, too.

A small food chopper that consists of a glass jar with a screw-on top with four blades is handy. You can finely chop onions, green peppers, and nuts.

Are you tempted to plunk sticky fingers into a cannister when sprinkling flour on cake pans, fish, and poultry? Try filling a larger salt shaker with flour. It isn't wasteful because you spread only as much flour as you need.

One student wondered how to refill ice cube trays without re-creating the Youngstown flood on the kitchen floor.

"I never thought about it," I answered. "But why don't you fill the tray, put it inside a bread wrapper, and then into the freezer? When you want ice, empty the tray into the bag and seal it."

She happily saves bread wrappers and doesn't send cubes flying as she empties trays.

Another gadget worth checking from the American Foundation for the Blind is a cake cutter. Its two handles can spread as wide as the wedge you require. Just press down and there's your slice.

A friend gave me a butter spreader, maintaining that every household should have one. Its short, broad blade is about an inch wide, making spreading of butter and sandwich filling a snap with one or two swipes. After comparing it with the narrow blade of a table knife, I agree with her. Don't confuse it with a butter knife, which has a much narrower blade.

Make a quick assessment of your kitchen appliances to be sure you can operate them safely. A food processor is no way of proving your mechanical ingenuity. Any time you buy a new appliance, get the instructional manual read. If the kitchen is a new adventure for you, you owe it to yourself to corner someone to show you how to run the gadgets. When you know what to do but not how to set, mark the dials (see Chapter 11).

A totally blind woman who lives alone bought a hamburger cooker that she was anxious to try. Having no one around to run through the instructional booklet, she thought that plugging it in was all that was necessary. She couldn't understand why the counter became coated with grease each time she cooked a patty. A friend pointed out that the cooker was upside down — excess fat couldn't drain into the drip pan.

Since we're talking about modern marvels, let me put in a plug for microwave ovens. They top my list of labor and time savers and are especially a boon for blind people. As food becomes hot, it conducts its heat to the cooking utensil, so don't be fooled by thinking that you won't need to protect your hands as you reach inside a microwave oven. It's not the same as reaching into a conventional oven, though. Once you get the hang of microwave cooking, you literally set and forget until the appliance turns itself off. Because this method of cooking is so exacting — time and temperature make a difference — you should be able to set adjustments accurately.

One woman told me sheepishly that her family gave her a microwave several Christmases ago.

"Great," I responded. "What do you prepare in it?"

"I was afraid you'd ask that," she muttered. "I use it for a breadbox because I don't understand the damn thing."

It is a breadbox no longer. This lady took my advice about having her daughter go through the instructional manual and cookbook with her. She started out by memorizing cooking times and temperatures for easy-to-prepare dishes. A cup of instant coffee was her first try. Then she heated soup and cooked fresh and frozen vegetables. So taken with the speed reduction in work was she that the lady enrolled in an adult education cooking course.

A partially sighted woman who is a microwave enthusiast insists that she prepares almost everything in hers. She bought a small browning skillet mounted on legs. Although this utensil gets quite hot, the handle prevents her from burning her hands. She cooks chicken, minute steaks, fish, and roasts. Sprinkling a powder called Microshake® turns meat and fish into an appetizing brown. One shortcoming is that unless you take special pains by adding Kitchen Bouquet® or using a browning skillet, food remains pale in color. One student thought she'd delight her family with a pineapple upside down cake baked in the microwave. How disappointed she was when the gang didn't tear into it. They couldn't quite get past the stark white appearance.

Microwave classes might not be the route for you, at least not now. Round up somebody who is knowledgeable and can impart this expertise. The consumer relations department of your local electric company is a possible resource. A totally blind man, vowing that he wouldn't cook after losing his sight because he avoided the kitchen when he could see, learned from one of these experts. When his wife is away at mealtime, he warms in the microwave whatever she has prepared for him. Because he is diabetic, it is essential for him to eat at regular intervals.

Are you in the market for a microwave oven? Avoid those models that are programmable: from defrost to complete cooking with a few flicks of the finger. The warmth of the finger (and yours might be searching) is enough to set off controls. A dealer told me that a customer's cat, curious about the gadget, used to screw up the works by snooping near dials. You should also check to see if a manufacturer will provide tactile markings. Some companies will provide this service upon request. Your appliance can be simple with settings for low, medium, and high power. If space is limited, think about a small microwave.

As for plunging into the newfangled cooking method, there are several Braille and cassette microwave cookbooks. They can serve as a guide until you work out your favorite standbys.

Perhaps you can't afford or don't have space for a microwave oven. Don't toss in the apron and concede the end of your culinary career. Most people, sighted and blind, don't own this appliance.

Other electric gadgets that might grab your fancy include an electric knife. Hamilton Beach makes one that cannot be accidentally started. You must deliberately turn the button. You can stop the knife to check progress, then resume carving. General Electric markets an electric can opener that starts when the lid is engaged and shuts itself off when the lid is removed. The Hotshot®, made by Sunbeam, is meant for boiling water for instant coffee, tea, and heating soup. A button activates heating. After setting your cup under the spout, you press another button to pour. You don't heft a kettle for pouring hot liquids.

Whether you're slapping together a peanut butter sandwich or rolling up your sleeves to start a seven-course dinner, you need to methodically arrange ingredients and utensils. Your tray can serve as a focal point on which you can mix, pour, and catch any spills. Your kitchen won't look like an explosion in the flour factory. Ingredients can go to the left, trash such as eggshells and packaging to the right. Small utensils such as measuring cups and measuring spoons, mixing spoons, and spatulas are easier to find within the confines of the tray. If interrupted, or when clean-up time comes, everything is together before you.

Resign yourself to requiring more time because of your visual limitation. Yes, you may once have prepared dinner for six in less than an hour. Now that you don't see as well, those few minutes that it used to take to chop celery and onions for tuna salad can stretch into more than a half hour. Don't expect too much of yourself or allow others to imbue you with unrealistic powers. Start easy. Maybe you will toss the salad for tonight's meal; then prepare pudding for tomorrow night. You can't discount the fatigue factor, especially when starting again after not having done your stint for a long time. Perhaps you haven't done it at all previously. Would-be chefs give up because they give out, biting off more than they can chew.

Allow yourself disasters and forgive yourself for them. The cook who hasn't added too much salt to the stew, fried bacon to a cinder, or baked a cake that fell is a cook that hasn't really been adventurous. Blindness probably isn't to blame in these instances. People with normal sight have tried and failed. If you create a catastrophe, dump it out, have sandwiches for supper, and try again tomorrow. It's not fair for others to remind you of your mistake, either. If they think they could have done better, why weren't they doing it in the first place?

Let go of those meals that are too difficult or time-consuming for you now. So you can't flip pancakes, or lasagna demands too much preparation. Order such foods when you're dining out. Another point in letting go is knowing if fresh vegetables are absolutely free from blemishes and other defects. Bill suffered from this "what if" quandary. What if there were brown spots on the celery stalks? What if he didn't peel potatoes perfectly? Lettuce leaves can feel firm and crisp, but what if they bore brown spots?

My reaction to the what if worries is, "So what?" I never heard of anyone succumbing to brown spots on celery or lettuce. If these vegetables really have taken a turn for the worse, they'll be limp and mushy and you'll know it. I defy anybody to fish out a few shreds of peel from mashed potatoes. Besides, people who are that fussy deserve to prepare the spuds themselves.

Even if you have time on your hands, don't always think that from scratch is the best way. For you, from scratch may mean so much time and effort that you'll be less likely to cook, reducing the frequency of your times in the kitchen. Do you really need to peel carrots and potatoes to flavor the roast? Is prepared spaghetti sauce really such a far cry from what you make from scratch? (Doctor up the prepackaged sauce if you find it bland.) Sure, you already know about these helps for harried cooks, but may not be aware of other convenience foods in the market. If you shop for groceries alone, you may be gliding by shelves, dairy, and frozen food departments burgeoning with prepared foods you never dreamed existed. A trip to the supermarket with someone who has time to run through these displays will give you new options.

Marketing is another factor to consider when you're menu planning. Whether you or somebody else does it, you can't jump into the car and zip over to the corner if you're missing a bottle of olive oil for a recipe. Keep in mind, if not on paper, a good idea of what meals you will be preparing when you shop so you won't have to scrap intentions for making chili when you're out of chili powder.

Whether you are the experienced cook learning to adapt or the rank beginner learning to cook, your hands will be among your primary aids. The less sight you have, the more you'll be relying upon them. You'll have to wash often—a bar of soap or bottle of liquid soap on the sink and hand towel nearby will take care of that routine.

Georgia, a totally blind woman in her late thirties, told me her brother-in-law lived with their family. He didn't want to eat meals she had prepared because she touched the food so much during its preparation.

"Do you wash your hands frequently?" I asked.

"Of course," she responded indignantly.

"Then tell your brother-in-law to fix his own meals or eat out. If he goes the restaurant route, he'll be appalled by the lack of sanitation in some eateries."

Cooking in larger quantities also saves time and effort. Why fry a few strips of bacon? Fry the whole package and use it as you need it. That trick also works for sausages. Make twice the amount of mashed potatoes you will serve at one meal; serve the rest tomorrow. You can freeze most leftovers if you or your family resents repeats. Store your leftovers on the same shelf in the refrigerator if you don't consign them to the freezer. Before serving, give them the sniff test. When in doubt, throw out. Food poisoning is much costlier in suffering and expense.

"I would like to help with the cooking but I live with my grandmother," said Keith, a twenty-six-year-old man who recently became totally blind. "She's queen of the kitchen. Although she doesn't always put everything back precisely, she can find it. It takes me too much time to find utensils and ingredients—I'd give up before I started."

Keith's complaints are justified. If you are not monarch of the kitchen, your forays into this realm aren't regular. You can hardly demand that others comply with your arrangements for appliances, utensils, and food. When the urge comes, I suggest that you ask specifically for what you require; someone else can dig out supplies and set them on the counter for you. (Nobody of sound mind is going to resist assistance with a meal or resent your baking a treat.) When through with your task, you can clean up, but leave the putting away chore to your helper.

The mother of a blind teenager asked me about her son's complete ineptitude in the kitchen. Blind children deserve their turn just as much as their sighted counterparts. Because they may not be able to watch an experienced cook, terms such as *beat, whip, stir, or parboil,* or elementary tasks such as spreading butter, might be meaningless. At these times, someone should be in the kitchen with Dinah or Don to teach some of these basic concepts.

When teaching a partially sighted youngster, let him hover as near as necessary to watch what's going on. For the totally blind learner, hands-on demonstrations mean the hands of a patient adult literally manipulating those of the youngster through an operation. Sure, there will be more spills and messes than ordinary, so pick a time that isn't rushed. Repetition and plenty of opportunity will make up the deficit of being unable to imitate by watching.

The parent will have to be specific—show the youngster what a dab of butter is, or a pinch of salt. The experienced cook will have to be imaginative, too. Teaching a kid to turn meat may be a demonstration using a piece of bread in a cold frying pan.

Of course it's easier and faster for a parent to do it, but that kid eventually will have to fix meals, be they ever so simple. Begin with minimum tasks such as making a sandwich, heating a can of soup, and pouring a glass of milk. Parents of blind youngsters ought to know that functioning independently in the kitchen is one of the most glaring deficiencies of children blind from birth. The sooner these deficits are attacked, the easier will be the corrections.

Some books that are helpful because they contain simple recipes are *Cooking Without Looking* by Esther Tipps; *Pre-Primer for the Blind Cook* by Sally Jones; one book with adaptive techniques is *When The Cook Can't Look*, a cooking handbook for the blind and visually impaired by Ralph Read (RC 17940); and *A Student Notebook: Manual for Teenagers Who Like to Cook* by Eleanor B. Martin. They are available in Braille or large print from the American Printing House for the Blind. They give detailed step-by-step instructions as well as precise cooking times.

More experienced cooks usually have a few favorite dishes, those dependable standbys. You can accumulate your own recipe file either in large print or Braille. Copy only bare essentials when noting recipes. Print users can keep a notebook with ingredients listed on the left page, method on the right. Braille users will find it easier to write ingredients in a column with notes about method below. Three-ring binders are handy for Braille because index cards usually aren't large enough for one recipe. These self-made recipe books also work for directions for prepared foods such as cake mixes or instant potatoes. Common sense tells you to beat well, cut brownies into bars, or cool cakes before cutting.

No, you don't need a whiz kid's memory if you can't read print or Braille. Marge, a middle-aged housewife, was looking for new recipes but couldn't learn Braille. She asked her family and friends to dictate slowly onto cassette tape. The reader dictates ingredients slowly enough for Marge to gather them while listening. The method is read slowly with pauses so that she can stop the player to carry out directions. Marge reserves one cassette for main dishes, another for desserts, a third for cookies. To avoid gumming up the works with sticky hands on the cassette player, she places a dish towel over it. She sets the machine away from the field of action so she won't spill food or liquid on it. As a matter of convenience and safety, she operates it on battery.

Besides basic cookbooks, Braille and large-print users will find a wide variety of advanced books in both forms. They include cooking for one person, convenience foods for quick meals, international cooking, and preparing food for large groups. Several magazines, such as *Good Housekeeping, Family Circle, Better Homes and Gardens,* and *Ladies Home Journal* are in Braille, disk or cassette form, offering a never-ending fund of ideas. Braille users should stash a damp cloth near the book to wipe hands before referring to a recipe. Otherwise, you might have more dots than you bargained for. Large print users could try a hint I ran across—an inverted glass pie plate protects pages and also slightly magnifies print.

Once you feel more at home in the kitchen, you can consider inviting guests. You can begin small with coffee cake (from the bakery) and coffee. Be extravagant later with a seven-course dinner if you're so inclined. Don't feel as though you have to prove yourself as the perfect host or hostess. Ask a guest to pour coffee and serve pastry if it's hard for you to pull it off neatly.

Think about it. Guests are always padding through the kitchen of someone else's house, regardless of sight, wondering, "Is there something I can do?" They will rise to the occasion with delight when your answer is yes.

Memories of my first show-off dinner are vivid. Almost a stranger to the range, I slaved over it all day. Determined to pull off the extravaganza singlehanded, I transferred food from pots and pans to serving dishes. Letting offers of help fall on temporarily deaf ears, I carried them into the dining room. Conversation ceased suddenly as I began placing platters—one nervous diner told me later that the gang collectively held their breath as I narrowly missed mashed potatoes with the gravy boat. I cruised by the candle with the salad bowl with barely an inch to spare.

Those close calls left a lesson in their wake. When I organize serving dishes and utensils on the counter, everything is ready for a guest to serve. I settle with the rest in the living room while a helper or two handles last-minute details. Shucks, I cooked the meal, which won't land on some poor soul's head or lap.

Appointing a clean-up committee isn't such a bad idea either. Thelma, a woman having low vision, was entertaining a few friends when her husband was out of town. She remembers with chagrin the cocktail glass that nestled between couch and end table on the floor, which she found three days after the party. She discovered it while vacuuming, when it was nearly too late. Visitors can find the most ingenious, out-of-the-way places for ashtrays, glasses, napkins, and dishes. If you are totally blind and alone, check which lights are still on before the crowd disappears.

If your clean-up committee clears the table after a meal, stay on top of the situation. Despite their insistence, it isn't necessary for them to do dishes. When they rinse and stack, know what's put where. You can't expect guests to intuit where everything belongs, nor should you psyche out the whereabouts of the soup ladle later.

A blind couple of my acquaintance leaves bar tending entirely up to sighted guests. They lay in a supply of beverages. Glasses and ice are also well stocked. That couple's philosophy when it comes to freshening drinks is that the gods help those who help themselves. John also contends that were he to taste to identify, he wouldn't last five minutes into the party. Since they entertain often, their friends don't mind this arrangement of self-service at all.

No how-to book will turn you into a gourmet. These ideas may help to modify techniques and suggest useful devices. Your powers of organization and attitude toward feeding yourself and others will determine your comfort in the kitchen. Whether you started sixty years ago or are a rookie, you can master enough to keep yourself safe and well fed. Be it ever so humble, your first meal can serve as a gift to yourself and perhaps to others. Your health permitting, allow yourself the pleasure that comes with creating in the kitchen. Past flops and future failures are water under the bridge. Sure, be watchful of the dangers that exist and learn how to circumvent them. Uncertainty and lack of confidence work their way out with time and experience, and the joy and satisfaction will outweigh your initial uneasiness.

Chapter 15

YOU CAN EAT IN PUBLIC
AND NOT BE THE STAR DISTRACTION

A totally blind woman of twenty-four, mother of two pre-schoolers, tearfully reported that she refused to eat in front of other people, even her children. In the six months since she had lost her sight she fixed simple meals. But she remained alone in the kitchen while the rest of the family gathered in the dining room. Her solitary eating habits developed because she was so nervous about actually putting food to her mouth that she used only a spoon.

Treading close behind this unfortunate lady was a forty-nine-year-old professional man. Blind for fifteen months when I first saw him, he admitted sheepishly that he dreaded eating in public. He turned down an invitation to attend a banquet with his peers because his wife wouldn't be there to accommodate his needs.

Although we generally eat three times a day and think nothing about it, this area ranks among the most sensitive for some people who are newly blind. Unless you turn into an instant hermit at mealtime, you'll be eating in public, even if it's your three-year-old sitting across the table from you. Somehow people think that any miss between plate and mouth will be witnessed and looked upon aghast by everybody within a hundred feet. I'm afraid that many recently blind folks, like the young mother and the middle-aged man, lose out on enjoying good food and good company in a friend's home or at a restaurant meal for fear of rolling peas off a plate or tipping over a cocktail glass. Armed with a few ideas of how to avoid obvious pitfalls and the conviction that everyone makes miscues, you should feel more comfortable in these situations.

If you forget all else, when in doubt, ask for help. Cutting a pork chop from its bone could be a challenge you're willing to meet at home, but not one with which you'd like to wrestle in a restaurant. I've dodged the meat-cutting problem by simply saying to a waitress, "I'm blind, would you please have my meat cut in the kitchen?"

Knowing the chef has sharp knives at his disposal, I don't consider this request unreasonable. It takes about a minute for him to finish the job. Apparently the waitress doesn't think it out of line either. None has ever thrown down an order pad in disgust. When my plate is served with the meat cut, it is often pushed together to appear as a whole piece. I can merrily eat in peace. My companions can tend to their own dinners without worrying about offering me help. Their food doesn't become cold because they are providing assistance.

I remember dining with a totally blind man. The waitress reminded him that pork chops were the special of the day and offered to cut them before she brought his meal. He declined the special, although the meat is among his favorites. When she left, he said to me that he thought her assistance would be an imposition upon her time. I mused to myself how unfortunate it is to forego a favorite just for the sake of pride.

You will probably want to cut your own at home, and perhaps in public. Start as the chefs do, with a sharp knife in hand. Even if you're eating meatloaf or fish, a keen blade makes the job easier. (A table knife will do for spreading but isn't satisfactory for cutting.) Locating the edge of the meat with your fork, place the knife behind it and cut as you always have. If you have whacked off a chunk instead of a bite, you'll know by the weight on your fork. You will learn to judge the size of the piece cut also by lightly touching with the knife blade. Since most people are right-handed, you're likely to wield the knife in your right hand. Some people eat European style. The fork remains in the left hand, lifting the bite, saving switching the utensils back and forth. Whether you are dining in Paris or Podunk, this method is acceptable.

"How do I know if food is still on my fork?" asked a student frustrated by many empty passes from plate to mouth.

I told him to be aware of the weight of the fork. A utensil filled with food balances differently from one that is empty.

To discover if you have joined the Clean Plate Club or still have farther to go, make a quick search by moving your fork lightly. Starting at the rim and moving toward the center, you won't send a mushroom flying. If you're still edgy about sending food over the edge, hold a pusher in your left hand at nine o'clock. It acts as a barrier and is still among the okays of etiquette. Long ago a sterling silver pusher was part of the table service. You can get by with a half piece of bread or a roll.

Another student, especially conscious of good manners, was concerned about digging in before everyone else had been served. I reminded her that she could listen for the familiar clink of silverware. Were she among silent diners, the most obvious solution: Just ask if others have received their food.

Not even Emily Post wrote all the answers for which utensils to use for what foods. Of course you remember looking around to see how other people were managing. If you can't, ask and ye shall know if folks are picking up fried chicken or cutting it from the bone. When uncertain about attacking dessert with fork or spoon, again it's allowable to inquire.

Some foods may give you more fight than you bargained for. Spaghetti strands sometimes appear to go on forever. To secure them on a fork, try an adaptation of the classic Italian style spaghetti twisting. Spear the spaghetti in the middle of the plate with fork tines, take a few quick spins of the fork and zap, you have it. In case your wad is too big, it's time for the knife.

You might innocently order a sandwich, thinking it is the closed-face kind. Alas, it comes to you open face, smothered with sauce, gravy, or sour cream. When there's the least suspicion that you might be so booby-trapped, ask before making your order. If you don't want to give up on the sandwich, request that the sauce or sour cream be served to you in a small cup on the side. Some vegetables seem to have a mind of their own. Why chase around whole kernel corn, peas, and lima beans? Have them corraled in a small dish on the side.

Salads are fast gaining in popularity. If including one with your meal, it will be easier to handle when in a bowl, not a plate. You won't be playing hide-and-seek with cherry tomatoes, or popping chick peas out of bounds. If you suspect that half a head of lettuce is the main ingredient, ask that it be cut or torn into small pieces. Chicken, tuna, and potato salad frequently top a bed of lettuce. Leaves are mostly decorative. Since many people don't eat the lettuce bed, you can suggest that it be omitted. You'll save yourself from probing among nooks and crannies. Salad bars can be tricky, too. Unless you see well enough to be confident about making your own, pass the task to someone else. When you are picky about fixings, a quick rundown of possibilities usually suffices.

Grapefruit halves can be potential geysers. When you don't wish to spray yourself or companions in the eye, ask that it be sectioned and served in a small bowl. At home I just peel a grapefruit, pulling apart sections as if it were an orange.

Other possible trouble spots can come when adding condiments — catsup, mayonnaise, steak sauce, mustard, relish. A heavy hand could ruin your hamburger. Be an arch conservative if you do it yourself, or ask someone else. At home you can spoon out what you want. Adding cream and sugar to coffee or tea and buttering a roll can also be unnecessarily challenging. Don't despair — these are times when it pays to ask for a hand, even from the waitress, if you are alone. You can season your own food with pepper and salt by allowing grains to pour through slightly spread fingers. Incidentally, salt shakers weigh more than pepper shakers. Holes in salt shakers are also larger.

Spilt milk at home or while dining out isn't worth crying about, but does merit avoiding if possible. Keep your hand low, fingers curved. When you reach for a cup or glass, move slowly. Quick movement with fingers extended is inviting an upset. (By holding a stemmed glass by its bowl, you're better able to judge its rim.) Partially sighted folks are almost as prone to accidents because of poor depth perception, dim lighting, inability to notice clear glassware, or plain overconfidence. They need to employ the hands-down policy just as rigorously. When you want salt or cream and it isn't within your seeing distance, it's safer to ask than go ranging about the table.

No matter how accomplished you become in acceptable eating habits, some challenges will be more than you want to risk, so why tempt fate? Take a large gathering at home, for instance. Because table space is as scarce as grass in New York City, most people find a seat wherever they can and balance a plate on their knees. The odds of getting through that dinner unscathed are stacked against you. It's no breach of etiquette to ask unobtrusively for a snack tray or a corner of the kitchen table on which to place your plate. In the bustle of the affair, host and hostess probably never thought about your predicament. So you won't feel like an outcast if you're eating in the kitchen, invite another guest to join you. That person will be relieved by not going through the balancing act, too.

Standing with a drink in your hand or, worse still, walking with one is also looking for trouble. Unless you intend to be a literal wallflower by leaning against a wall, your extended glass in hand might shower another guest whom you bump or who brushes against you. By all means, sit down to get out of the line of fire. Provided there is no handy table, put the glass on the floor between your feet. Just don't get carried away crossing your legs or leaping up. When someone hands you a drink, take the glass and put it where you want it. That's another troubleshooter because you avoid the seek-and-ye-shall-find game.

"What do I do when I'm alone in a restaurant?" asked Bob, a college student with low vision. He eats out most of the time. "How do I signal the waitress when I want more coffee, when I'm ready for dessert, or wish the check would come? When I have to get to class, I don't have the time to wait until she remembers I'm there."

I told Bob a story of handling that situation several years ago—and ever since. Somehow friends and I crossed wires. They never showed up to meet me at a large, well-known restaurant where we planned to have dinner. I had two choices: hailing a cab to go home to a solitary peanut butter sandwich, or staying put to savor the fine fare. I was sure I could enjoy the atmosphere and eavesdrop on nearby conversations. I decided to turn the event into an adventure. When the waitress came to my table, I informed her, "You can be the difference between my having a miserable meal or a delightful evening. Would you please check periodically to see if there's anything I need? Just remember that I can't signal to you."

I never stewed about having more coffee, or what was on the menu for dessert. Upon returning to that restaurant later, I stopped to chat with that waitress who saved the dinner from disaster.

When dining alone, state your needs immediately. If the waitress still forgets, you can make your request for her attention to another nearby diner. It may be easier for you to have the waitress take your check to the register—she'll be glad to do it if you ask. While you're at it, you might suggest that someone show you the way to the door if you are uncertain of its location.

You'll find that dining in a cafeteria is even more demanding of your ingenuity than a restaurant. Cafeterias certainly weren't designed with blind folks in mind. Since many large companies and hospitals feed the throngs this way, you'll have to resign yourself to them in some instances. Unless your vision allows you to comfortably read the menu, carry the tray, pick up utensils and napkins, and choose from the help-yourself dishes, you are better off to leave these matters to somebody else. If another person is handling your tray, it might be less awkward for you to take a seat at the table, waiting for the food to be brought to you. Provided you and your companion are light eaters, it's possible both meals will fit on the same tray. Your grip on your friend's arm should be gingerly. Be prepared to readily release to let him reach to the counter or pour coffee. If you eat regularly by yourself in a cafeteria, members of the dietary staff will learn the routine and come without bidding to your aid. Remember that they are like anyone else who hasn't had contact with a blind person. In the beginning, you'll have to suggest the best ways for them to help you.

The same rules of thumb for eating in a restaurant also apply in a friend's home. Asking for a bowl for your salad or vegetables won't send the hostess into a tailspin. The trusty steak knife is standard table ware. (You might explain that it's easier for you to cut food with this implement, so you don't imply that the meat is tough.)

Relax, relish, and enjoy yourself. Remember, you're among friends.

Sure, there will be times when you feel on the spot or in the spotlight. It might be a date with someone you want to impress, dinner with your boss, or lunch with your colleagues when you have returned to work. Asking for assistance when you're eating isn't childish—it's plain good sense. Recently I attended an awards dinner at which I was among the honored recipients. My guest was the president of the hospital for which I work. I would do anything to avoid the horror of slithering a slice of meat onto his lap or sending a sauce-covered broccoli spear off into oblivion. The point at issue was retaining my dignity while seeking assistance from my boss without drawing undue attention. Not being one to agonize over decisions or possible consequences, I turned to him and quietly said, "Would you give me a hand by cutting my food?"

He gladly complied. Later, when I came to know him better, I questioned him about this incident. He admitted that he would have felt uncomfortable watching me struggle, uncertain whether or how to offer a hand. He actually felt relieved when I stated my needs. His quick manipulations of knife and fork were so unobtrusive that they went unnoticed by others at the table.

Are you still chagrined about your reluctance to eat in public? Two sighted friends, each on a different occasion, agreed to don a blindfold before accompanying another sighted person and me to a restaurant. Fred found the half-mile walk to the restaurant with his guide a harrowing experience—traffic sounds seemed magnified, and the uncertainty of the terrain underfoot gave the sensation of walking off a cliff. It was hard for him to concentrate on food. He didn't savor his selection, and his mind was probably elsewhere with distraction and preoccupation. Pete, on the other hand, rode several miles to the restaurant of our choice in a car. After futile attempts at cutting a sliced lamb sandwich served in pita bread, he gracefully accepted help proffered by my boss, the same man who had seen me safely through the awards dinner. He enjoyed his meal more when he realized he didn't have to fight it alone.

After finishing their meals, each man wondered if he had spilled anything on his clothes. They knew equal relief when assured they weren't creating spectacles of themselves. Upon taking off their blindfolds, Fred and Pete readily understood why many blind people undergo qualms about eating in public.

It is probably more than coincidence that these friends, having such a spirit of adventure, are newspaper writers, ready to undergo the unknown for the sake of experiment. Chances are that if you make that offer among your friends, you won't find many takers. But you can learn from the story.

Partially sighted people waver between wondering about occasionally seeking help and being completely self-sufficient. One woman with low vision takes a battery-powered lamp with her. She thinks of dimly lit restaurants as blackout areas. Another man with just a little sight always requests a steak knife to cut his meat, regardless of how tender the cut. Slip-ups occur when they reach for an item that isn't quite there, or mistake one substance for another because of similarly shaped containers, thinking that cream is in a pitcher when it turns out to be syrup.

"But I can see what I'm doing," objected Paul, a young man with usable sight. "I shouldn't have to bother learning these techniques."

Paul and many more like him can manage quite well in most instances. But those odd situations in which lighting is poor or in which fluctuating vision has ebbed to its lowest point should be considered. Some people with residual vision compensate by lowering the head toward the plate to see what they are doing. If you are likely to face such predicaments, you would be wise to develop eating habits similar to those employed by someone without sight. Then you can derive full satisfaction from a meal without concern, just as anyone else.

Despite precautions, you are bound to encounter spills and upsets. To attempt to sop up the mess will probably cause more confusion. The best reaction in case of an accident is to apologize quietly.

I've been with blind people who tipped a glass of wine or cup of coffee. Their expansive explanations and exclamations simply magnified the mistake. One man blamed himself for being a clumsy oaf, drawing more attention to the mishap and making others feel uneasy. As the song says, what can you say, after you say you're sorry? Of course, good manners dictate that when your accident results in a cleaning or laundry bill, you offer to take care of it.

One student, a man in his midtwenties, follows a philosophy that should put most worriers' minds to rest. "Why should I feel that people in a restaurant or in a friend's home are always looking at me? They're out for dinner and a change of pace. They become absorbed in conversation and the meal before them. Why should I be so self-centered that I think all eyes are glued on me with every mouthful?"

Eating is a social occasion, a time to enhance good food with fine company. Come out of the closet, if that's where you've been hiding, and enrich your life with both.

Chapter 16

CHALKING UP SOCIAL GRACES, NOT DISGRACES

W e're entering a gray area, the expanse and depth of human relationships, which defies definite answers because individual personality, circumstances of the moment, and the reactions of others are so unpredictable. Your general outlook on life, your mood at the time, and how you have been reared all color your interaction with others. Even with a firm grip on your own feelings, you can't anticipate how other people will view you. Throw blindness, an unknown entity to other people, into the picture, and the initial impression others have of you can be distorted.

Through history, blind people have made monumental strides forward. In the times before Christ, blind infants often were left on the mountainside to die because they were imperfect. In China they were considered to have extraordinary powers and were appointed fortune-tellers. Even in our own country, as late as the nineteenth century, there were institutions for the blind, called asylums.

Consciousness raising has swept the United States in the last few decades, hurling in its wake everyone from the liberated women to children to minorities to the disabled. Public education about blindness often begins with the first contact between one sighted and one blind person, and every such exposure paves the road to understanding.

In some cases, the onset of blindness can isolate a person, as it

143

did with Isabel, fifty-eight. Her degenerative eye disease caused her to retire. It was she who literally retreated, not those around her. She went to bed, staying there most of the day, rising only to prepare simple meals for herself.

Other students report similar reactions upon losing their sight—bed becomes a haven for hiding; sleep is an escape. With the perception of hindsight, Isabel realized that she was depressed and that her friends were coming to visit her out of concern, not disguised curiosity. Had she not crawled out of her cocoon of covers, she probably would have lost that circle of people reaching out to her. Luckily, it wasn't too late.

Emile, an engineer of forty-nine, suffered gradual sight loss, too. Taking a year off from work to learn to cope with his disability, Emile found himself falling comfortably into a routine around home. At last he had time to putter in his workshop, to plant fruit trees, and play with his two active sons.

"What about your work associates and close colleagues?" I asked. "A year is a long time if you're not among their company. Sometimes it's hard to pick up where you left off, especially if you're physically different from when they saw you last."

Emile mulled over that bit of advice for a week. Then he announced he wouldn't be in the next day for training. He was going back to the office to have lunch with the guys. He told me afterward of their initial uneasiness—colleagues weren't sure of when or how to help him. Could he read the menu? Was he able to find his way to the men's room? Because we had talked at length about these quandaries, Emile was ready for them. He explained what kind of help he needed, and that he wasn't totally blind, being able to discern large objects and manage by himself most of the time.

"I used to be quiet, staying pretty much to myself," admitted Mary, thirty-six. Her diabetes left her with vision that varied from day to day. Not only could she not count on it, how could she expect others to catch on?

"Now I find myself talking with people, even strangers on the bus. Because I can't watch what other people are doing and read their expressions, I'm moving toward them in the only way I know," reflected this woman who had returned to college to complete her degree.

Like Isabel and Emile, Mary plunged in by reaching out to others far more than ever before. These three people haven't let themselves tumble backwards into the abyss of withdrawal, that murky hole in which they could wallow for the rest of their lives. They have recognized that sighted friends and strangers, facing them as blind people for the first time, could also be backing up a step.

Have you taken a good look inside yourself recently? How does your self-esteem measure up? Do you see yourself as being less of a person because you see poorly or not at all? Do you bill yourself as second-best or damaged merchandise because of a visual impairment? Does your attitude of low self-worth express itself in posture, tone of voice, manner of speech, or facial expression? You may be unconsciously apologizing for the immutable fact that you are legally blind. If blindness is incurable, it's as unalterable as your build, sex, or age. Recognizing it as such, compensating when you can, and accepting assistance when you can't will make you more comfortable and other people more at ease.

Perhaps this misconception that everyone has to measure up to the mythical ideal accounts for many partially sighted people who try to slide by, passing themselves off as being normally sighted.

"Why didn't Joe tell us that he was legally blind?" said a mutual friend, somewhat angry and hurt. "We always wondered why his wife drove all the time. When we were last with them at the lake, we were exclaiming about a freighter coming by. Why did Joe pretend that he saw it, too?"

Joe was doing a disservice to himself and those close in his life. Because he can move around independently, recognize people when they are near enough, and outwardly appear totally self-sufficient, he is confident that he has pulled the wool over his friends' eyes—his bluff kept his visual impairment a secret.

When I speak with people like Joe, I ask what happens when the neighbor across the street waves and they fail to acknowledge the gesture or when the kids' car pool needs a driver unexpectedly? Doesn't the excuse that he needs stronger glasses so he won't have to hold the newspaper so close wear thin after a while?

People with partial sight counter by insisting they don't want to be dubbed as blind, as the word rings sourly in the ears of the sighted, and they don't want to be doted upon when they can handle themselves quite well. In many cases, those points are valid. But the flaw is that no one with limited vision can expect to perform with the precision or accuracy of one with normal vision in some instances. By failing to explain your restriction, you are setting yourself up for expectations you can't possibly meet. Instead of accepting the fact that you don't see well, others may think you aren't very bright, or are uncooperative, or a snob.

Ruth is in her early fifties. Tunnel vision allows her to read a newspaper slowly, yet she uses a dog guide.

"That's a toughie to get across," she told me. "I'm sure some people think I'm a fraud. I just tell anyone curious enough to ask that I can see in a very narrow field but not straight ahead. When I'm walking, my field is so limited I may not notice an obstacle. That's why I have a dog."

How would you react if a good friend approached you with this story: "I've just been diagnosed as having a serious eye disease. I can still see well enough to get around by myself. I can read some print. Some days are better for me than others. My vision comes and goes. I might spot a dime on the floor ten feet away, but may not recognize a neighbor who toots as he drives by."

Would you think less of that person? Probably not. You might ask a few questions about whether surgery would help, wonder if you yourself could lend a hand, and let it go at that. If this person were a dear friend, naturally your concern would increase. Certainly you wouldn't lose sight of him as the neighbor, colleague, or friend you had before. As you became accustomed to his functioning with decreased vision, you would accommodate when necessary and forget about it, accepting him as the human being he is.

Now consider giving other people the credit you attribute to yourself in such a situation.

At twenty-four, Bob became instantly, totally blind from an industrial accident. Months spent in the hospital served as a buffer between him and the outside world. Nurses, doctors, and therapists quickly adjusted to his blindness. They picked up on such cues as identifying themselves upon entering his room, placing objects directly into his hand, and letting him know as they left so he wouldn't be speaking to thin air.

When discharged from the sanctuary of the hospital, Bob realized that the rest of the world didn't operate on the same wavelengths. The awakening of constant accommodation to sighted people who were unsure of what to say and how to act developed into frequent frustrations and painful moments for Bob.

"It seems as if every time I meet someone new, it's the first time that person has run into someone blind," he maintained. "Do I always have to answer those probing questions—details of my accident, that I'll never see again, how it feels to live without sight?"

Bob can stand up for his own right to privacy. When he doesn't feel like discussing anything related to his loss of sight, he can make that point clear. A total stranger wouldn't ask another why he is fat, how long he's been divorced, or what his annual income is. If Bob considers his blindness a personal affair, he doesn't have to share it with a casual acquaintance. An open, forthright statement to the curious pedestrian who walks with him across the street could be, "I think that is quite a personal question." Such encroachments often begin by a stranger softening the blow with the remark that he hopes you don't mind a personal question. If you do object, say so.

I heard a story about a psychiatrist who was seeing a woman whose deteriorating vision had thrown her into a state of confusion and despair. During one session she complained that people stared at her, especially when she was carrying a white cane. "Don't be silly. Why should people stare at you?" chided the doctor. The good doctor apparently wasn't attuned to such reactions when people encounter anyone different—unusually tall, in a wheelchair, or on crutches—or even a ravishing woman. When others stare at you or, worse still, talk about you as if you aren't there, naturally you feel uncomfortable and resentful. One partially sighted woman who noticed a fellow elevator passenger eyeing her with her cane turned to him and said, "Excuse me. I notice you've been staring at me. I don't think we know each other." That fellow and the others caught the message. He shifted uneasily as attention fell upon him for this breach of etiquette.

Often a blind person has to bend a little, even with the most flagrant violations of decorum. Remember how it was when you were sighted, and how little you knew about blindness. Putting yourself into the other guy's shoes gives you a sense of his trepidation. Sometimes a sighted stranger makes an untoward remark simply because he's rattled.

Speaking to the companion of one who is blind is an example that frequently happens. "What does she want for dessert?" "Where does he want to go?" "How did she get here?" Taking the third person approach is a signal the stranger just doesn't know how to handle the situation. By just saying, "Please speak directly to me so I can tell you what I need," you'll be letting that stranger know you're able to answer perfectly well yourself. No ego suffers damage. Some blind folks, irritated by this occurrence or in a bad mood themselves, resort to this tactic: "She wants cream in her coffee."

That's a rather rough put-down. But you have your foul moods, too. When annoyed enough, you might go that route. Just don't make a habit of being surly.

Sure, there will be times when you feel these affronts are assaulting you like a battering ram. If you allow yourself the false luxury of being constantly caustic and cynical, a reputation of hostility soon will build around you. Then your social contacts will drop off like autumn leaves, perhaps never to spring to life again.

In the same vein, don't become an injustice collector. You don't want people to be wary of you, fearful that you will deliver a stinging attack because of some oversight from the past. One friend confided that once he caught on to the what-to-do's and what-not-to-do's in our relationship, he was chagrined at some of the faux pas he had committed. Our friendship grew even deeper when he realized I wouldn't remind him of his past failings. Most folks begin with good intentions. It is in executing these intentions that they bungle. Brace yourself for these bumblers, remembering that their feelings and ego are just as sensitive as yours, and everyone will come out on top.

Regardless of your degree of sight, there will be times when you don't recognize someone who speaks to you. Your spouse's identity could conceivably bewilder you if you didn't expect that person to be in a particular place at that time. Your spouse would probably say his name, knowing that these circumstances could be mystifying. Otherwise, guessing games can be hazardous. I muddled hopelessly through a conversation with a woman who plainly thought I knew who she was. Fishing for a clue, I inquired about her children. "Kids!" she exclaimed indignantly. "You know I'm not married."

Just 'fess up and tell the mystery arrival you don't recognize him. If your acquaintance or friend appears crestfallen, remind him that you announce your name when calling by phone. They'll catch on and identify themselves when there's doubt. The few who insist on playing the guess-who game are unwittingly taking advantage of your lack of vision. Unless that is a challenge you enjoy, bow out. The guess-who'er puts a name to you because he sees you. Why should he expect you to do the same when you hear only a word or two?

Awkwardness may be a measure of self-defense. By letting a stranger immediately know how to help you, you are relieving his anxiety. Tell the pedestrian that you will take his arm. Ask the waitress to read the menu. Explain to the clerk that you can see most colors but you can't decipher price tags too well. Then the stranger has a better grasp of what to do. The dilemma of wondering, which causes many sighted people to back away or to come on too strong, is resolved.

"I hang back when it comes to helping a blind pedestrian," said a businessman who worked in the congested downtown area. "I've been rebuked sharply several times. Nobody deals well with rejection."

Frankly, I don't blame that man for being reluctant. Attempts to lend a hand by those who are uncertain of how or what to do might be irritating, but to snap at the hand that reaches out to you is even worse. You or another blind person might desperately need that hand someday, only to find it isn't extended. If assistance would confuse or delay you, you can dismiss it but not put down the prospective helper: "Thanks, but I can manage now. But there are times when I'll need to count on you." A no-lose exchange. You are asserting your ability to cope, but not destroying the other person's well-meant intention.

What about those boners that make you want to vanish into thin air? You hugged the wrong person in greeting, knocked a cocktail out of your hostess's hand, or sat on somebody's lap instead of an empty chair. Prolonging your apologies magnifies the blunder. Embarrassing moments don't visit themselves only upon blind people—they crop up in everyone's life. Downplay them as much as you can. If others dwell on your mistake, try changing the subject: "No, I didn't burn myself with that spilled coffee. Let's get on to more interesting topics—what do you think about the upcoming election?"

At a large gathering or party, a boor might latch onto you. He may mistakenly think that since he and you are different, differents attract. When you can't escape under your own steam, do you have to suffer through the entire evening? A foolproof escape hatch I've discovered is to excuse myself by saying that I'm going to the bathroom. That's a nonnegotiable statement, and one that nobody will try to dissuade you from executing. If the boor offers to show you the way, the dodge is to remark that you would feel more comfortable if the host or hostess went with you. When well out of earshot, you can confide in your companion, suggesting that on the return trip you sit somewhere else.

Other guests circulate in a friendly group; why shouldn't you? Sometimes your spouse or companion drifts away to visit with other guests. You have that option, too. The people with whom you have been chatting may not be boorish, but tell them that you would like to mingle. There is nothing wrong in your saying that you would like to dip into the conversation at the other end of the room, and would someone go over there with you.

Speaking of earshot, be careful of who's within and who's without. You'd feel chagrined complaining about your neighbor's brats if their mother were sitting within six feet of you. Nor would you wish to whisper sweet nothings in someone's ear when those words could carry farther than you thought. When in doubt, quietly and discreetly ask who is close enough to hear.

Although blind people complain that sighted folks sometimes raise their voice as if they were deaf, some blind persons lapse into the so-called broadcast voice. Perhaps excitement, pleasure at seeing old friends, or plain forgetfulness causes them to veritably shout. That characteristic is a virtual flag waver.

I mentioned the bathroom as a way out. For everybody it's a

must every so often. Some folks would rather suffer in silence than to make this need known to anybody. No one will be stunned speechless if you ask to be shown to the bathroom. Don't be shocked, either, if your guide flicks on the light. It's just a sign that he thinks of you as he does anyone else. It's actually a left-handed compliment. To make an issue of this oversight would result in drawing unwanted attention to your disability.

"I hate to dwell on the bathroom business," reluctantly admitted a student, "but what can I do if I'm out with a woman, or I'm in a public place by myself? It seems like such a personal request. Besides, I may not know my date very well."

I cautioned him with a story about another male student who occasionally took his wife to dinner. When he wanted to use the restroom, his wife accompanied him inside. Up to that point they had been fortunate in not finding another man. But that luck was bound to break, causing a most embarrassing situation for all involved.

When seeking help from someone of the opposite sex, you can suggest that your friend show you to the door. Unfolding a collapsible cane when you step inside, you can signal to others that you might need to be shown to the facilities. That's more dignified than fumbling around on your own. If you're alone, there is no choice. Your friend can wait for you a discreet distance from the exit. Once inside, women would do well to find toilet paper before sitting down—it can be in the least expected places. They might also check the position of the toilet seat—it's quite a jolt when it's up. Before washing your hands, round up soap, paper towel or hand dryer, and wastebasket. It's miserable searching with dripping hands.

As in the example of someone turning on the bathroom light, people will forget at times that you are blind. They may point to an object, exclaim about an unusual sight, or hand you something to read. I visited an executive recently who gallantly showed me to the first floor exit at the end of our interview. As I stood with him on the crowded elevator, I held his arm with one hand, my dog's leash with the other.

"Where did you park your car?" he casually queried.

"I'm taking a cab this time," I answered, not even cracking a smile. I'm not sure yet that he realized what he said, but I wouldn't dream of humiliating him, especially among a group of strangers.

"How do I get back into the mainstream of socializing with friends and colleagues?" mused Kay, the social worker whom we met at the beginning of this book. "Some people turn away from me as if I had the plague."

Kay expressed sentiments echoed by many people who have lost their sight, as well as some who have never seen. Some blind people gravitate toward others with a visual impairment. Perhaps there is a feeling of camaraderie, a common denominator that binds them together. Certainly the need to explain, defend, or rationalize doesn't exist. Nobody will wonder how you get dressed in the morning or if you always find your mouth when you eat. Only you can decide whether your social contacts will be among other blind folks, those who can see, or both. Most important is that you make and maintain these relationships. That won't happen if you're behind closed doors, shut in your house, or closed within yourself. I advised Kay to reach out to friends. She could come up with ideas for social engagements instead of waiting for them to step forward. Though she may not feel ready to attend a wedding reception of 200 people, an evening at home with three or four friends for cards or conversation would seem more reasonable. I counseled her not to wait for friends to draw her out, but to consciously extend herself to them.

By being the initiator and starting on a small scale, word will filter out to others in your circle that you are back in circulation. Sure, people will talk and speculate among themselves about your sight loss, but what do you expect? Would you remain tight-lipped if a close friend lost a spouse or child? Of course not. With mutual friends you would express your concern and perhaps curiosity about the event. Don't count on the majority of people being different.

"I still feel uneasy in a group, especially when I don't know anyone else," confided Bill, twenty-six, who had been partially sighted all his life. "Yet I want desperately to make friends."

Bill lived by himself and remained pretty much to himself. I pointed out that his world wouldn't widen unless he put himself into places where other people are. His vision enabled him to move about independently. Why wasn't he taking part in groups in which he might meet people with similar interests? His range of social activities might take him to groups of other blind people for recreation, to civic, church, or singles organizations that form around hobbies or goals. He had to agree when I reminded him that the world wasn't stampeding to his door to befriend him—he had to throw that door open wide.

At the other end of the spectrum are senior citizens whose loss of sight assails them late in life. These times become even more painful when lifelong friends and other family members die. An older person can feel really isolated. "I can't be bothered with those senior citizen clubs," complained Robert, sixty-five. "I don't give a hoot about playing cards or square dancing anyway." "Don't you find time heavy on your hands and sometimes feel lonely?" I prodded. "Once in a while," he answered grudgingly. He quickly defended himself. "I have the TV and the cat."

Robert had been a maintenance man in the public school system. He liked to tinker around the house. From an over-the-fence conversation, he discovered that the working couple next door had neither time nor know-how to do some minor repairs their home required. Robert offered his skills and refused payment. His neighbors occasionally invited him to dinner and included him on family outings for picnics and trips to the zoo.

Some blind people are housebound because of other disabilities. If this is your dilemma, then friends and acquaintances have to come to you. An eighty-two-year-old woman I know is legally blind and unable to walk because of arthritis. She rarely suffers from lack of company. Her constant stream of visitors delights in her attentiveness to them. Through radio and TV she keeps well-informed about what's happening in the world, and by listening carefully to those who visit she keeps track of the ups and downs in her friends' lives. No one minds making a cup of coffee or taking a bottle of beer from the refrigerator. This lady operates on the "help yourself" philosophy, and everyone's happy. An avid poker player, this woman knows when to hold and when to fold, whether it's a card game or the web of human relationships.

Perhaps we might learn something from her. What are you proving when you decline offers such as a hand through the cafeteria line, a friend reading a large amount of printed material, or an arm extended to you in crowded conditions? There is a thin line between personal dignity and allowing others to take the rough edges off a difficult situation. It may come down to permitting somebody the satisfaction of providing assistance. One line from the movie, *Wait Until Dark* sticks with me. A frustrated friend said to the central character, who was blind, "What do you want to be—the world's champion blind woman?"

You may want to be the champion chess player, gardener, speller, or woodworker. But being the world's champion blind man or woman is a goal not to be sought. Nothing will turn off other people quicker than the attitude of total independence, of being always able to do it yourself.

Regardless of where and under what circumstances, there are a few innuendos that can escape your limited vision. Most people prefer eye contact. If you cannot maintain eye contact, at least look in the direction of the person who is speaking with you. Nothing is more distracting to a sighted person than to have a conversant's head turned in the opposite direction, or looking down or up. As much as possible, try to match your facial expression and gestures appropriately with the conversation. You'll want to avoid the blank, vacant stare or the ever-present smile that sometimes is characteristic of people who have never seen. Tune in to other people's nonverbal communication. Body language can speak many words, such as "I'm bored," "I want to leave," or "I'm nervous." Shuffling feet, rustling papers, or a head turned away from you are all such signals.

There may be times when you'll be uncertain if it is you being addressed. You would feel foolish if another person is the object of a question to which you answered. When you're not sure whether it is your turn to speak, just interject, "Excuse me, were you talking to me?"

"I'm ready to get back into the dating scene," confided a man in his late twenties. "I'm afraid of being rejected by a woman because of my poor vision, but I enjoy the company of women just as much as I did when my vision was perfect."

That's a toughie. My reaction was to encourage him to approach a woman he wanted to date, suggest that they go out for dinner or a movie, and then to matter-of-factly add that he has a visual impairment. He could allay any apprehension on her part by openly stating what his needs are, including the obvious fact that she must drive. Just as in any other dating situation, the final decision is up to her.

Many blind people complain that dating is extremely difficult because visual disability is a turnoff to most uninformed sighted folks. They maintain that it's impossible to flash the "I'm interested in you" signal, which is purely visual, or to realize when it is being sent to them. If you are in this predicament, you probably find that relationships don't occur with a one-time encounter. It may take several contacts before another person catches on that blindness has little to do with your personality. That means getting yourself out among eligible members of the opposite sex through social activities and cultural events. It may call for more initiation on your part than you would ordinarily consider making. Women's liberation is on your side if you are a female. Introductions through friends are always helpful because they can sometimes resolve the discomfort that an unaware sighted person might register.

As you can see, there are no pat formulas for dealing with social situations, no stockpile of ready answers, no ready-made comebacks or guaranteed salves for your bruised ego. Some folks, blind and sighted, develop more self-confidence and poise by taking assertiveness training classes. I know a blind man who developed more social presence by taking a Dale Carnegie course. You weren't an island before losing your sight; you cannot afford becoming one now.

It's natural to feel somewhat intimidated or threatened at first during social encounters. Pull yourself together, think positively about your own image, and force yourself forward. Forget about the faux pas and concentrate on the satisfaction of human contact. Remember that the more you hang back, the farther you slide into that bottomless pit of withdrawal. The only way is up and out, even if you edge ever so slowly.

Chapter 17

YOUR SUPPORT SYSTEM
IS PEOPLE, NOT MACHINES

S o you've come around to the realization that you can't do it all alone. Everyone, regardless of visual acuity, is somewhat adrift in the same boat. Perhaps that unbending ideal of bullheaded independence is a carryover from the pioneer days when the family gleaned almost everything from the land. Remember reading in history books about huskin' bees and barn raisings? Our forefathers probably weren't as self-sufficient as historians would lead us to believe.

The loss of your sight, whether it has been gradual or sudden, partial or total, is probably the greatest crisis in your life. Your reaction could be one of utter disbelief, depression, or bitterness—or a combination of all three. Discussing your feelings of frustration and disappointment is one way of recovering from this staggering blow. If you choose to seek professional help but cannot afford regular fees, community agencies often can refer you to resources that charge according to ability to pay. Health insurance may cover the major portion of such costs. Rehabilitation centers for the blind frequently include social workers and counselors who deal specifically with people suffering sight loss. Families and friends also might be included because blindness does not affect the life of one person exclusively. Sessions can be individual, or group therapy, in which people facing the same difficulties air their feelings and learn coping mechanisms from each other.

Don't consider yourself weak-kneed or, worse still, missing a few marbles if you enlist professional help. The objectivity of a trained counselor may be enough for you to see your way clear in living with this disability and its ramifications. You wouldn't hesitate to see a dentist for a toothache or an auto mechanic if the brakes on your car gave out. Should your depression continue month after month, for a year or more, it's time to do something about it. Nobody can make the world go away for you, but some people can help make it more bearable.

Your route to set emotional turmoil to rest may bring you to a confidant, possibly a spouse, child, clergyman, or trusted friend. Probably this same person has turned to you in the past for entirely different reasons, but now it's your turn. You were there and will be there when needed. You'll have to be careful not to dump upon the same person all the time or too often, because even the most patient run out of emotional support. Since your confidant may have problems of his own, and moods that vary, your time to unload might not be his right time. Someone who is burdened cannot assume your troubles, too. In short, before leaning upon someone else, assess his mood first.

Keeping your own counsel (some people think they must) isn't a sign of rugged individualism. It can be a painful denial of the comfort and consolation that another can provide. Obviously, your counselor or friend can't restore your vision. Sometimes sharing that grief is enough to make you feel better able to face yourself and life.

Besides psychological reinforcement, what about compensations for the gaps left by decreased vision? You have performed some of these everyday tasks without thought because you could see what you were doing. Now some of them lie in the realm of the impossible (such as driving), or are extremely difficult. Sewing on a button could have taken five minutes when you could see well. It may now develop into a forty-five-minute marathon of pricked fingers, tangled thread, and jangled nerves. Your first two years of college might have been an enticing challenge. Because reading takes you twice as long now, it stretches into periods of fatigue, bordering on exhaustion.

A question I usually pose to my students is, Whom do you consider to be your support system? That query frequently puzzles people—they think of support systems as equipment employed to sustain life, to take over when body systems cease functioning. The light dawns as I explain that when eyes shut down partially or totally, others have to take over in some instances to make up what they can't accomplish with this vital operation.

"My fifteen-year-old son and I get along fine," boasted a forty-one-year-old woman. "He's so good about taking me shopping, reading the mail, helping with the housework, and lending a hand in the kitchen. Life has been smooth since my divorce. I don't know what I'd do without my boy."

The flaw is obvious and tragic. This mother depends only on one person, and her support system is one link, not a chain. What will happen when her teenager strikes out on his own in three or four years? Right now he's in the throes of adolescent turbulence. Although every youngster should shoulder responsibilities, are too many too much?

"My wife handles everything—she always has," confided a man in his late fifties. "She drives me anywhere I want to go, does the paperwork, and keeps up our home. She's kept busy, though, because we have a daughter who is legally blind and has two children that she's raising by herself. My wife often helps them out, too."

Not until he actually put it into words did this man comprehend the full impact of what he had said. His spouse was carrying several burdens singlehandedly. Apparently she isn't a complainer; he would have probably sought alternatives if she were.

If your loss of sight involved illness, surgery, and hospitalization for long periods, you'll recall that family members hovered close. They anticipated your needs before you expressed them. A hand reached out to guide you around the bookcase. The coffee cup appeared in your hand before you asked for coffee. When you were recovering, family and friends began to breathe easier. Fears surrounding your disability and their insecurity started to fade. Feeling stronger and better able to manage, you probably tried fending more for yourself. Perhaps you had to literally brush away those hands so eager to help, or quiet the voices questioning your independence. If you haven't taken a few steps on this road back, I hope that some of the suggestions in this book will give, you the know-how and confidence to try.

Yet you still have those impossible or hard-to-do tasks with which to contend. Are you asking the same people all the time, like the mother of her son or the husband of his wife? Have you detected any resentment, maybe half concealed? Tone of voice or demeanor can say more than "I don't want to," or "I'm tired (or busy) right now." Just as you ought to be sensitive to the confidant who can't handle your concerns because he's weighed down straightening out his own life, you need to tune in to the demands you place upon others, no matter how close they are to you. A partially sighted man put it well when he said, "It becomes a case of diminishing gladness."

How about expanding your support system and adding a few links? Start with yourself. Can you reasonably carry out some of the responsibilities you have laid upon others? If you're not working, time isn't such a precious commodity. So you take the bus to the shopping center instead of asking somebody to drive you. It may be that your partner has returned to work because you are unable or don't have a job. Sure, you might bungle and balk at first, but can you try your hand at keeping the house going? In many instances trade-offs are an answer. Previously you paid bills, kept records, and tended to the taxes. Now your spouse has assumed these duties because you can't read well enough. Doing the laundry could be your contribution or share of the bargain.

Have you thought about stepping outside boundaries of household and immediate family for helpers? By going to the store with a neighbor instead of your partner, you allow your partner more freedom. If taking the bus or cab is out of the question, you can work out arrangements for running errands. One friend could drop you off at the dentist's office, another could pick you up.

Although your son or daughter wants to please, occasionally asking another youngster to pitch in with routine tasks relieves your offspring and gives somebody else's kid a chance to reap satisfaction.

I have a sighted colleague who read to a fellow student while they were both in college. When they graduated, she continued to come to his apartment two hours a week to go over mail, check his clothes for cleanliness, and assist with filing. When the man married, she continued to provide assistance.

"He just didn't want to pile it all on his wife," reported Linda. "She also worked. I really enjoyed these times with him because he is such a cheerful fellow, involved in so many stimulating activities. We accomplish a lot in those sessions, and the three of us benefit from them."

Linda touched upon a point for you to keep in mind: Everybody needs to feel needed. Of course, that doesn't mean all the time, by the same person. Many people will be flattered, even delighted, if you would call upon them.

If you don't have distant relatives or friends upon whom you can depend, don't consider volunteers active only in hospital auxiliaries and political campaigns. Many folks would welcome the opportunity to work on a one-to-one relationship, even though you're not a member of any organization. College fraternities and sororities, churches, senior citizen groups, high school students, United Way, public service agencies, and high school counselors are sources you might not have thought of tapping. You'll need to meet and screen would-be assistants. Despite best intentions, personalities can clash; your expectations and your helper's capabilities won't necessarily match.

Many of our students balk at increasing their support system, afraid of being a nuisance to an outsider. They rationalize that spouse, children, or parents are somehow obligated to perform services. They conjecture that to branch out might imply troubled waters at home or could cause family members to feel unwanted or unsatisfactory. Perhaps these skeptics never considered that, given the option of relief from expected duties, one's family might well feel released. You would be wise to lay your intentions out in the open, to explain why you are seeking others' help, and then test the winds.

Your approach to seeking a hand, whether from family, friends, or volunteers (volunteers can develop into friends) should not border on the conviction that you are a bother and a burden.

"I don't suppose you'd like to take me to the shopping center tomorrow night?" or, "Could I bother you to write some checks for me?" smack of self-pity and anticipated rejection.

Make your request direct but not demanding. "I have to go to the shopping center tomorrow night. Would you be interested in going with me—maybe you have errands to do too." Or try this: "Bill-paying time is rolling around again. Could you give me a hand in writing checks—at least they aren't yours."

Tony is thirty-two, partially sighted, and in poor health from diabetes. He is divorced and lives with elderly parents. He justifiably is reluctant to prevail upon his mother and father too often and is also hesitant to farm out his errands to his two married sisters.

"How do you manage when you have to go somewhere and can't get there on your own?" I questioned.

"I guess I still go back to my parents," Tony admitted. "I've called on other people, but when they tell me no, I don't try again."

Tony might abide by another maxim: no doesn't mean never. Most people claim to be busy—it sometimes happens that the busiest folks can find time for you. But conflicts in schedule can occur, or the proposed jaunt or task is something that they would rather not do. When making your request, give a person room to say no. Being turned down once doesn't necessarily mean you'll be refused again and again. You'll catch on quickly enough if the one who denies your request would prefer not to be asked at all in the future.

Nor should you lay a sense of guilt upon a person who says no.

"But I was counting on you to go with me to the auto show. I don't know how I'll get there now."

Your would-be companion might soften to comply with your wishes because he doesn't feel right when confronted with leaving you in the lurch. By spinning him off on a guilt trip, you're setting up a roadblock he'll attempt to avoid in the future. He'll be dodging that barrier—and you. You'll have to hide your disappointment, pass it off with assurances you can find someone else, and let it go.

You are more likely to receive yes responses if you plan ahead and choose a companion who doesn't have an aversion for the tasks or errands you have in mind. Of course, it's fun to operate on the spur of the moment. Unless you know kindred spirits who will drop everything for your whim, your intentions will have to fit into somebody's routine.

Unless it's an emergency, calling someone at the last minute can be inconsiderate. It's just as thoughtless to urge a friend to accompany you to a jazz concert, or to sew for you, when you know that activity is at the bottom of that person's list.

"I don't like being always on the receiving end."

That's another objection. You won't be able to reciprocate in kind, as in driving or doing paperwork, but there are other ways of evening the score. Friends who take me shopping come to expect dinner afterward—it's a treat for people who cook for themselves. People who do little favors often delight in unexpected small gifts, such as home-baked cookies or a bottle of wine. The fact that you can be a pleasant companion, who listens attentively to a friend's concerns, frequently is more than enough.

Some blind people are able to pay for routine services that would otherwise be handled by those close to them. If you can afford to hire someone to cut the grass, do household maintenance, or drive for you, again you are freeing up links in your support system for more intimate help, for which you wouldn't want an outsider.

Single parents and single persons living alone are no longer uncommon. I have noticed this phenomenon among students I meet. The question I pose to folks in these circumstances is, "What would you do in case of an emergency?" Suppose your eleven-year-old daughter had an appendicitis attack at 2 AM, or you cut your hand seriously while washing dishes. Since you don't drive, would you call the police for help? Wouldn't you want someone with you—relative, friend, or neighbor—to provide you moral support? You can get to a hospital emergency room or a loved one's bedside in an ambulance, police car, or taxi. After you're there, would you feel equipped to face the crisis by yourself? Most students haven't covered this possibility in their planning. My solution is to establish an emergency reserve list, consisting of a few people you could call without warning and upon whom you could rely to confront a crisis with you. Ideally, these people would live within a few miles of you, because time is essential in an emergency.

When you start to build your emergency reserve list, it's only fair to ask people whether they can come through under such circumstances. Assure them that, even though it is highly unlikely, you could call in the middle of the night. While making your inquiries, find out whether friends or neighbors abhor the sight of blood. I had one friend bow out because he couldn't stand to see blood. Another couple I know admitted that neither remained cool in a crisis. With these reservations in the open, you can move on to others better able to cope with the unexpected. Having three or four names on your emergency reserve list is common sense — people may not be home when you need them. I tried four different friends until finding one at home when my father became seriously ill at 9 PM one Saturday. Posting your list by the telephone eliminates searching and frantically wasted moments.

Establishing and using a support system for routine tasks beyond you, and extraordinary events outside your control, is one of the greatest barriers blindness can bring. Besides considering others' needs and feelings, think about your possible subconscious resentment of depending too much and too often on the same few.

Start out by doing what you can reasonably expect of yourself. Then, by diffusing your requests, accommodating them when possible to others' convenience, and compensating either by pay, little gifts, or the all-important giving of yourself, you won't be putting undue pressure on any one link in your support system. You, in turn, become a living link in the support system of those dear to you.

Chapter 18

THE THREE R'S
AIN'T WHAT THEY USED TO BE

L osing my sight meant not being able to read," recalled Alan, a man in his early twenties who had earned a master's degree in American history before an eye disease took its toll. "That was the hardest blow of all because most of my life had been spent poring over books."

At the other end of the spectrum was Robert, nearly seventy. He had enough vision to read newspapers for a short time.

"You can't tell me I'd sit still long enough to enjoy reading," he grumbled. "I wasn't much for messing around with books and papers—maybe the sports page once in a while. I always had too much to do, so books never caught my fancy."

Alan and Robert are two among thousands of participants in the Talking Books program under the Library of Congress. They select from over 33,000 books and forty-three recorded magazines on four-track cassettes or long-playing discs. Their selections can range from astrology to zoology, mysteries, Westerns, historic and modern romance, science fiction, books for children and young adults, adventures, and best-sellers. Nonfiction works include politics, health, psychology and self-help, travel, sports, biography, and science. The entire Bible has been recorded. Some of the more popular magazines recorded are *Reader's Digest, National Geographic, Sports Illustrated, Ebony, Good Housekeeping,* and *Newsweek.* There are special-interest magazines on music, foreign affairs, and blindness.

If you're not already on the Talking Book bandwagon, you might give it a whirl. 'Tis true: Some of the best things in life are still free. Equipment on which to play recorded books is lent without charge. Think of these books, which come through the mail postage free, as library books. You have to return them, but you don't pay postage. Ordering a list of Talking Books is usually as simple as picking up the phone to call the Talking Book library nearest you. Returning them requires reversing the address card on the front of the mailing container and dropping it into a mailbox. Some obliging postmen pick them up as they make mail deliveries at your home.

To find one of the over 50 regional Talking Book libraries or one of the nearly 100 subregional libraries still means you have to know the name of the specific library you want. Call your closest public library to learn which Talking Book library serves your area. Upon hearing of this service, some eager students assume that they can play cassettes on a home tape deck or records on a stereo. Not so. Talking Book cassettes are recorded at $15/16$-inch per second, twice as slow as the speed of commercial recorders. The cassette player's four-track capacity allows up to four hours of listening per tape. Library of Congress players can only play back, not record. Discs are recorded at $8\frac{1}{3}$ r.p.m., twice as slow as the stereo's lowest setting, 16 r.p.m.

You have the option of requesting a cassette player, disc player, or both. It's likely most books you'll want will have been recorded on cassette. Because of timeliness and reduced production costs, most magazines are on disc. Some come directly from the publisher and do not need to be returned. New books generally are recorded onto cassette. The cassette player can operate on rechargeable batteries. An ordinary earphone for a transistor radio permits you to read without distracting others, or you can order a headset from the library. An extra cassette player or disc player can be purchased from Science for the Blind. The disc player is much smaller than that issued by the Library of Congress.

Anyone legally blind or physically unable to hold a book or turn pages is eligible for Talking Book services. If your equipment breaks down, return it to the public library where it will be picked up for repair. A replacement will soon follow in the mail.

Your Talking Book librarian will send you an application. You must have it signed by someone who can authorize your status of legal blindness. When your equipment arrives through the mail, listen to the cassette or disc of instructions. The cassette player could initially puzzle you because of its four tracks, two speeds, and control to increase or slow reading rate. I've known students to miss half of a book (they never found out who did it) because they didn't change the side selector switch to hear all four sides of the tape. Control buttons, which bear raised markings, are brightly colored, so you don't have to be a mechanical wizard to operate the machine.

Boundaries of the world of recorded books and magazines extend beyond the Talking Book program, which has been in service since 1934. In the past few years, radio reading services have been springing up to help combat the information gap for the print handicapped. Volunteer readers broadcast over subchannels of FM radio stations as they read daily newspapers, current magazines, installments from books, ads from local stores, recipes, and cooking hints. Some programming features interviews with local celebrities, hints on coping with blindness, and call-in shows.

You can't tune in on your regular radio. You need a special receiver for the subchannel and the station that is its main carrier. Because broadcasts reach from fifty to seventy miles, you might be out of earshot. Contact your Talking Book library to learn if your area is covered. Over 100 services exist today, and their number is constantly increasing.

"I used to think I kept up with current events through TV," admitted one student. "But the newspaper is far more complete, especially with editorials and ads. Besides, now I don't miss Dear Abby."

Some reading services broadcast up to sixteen hours a day. You can choose your listening by following a program guide. Newspaper reading breaks into segments so that you can read sports, national and international news, or business by tuning in at the appointed time.

Most radio reading services charge a nominal annual subscription fee. Although readers aren't paid, costs mount for receivers, engineers, and studios. This charge wouldn't cover the cost of a daily newspaper. No listener is turned off because he can't manage the fee.

A partially sighted colleague came up with a marvelous suggestion for storing all of this equipment. She bought a three-shelved utility cart on wheels. A power strip is attached. On her mobile sound unit are her Talking Book machine, cassette player, radio receiver, and books. She rolls it around the house, plugging it in wherever she wants to read or listen.

The Bible is still among the most popular books sought by readers, sighted and blind. Should you want your own copy, you can buy it in several forms from several resources. The American Bible Society sells an 18-point edition of *The Good News*. The paperback copy costs $4.50. The hardcover edition in large print (including the Old Testament) comes in two volumes at $16. The entire Bible in Braille is in 18 volumes, costing $235, or $13.50 per volume.

Perhaps you'd rather settle back and listen to The Good Book. You can buy the King James version on flexible disc from Talking Book Bibles—its price is $7. The New International Version is read by Bill Pearce. Published by Bethel Publishing Company, this cassette edition of the New Testament also features background music. The "Living Bible" is a paraphrasing instead of reading word by word. Different readers take the parts of Biblical characters, and it is easy to understand. Your religious bookstore should be able to order cassette and large-print editions for you. Another resource for Braille and recorded Bibles is the John Milton Society.

"I still enjoy contact with the print word," said Beverley, fifty-six, who continued her job as high school English teacher after losing much of her sight. "But I find that regular-sized print tires me so fast. Can I find large print books anywhere?"

I told Beverly that public libraries are picking up on large print requirements of patrons. Many have extensive collections that borrowers can browse through and take home. Some Talking Book libraries also will send large-print titles through the mail. Some public libraries will bring books to people who are homebound or in nursing homes. Just as in Talking Books, the variety isn't as broad as in ordinary print. You also can subscribe to two large-print publications. The *Large Type Weekly* from the New York Times provides news capsules and crossword puzzles. *The Reader's Digest* is published monthly and also can be ordered directly from the publisher.

The National Library Service, the department of the Library of Congress that distributes Braille and Talking Books, hasn't overlooked music buffs. Scores in large print and Braille cover a wide range of music. Instructional cassettes teach rudiments to those who can't read musical notation. For further information, write to the Music Section of the National Library Service.

"I have a whole shelf of books that I never got around to reading," said Lynn, a thirty-five-year-old housewife whose sight loss happened suddenly. "I'm sure that many have not become Talking Books. Should I pack them up for the local charity and give up on ever having them read?"

Lynn is likely to find that her local Talking Book library has a volunteer group that would gladly record books of her choice. She won't have to pay for the service, but she must return cassettes. If she can't find a local organization, the National Library offers a listing called "Volunteers Who Produce Books." It is broken down by state, noting groups and their specialties: recording, large print, etc.

Recordings for the Blind, a national organization that cassette-records mostly textbooks for students, will be discussed more fully in Chapter 23. Don't run away, though—you don't have to be a student to use this service.

If print is still your primary means of communication, are you making access to it as easy as possible? If you're a bit fuzzy, review Chapters 6, 7, 8, and 10. There's no point in burying your nose in a book unless you must, or staining that schnoz with a felt-tip pen unless you can't read what you write with any other instrument.

People who take extensive notes may stay on the line better by using dark-lined paper. Heavily lined paper also could help those who dabble in accounting. You can order both from the American Printing House for the Blind.

Even if you haven't enough sight to see what you write, you should maintain your longhand because it can be immediate communication with sighted folks. You can buy writing guides from the American Foundation for the Blind or American Printing House for the Blind to keep you on the straight and narrow. Raised-line paper with ridges that can be felt spaced 3/4-inch apart serves the same purpose. When in a pinch without a writing guide, fold a sheet of plain paper into widths about 3/4 inch wide, unfolding it as you write.

Since your John Hancock will be demanded more than any other sample of your penmanship, you might consider a signature guide if you can't see where to sign. Either the American Foundation for the Blind or the American Printing House for the Blind is the place to purchase. The best guide is about two inches long, and an inch high. An elastic band runs horizontally near the bottom, giving you flexibility for letters that come below the line, such as g or y. Use one of these, and your signature will be straight and contained within a reasonable space.

"I always thought that all blind people learned Braille," maintained Dick, a former dock worker, now fifty-eight. "My hands have had a lot of wear and tear. I can still read some print, especially when I write it. Do I have to learn to feel those bumps?"

Dick shared the misconception that most sighted people and many blind people have: that blind and Braille are linked. It surprised him (and probably you) that less than 20 percent of the blind population knows Braille. Since so many people lose their sight in later life, and another hefty chunk see well enough to use print in some form, Braille users are a definite minority.

Braille is a system of six dots contained within a cell three dots high and two dots wide. By relying on various combinations within the six-dot limit, all letters, numbers, and punctuation marks can be reproduced. When Louis Braille invented the system in the midnineteenth century, his intention was that symbols could be felt easily by moving fingers across them. Louis didn't count on people who, like Dick, had injured nerve endings in their fingertips, or physical problems such as those caused by diabetes or poor circulation that prevent people from feeling letters.

Braille consists of two levels. Grade One is enough for self-communication because it includes alphabet, numbers, and punctuation. Comprising Grade Two are nearly 200 contractions that represent whole words or parts of words. Practically all Braille publications are in Grade Two because it conserves so much space. It follows that your notes will be much quicker and concise in contracted form.

You can write Braille either with a slate and stylus or Braille writer. A slate is a hinged piece of metal with openings, each of which has six niches for the dots of the Braille cell. Sliding a heavy sheet of paper between the hinged metal, letters and contractions are punched with a pointed instrument—a stylus. Because you punch the stylus downward into indentations on the underside of the slate, you begin from the right. You read the Braille that results by turning over the page to scan from left to right. A Braille writer (not a Braille typewriter as it is frequently misnamed) is a six-key machine. You press combinations of these six keys simultaneously. Braille characters appear immediately, because paper feeds into the machine somewhat like a typewriter.

A slate and stylus for a blind person is as convenient as pen and paper for a sighted counterpart, being small and easy to carry. A Braille writer is faster, but its disadvantage is that it isn't conveniently portable, since it is about the size of a small typewriter. Expense is another factor. The Perkins Brailler, top of the line, costs about $250. You can buy Braille writing equipment from the American Foundation for the Blind, American Printing House for the Blind, and Howe Press.

"How could I learn Braille if I wanted to try?" That is a fair question. Rehabilitation agencies for the blind almost always include someone who can teach Braille. Some rehabilitation teachers will visit you in your home once a week or so. I have written two textbooks to teach blind adults. Both are available from the American Printing House for the Blind and could be used by someone who chose to study independently. They are *Getting in Touch with Reading* and *Getting in Touch with Reading: Grade Two*.

The Hadley School for the Blind in Winnetka, Illinois, is a nonprofit correspondence school. Among over 100 Hadley courses are several home-study Braille courses. As in any other Hadley course, lessons are mailed to an instructor. He returns them with comments and suggestions. There is no charge for this correspondence school, which is accredited.

If the conventional Braille cell is too small for you to feel, Jumbo Braille is another possibility. It is one-third larger and can sometimes be read by people unable to feel standard Braille.

"I'll probably lose the rest of my sight — I just don't know when," pondered Phil, forty-six. "Should I learn Braille now so I'll be prepared?"

Phil asked another of those questions without a black-and-white answer. My advice was for him to give it the old college try, at least to discover what it entailed. It takes about four to six weeks for someone to learn Grade One, another three or four months to wade through Grade Two. Count on a year or more before you become proficient, provided you don't let your newly acquired skills stagnate. If you have enough self-discipline to practice regularly, and if studying Braille doesn't drive you to drinking, give it a whirl. Don't let it develop into another source of anxiety for you. Remember, we're striving to wipe out as much of that stress as we can. If you do learn Grade Two, order a Braille book or two from your Braille lending library to sharpen your skill and increase reading speed. Otherwise, you'll forget many of those contractions.

Should Braille be impossible for you, and you still require some simple means of self-communication, Voxcom® might help. It is a machine that records brief notations onto cards bearing magnetic tape. It could be a method of noting phone numbers or labels. You can buy the recording device and notation cards for about fifty dollars from the Gladys Loeb Foundation.

Whether you rely on print, Braille, or neither, touch typing is another possible skill to add to your battery. Sure, you probably looked at the keys during those dreadful high school typing classes. You may now doubt that you could ever master the keyboard. You'll probably surprise yourself when you take to the typewriter, even for the first time.

When you dig the old portable out of the attic or ask the neighbor's kids to return it, you'll probably need some instruction. Rehabilitation agencies or rehabilitation teachers are good places to begin. You can also borrow instruction books on disc or cassette from your Talking Book library. Or you might take a typing course from Hadley. If you can read print well enough, buy a basic typing book and get started.

Despite typing teachers' protests, I still favor identifying the two major home keys: f and j. You can use tape or Hi Marks® glue. Especially in the beginning, you need to be confident about starting off with hands on the home row. If you move your hands to cassette player controls or consult Braille, your return will be quicker if those two keys are marked. Marking the numerals 4 and 7 also helps. Every secretary I know looks at numbers.

"I've been a secretary for years but can't figure out how to set margins without seeing the numbers on the scale," puzzled Hattie, sixty.

I reminded Hattie that the ribbon holder is a natural guide. If you're as unmechanical as I am, just determine where the keys come up to strike the page. Align the carriage so that were you to strike a character, it would print on the exact edge of the paper. From that point, space ten times per inch for a pica machine or twelve per inch for the elite. Repeat the same process on the right edge, but this time hit the backspace key to set the right margin.

Another mystery is how to make corrections. Executive Ko-Rec-Type® is small sheets of paper, each side easy to identify by touch. After slipping a sheet behind the ribbon holder with the shiny side toward you, backspace, restrike the error, and back space to hit the right character. Nobody will know you goofed. If you're among the blessed, your typewriter will have a correction key.

To insert your paper straight, roll it halfway into the machine so that both edges meet. After adjusting the paper so that both edges align exactly, roll the sheet back down to begin near the top. Use a backing sheet with about an inch cut off so that you'll know when you are nearing the bottom of the page. When the backing sheet slips out, you'll realize that you're near the end of the line. Address stickers save time in typing your return address on envelopes. If a service organization hasn't deluged you with them, you can buy them through mail order houses such as Sunset or Miles. They are often advertised in the Sunday newspaper.

To sign your name, turn the roller up three or four lines. Use the paper bail—the bar that holds the page against the roller—as a guide.

Now that you're keyed up about learning to type, or refreshing your skills, you may hang back about sending a letter to Aunt Susie because of your third-grade spelling level. Large-print readers will revel in a dictionary that doesn't have microscopic type: *Merriam-Webster Dictionary for Large Print Users*, published by G. K. Hall and Company, Boston, 1977. It's available in most well-stocked bookstores. Another help to those who hesitate with spelling is *20,000 Words*, published by McGraw-Hill Book Company. You can purchase it from the American Printing House for the Blind in large print or Braille or buy it in regular print from a bookstore. This book is an alphabetic listing of words that are syllabicated, with no definitions. Braille dictionaries are not very complete because they require so many volumes — *Webster's Unabridged* in thirty-three volumes is enough to engulf your living room. If you can't read print and wonder about a definition, you'd be wisest to have someone look it up for you or call your local library's reference department.

One final word about typewriters: ribbons wear out, get jammed, or dry up. Most typewriters have a stencil lever that you could inadvertently move, thus typing nothing. Occasionally ask somebody to see if your machine's print quality is good if you can't do it yourself. I heard of a college student who typed for two hours on a term paper, only to discover that the ribbon was faulty. I can't think of many things that are more discouraging.

To send those letters on their merry way, of course, you'll need stamps, unless you're sending Braille, tape, or large print to someone who is legally blind. Stamps in a roll are easier to handle, but if you don't have a bundle to buy a roll, try a book. You should be aware that not every stamp on a page is postage. Sometimes fillers are used to complete a page. If you have trouble getting to the post office, call to ask your mail carrier to drop off an order form for stamps. There is a minimal charge for this service, but they will be sent to your home.

Before leaving readin' and 'ritin', I'd be amiss by not mentioning electronic reading aids. Partially sighted people will find their fair share in Chapter 7. Technology is also advancing to resolve print reading for folks who can't manage print visually. The Kurzweil machine is the most sophisticated, converting printed characters into synthesized speech, sounding like a man with a Swedish accent. About the size of a standard typewriter, it reads aloud from many typefaces, although it falters on complicated formats. Its present price is prohibitive: almost $20,000. Schools and agencies for the blind have acquired these instruments, and a few are owned by individuals. For more details, write to Kurzweil Products.

The Optacon® is a device about the size of a cassette recorder. The reader feels letters beneath the left index finger. Tiny pins vibrate in the image of a print letter. A camera about the size of a penknife scans the printed line with the right hand. Because the Optacon reproduces exactly what the camera sees, poor print or complicated formats can be difficult. Despite its slow speed (average readers cover sixty words a minute) users of this device are enthusiastic. Computer programmers can peruse printout immediately without the twenty-four-hour delay of Braille transcription. Typists can proofread copy, fill out forms, and make corrections with a typewriter accessory. It is also handy for personal mail, packaged food directions, and short passages in books. The instrument costs $3,450 and requires intensive training and a good sense of touch. For further information, contact Telesensory Systems, Inc.

"I've always been lousy with math," reported Vivian, thirty-two. "I couldn't balance my checkbook without a calculator or figure out a tip without scribbling on a napkin. Am I out in the cold this time?"

Vivian won't have to count on her fingers. She'd be more accurate with a talking calculator, an innovation that hit the market several years ago. Sharp and Panasonic have developed several models, some combined with other features such as clocks, calendars, timers, and stopwatches. They range in price from fifty dollars to seventy dollars. If your local dealer cannot supply one, try Independent Living Aids, American Foundation for the Blind, National Federation of the Blind, or Innovative Rehabilitation Technology, Inc. When looking for a calculator with a visual display, shop around. Some displays in red are difficult to read with partial vision. Texas Instruments and other companies offer green displays with larger numerals, which are easier to see.

An upsurge in the use of the abacus blossomed about fifteen

years ago. This arithmetic device became popular in the Far East. In a modified version for the blind, white beads contrast against a red background. Beads are strung on wires resting on a felt backing so they won't move when touched. Once you've mastered operation of the abacus, you can perform the four basic arithmetic processes, as well as work with fractions and decimals. The talking calculator and abacus are both handy for temporarily recording telephone numbers.

If the abacus intrigues you, you can buy one from the American Printing House for the Blind. This source also sells the book *Using the Cranmer Abacus*, by Fred Gissoni, in large print or Braille. Hadley School for the Blind offers two courses on the operation of the abacus. Like the Orientals, you, too, can be speedy in your calculations.

A system of mathematical notations, called the Nemeth Code, is used by blind children, as well as those studying for a Ph.D. in mathematics. You can take this Braille course from the Hadley School or buy a textbook from the American Printing House for the Blind.

People who can't learn Braille or read print might feel out in the cold. A wide array of recording equipment is at their disposal. Handheld miniature cassette recorders can suffice for taking notes in meetings or class. The G.E. Modified 4-Track® cassette recorder, from the American Printing House for the Blind, allows up to four hours of recording time per cassette because of four tracks and slow speed. The tone indexer is a high-pitched beep audible only in the fast forward and reverse modes. By pressing the beep button, you can signal divisions within your recording. This machine's accessories include earphones, a foot pedal (to type from your own dictation), and a patch cord for duplicating from other equipment.

Your loss of vision might mean that you have to modify or develop other avenues of communication. Whether you gain access to readin', 'ritin', and 'rithmetic by looking, listening, or feeling, they aren't closed to you. You might feel like a first grader as you acquire some of these skills, but keep open these passages to self-communication, communication with others, education, and enrichment.

Chapter 19

WHEN YOU'RE ON THE GO, HOW DO YOU GET THERE?

T he four walls are closing in, and great misgivings hold you back, but frustration, isolation, and desperation push you forward. You figure it's time to strike out on your own.

What is the magic wand that will waft you safely through an everchanging environment unscathed? How well you realize that it is full of speeding cars, undetected curbs, sawhorses you don't see, and low-hanging branches that may go unnoticed. How will you find unfamiliar streets and addresses to which you have never been?

Sorry, there is no magic wand, no foolproof formula. Moving about safely with a visual impairment is so complex that the art and science of orientation and mobility have evolved. This specialty is taught in undergraduate and graduate courses at several colleges and universities. Graduates of these programs teach orientation and mobility to legally blind children and adults. Besides instructors who have had academic training, many professional workers for the blind have acquired knowledge and experience to provide adequate instruction to blind clients.

Just as you can't learn to cook or fly a plane by reading a book, don't expect to dash out the door armed with the necessary techniques by reading these two chapters. My intent is to explain independent travel, thus encouraging you to seek training from an instructor. You can find orientation and mobility instructors on the staffs of public and private rehabilitation agencies for the blind or school systems having visually handicapped students.

Three common aids to mobility exist: the human guide, the cane, and the dog guide. Because the training of the dog guide and master is so complicated, a separate chapter covers the subject.

"What about electronic travel aids? I've read about them and even seen them demonstrated on TV," queried Eliot. Totally blind from diabetes in his early thirties, he is enthusiastic about technological advances.

His mobility instructor conceded that technology has come close to perfecting an instrument that would alert a blind user to obstacles, drop-offs, and overhead obstructions such as low-hanging branches and awnings. Such devices aren't good enough yet, however, to be employed without a cane or dog guide.

The Mowat Sensor® is about the size of a transistor radio. It emits ultrasound beams that cause the Sensor to vibrate when the beam touches an object. As a pedestrian carrying this device approaches a telephone pole, vibrations intensify. When the Sensor is set for short range of three feet, the user can find a landmark such as a bus stop sign or an open doorway. Switched over to long range of twelve feet, it can detect oncoming cars or help zero in on a distant landmark such as a pole across the street, thus allowing the user to walk without veering. Some blind people rely upon the Mowat Sensor especially during heavy snow when landmarks are obliterated or hard to locate. Mowat Sensor owners usually pull out the device for occasional use. They don't wish to encumber both hands when cane or harness occupies the other. At present, the Mowat Sensor costs about $500.

A no-hands aid is the Sonic Guide®. Mounted on a pair of spectacles, two miniature earphones produce a variety of sounds as sonar waves bounce off different surfaces. A plate glass window literally *sounds* different from a bush. The wearer must learn to interpret this auditory feedback. Some complain that the extraneous noise distracts from necessary audible cues such as traffic noise and pedestrian footsteps and that its weight is uncomfortable. The Sonic Guide has been useful in teaching blind children to further explore their immediate environment. Like the Mowat Sensor, it doesn't warn of drop-offs, and once again a cane or dog guide must supplement. The price is about $3,000.

Now that we've made the circuit of technology, let's return to the first of the trio of mobility aids, the human guide. The sighted person, told and taught how to walk with a blind companion, is the most reliable means of mobility. Notice that I didn't claim that the human helper is the most independent method. Lack of sight, imminent danger, unfamiliarity of location and speed, and comfort in getting where you're going often dictate another person's guidance. When a family member, friend, or even a stranger is willing, and the situation is appropriate, a few hints on how to guide will make going smoother for both of you.

When instinct prompts a guide to grab your arm to propel you ahead, instinct has erred. It's time for you to do a bit of teaching. Just ask to take your guide's arm. Your hand will be slightly above his elbow, but keep your grip gentle. Don't give in to apprehension by hanging on like a vise. Not even your best friend relishes being clutched like a pump handle. Some pairs like to link arms, the blind person tucking his arm through the flexed arm of the companion. It smacks of the old days and appears more cozy. If you like your companion enough to be cozy, you'll be able to follow just as well.

Your guide walks a half step ahead of you. By the motion of his body, you can tell if the terrain is rough or smooth. Upon approaching steps or curbs, your friend can pause. Verbal cues such as, "Step down," are enough. As he descends or ascends, you can note height of steps because his body is slightly ahead. Usually it isn't necessary for him to tell you the number of steps because he will reach a landing before you.

Although manners mandate that a woman precede the man through the door, forget about Emily Post for the moment. Your companion can cue you in by swinging his arm behind his back, which is a signal to step behind. Your share in this maneuver is to hold the door so that it doesn't slam on you. It's almost an acrobatic feat for your friend to prop open the door while staying in contact with you. He might interject, "Door on your right."

Naturally you can't advance two abreast through narrow places such as between crowded restaurant tables or cluttered store aisles.

Again the arm behind the guide's back is a warning to walk single file.

Don't let revolving doors send you both into a tailspin. Wait until the door stops and step into an empty compartment, pushing slowly through. If you leave first, take a half step forward so that the spinning door doesn't make a sneak attack from behind with a wallop in the back.

Boarding an escalator shouldn't floor you either. Some blind people like to have a hand placed on the moving rail. Your guide is in front, telling you when to step on and off. Another approach is sliding a foot forward so that you feel the steps as they come to meet you. Bearing your weight on your heels and slightly elevating one toe will give you the information that you have reached the next floor.

Once a dentist nearly sent me head over heels backwards by trying to hoist and back me into the examining chair. (That just added to the heebie-jeebies of dental visits for me.) I stood my ground, firmly shaking my arm free. I explained that if she put my hand on the arm of the chair, I could manage from there.

This hoist-and-back maneuver is almost as instinctive as the seize-and-shove method by the well-meaning but ill-informed. Your helper can place your hand on the back, arm, or seat of the chair or sofa. You check it out. Take a swipe at the seat to be sure the cat isn't sleeping on it or that the kids didn't leave their roller skates. It's such a simple procedure when you both know what you're doing.

Getting into a car can be a graceful performance, too. Your guide can put your hand on the edge of the door or back of the front seat. This clue is enough information for you to know which way the car is facing. It's a bit embarrassing to put your foot on the seat because you thought the car was parked in the opposite direction.

"Do I have to go through all this educating business if I'm with a stranger, say, the nurse in a doctor's office?" wondered forty-two-year-old Phil. "I may never meet her again."

The answer to that question lies in how uncomfortable Phil is or you are in being guided improperly. If it doesn't bother you to be herded ahead, let it ride. Remember that you may never encounter that stranger again, but another blind person could. I tell a stranger that I want to take his arm before he has a chance to grab mine. If I'm not quick enough on the draw, I ask for a switch before moving forward.

"Why should I worry about these methods?" protested Dan, a student in his early twenties. "I'm just legally blind and can get around without somebody leading me."

Dan is right. Most of the time, he can walk independently. But some circumstances can be a challenge. What if he were leaving a football game with a few friends and 100,000 other people? Becoming separated would be more than unpleasant. When they stop for a beer and pizza after the game, odds are that the bar will be dimly lit, smoky, and crowded. Does the group wait until Dan, like many partially sighted folks, adjusts to the change of light, or does he take his chances on tripping over an outstretched foot or zinging the corner of a table? It's much less awkward to grab a wing and get settled. Besides, Dan may someday find himself acting as a guide for somebody who sees less than he does. These techniques don't take a genius's mind to learn or an athlete's coordination to execute.

Many partially sighted people can sail along on their own quite comfortably. But there are those whose vision fluctuates from day to day, who can't see a hand in front of their face at night, or who stumble over their own feet and everyone else's in dim lighting. These techniques are so simple to learn that the knowledge won't hurt you if you make the effort to acquire it.

Orientation boils down to knowing where you are in relation to your immediate environment. In your mind's eye, you have a map of your house, yard, place of work, and surrounding neighborhood. When becoming familiar with a new area, the key is to narrow down your landmarks. Don't bother about clues that don't affect your getting from Point A to Point B.

The get-acquainted game for the partially sighted should consist of those objects you see best. Look for buildings, changes of color of walls or floor coverings, and neon signs. Don't permit yourself the luxury of stargazing, or you'll miss the newsstand in front of the cleaner's.

If you don't see landmarks, it's even more important to weed out the extraneous. A totally blind person learning the way to the elevator in an office building shouldn't be concerned about doors beyond the elevator bank. It's significant that the tiled floor becomes carpeted when you turn left to the elevators. You need only such bare essentials, because otherwise your consciousness will be cluttered with trivia and you'll waste time by tracking them down.

Being conscious of compass directions can sharpen the outline of your visualized map. You may grumble that you're not a Boy Scout or a sailor and that you never knew north from south when you could see better. You can buy an audible or tactile compass from the American Foundation for the Blind or a commercial compass if you can read it visually. Confident that the main street in your neighborhood runs east and west, you know that intersecting streets run north and south. Sighted people can confuse rights and lefts when giving directions. It's not so bewildering to be told that the party store is on the north side of the street, two doors west of the laundromat.

Your remaining senses team up to supply some of the information gained through sight. You may nose out the bakery a half a block away before you see it. The exhaust system from the office building on the corner is audible before you smell it. The broken section of sidewalk underfoot is a sure clue that you have reached the street on which you live. If you suspect a hearing loss, your hearing should be tested. As your vision decreases, your ears are your most vital backup when traveling by yourself. If your hearing isn't dependable for localizing sound, such as approaching cars, and you don't see well enough to cross safely, make up your mind to seek assistance.

Totally blind people usually move around house, yard, and parts of work areas without a cane. If you don't have travel vision, (and in some cases when you do) a white cane can serve as being a probe that clears your path and an identification of your being visually impaired.

"Don't mention a cane," you may be muttering. "I won't carry one, I won't have anything to do with one. It's like carrying a badge of blindness."

This reaction and rejection are typical of people who are recently blind and are harbored by some who have been blind for many years. Some people resist the cane, feeling that it is an invitation to stereotypes of blindness as a state of helplessness, an object of pity. It also concretizes the final admission of a serious visual impairment. Those who are just legally blind or have light perception sometimes consider the cane synonymous with a beggar's violin and cup.

If you are in this camp, would you deny others a hearing aid or crutches if these aids were necessary? Worried about what others will think, are you unwittingly exposing yourself to danger by failing to alert drivers, pedestrians, and anyone else of your poor vision?

"I don't need a cane because I've been able to get along all my life without one," insisted Lynn, a nineteen-year-old college student who had 20/200 vision. "Sure, I get into binds sometimes in crossing busy streets or when looking for an address. But what would my friends say if I showed up with a cane? I'd want to hide with humiliation."

It's easy to empathize with Lynn's protests until we stack them up against her "sometimes binds." When crossing a busy intersection, Lynn can't always spot oncoming cars or warn drivers not to turn in front of her. She's operating as if she had normal sight, perhaps risking life and limb for the sake of this charade. Then there is the embarrassment of asking directions, only to have a pedestrian single out a landmark she can't see, such as the building housing the bookstore several blocks away. How is the stranger to guess that she couldn't see where he was pointing?

One measurement of partial sight is called travel vision. Some people see well enough to avoid obstacles, cross quiet streets, detect traffic lights, and read signs, if conditions are favorable. With a folding cane ready to open, they can be ready for the unforeseen around the corner. Winny, the sprightly seventy-five-year-old introduced earlier, welcomed the telescoping cane given to her. She could walk through the senior citizen apartment complex safely but was justifiably frightened about crossing a heavily trafficked thoroughfare nearby, even with a light.

"I open it whenever I need help—anytime I feel unsure of myself," she said enthusiastically. "I feel so much more confident knowing that it's just inside my purse."

As the degree of vision lessens, some people can move freely in familiar places, even along the street, but become jittery in an unknown territory. To have a cane for locating unexpected steps and unnoticed obstacles is comforting, much more relaxing than walking on eggs.

"I know the way to the building where my doctor is," reported Alicia, sixty-two, a woman whose sight detected large objects. "But I never can remember where the open flight of stairs is in the lobby. So I just unfold my cane."

Most partially sighted and many totally blind people like folding or collapsible canes. Folding canes, held together with steel cable, elastic or rubber tubing, pull apart into sections and can slip into pocket, purse, or briefcase. A telescoping cane retracts into itself even more compactly. It is less durable than a folding cane.

Straight canes are rigid, can withstand more banging around, and come with rubber golf-grip handles or crook handles. You can buy canes made from aluminum or fiberglass and, of course, the traditional wooden cane. If you're unsteady on your feet, you can purchase a support cane that is white. Some support canes are also collapsible. If you plan to be raising cane, check Chapter 30 for sources. A mobility instructor is your best resource to determine the kind and length of cane for you. If the cane you buy has replaceable tips, you'd be wise to stock up on a couple of extras, especially if your cane touches the pavement. The tip will wear out before the cane.

Some partially sighted people find that telescopic aids can make features of their environment more visible. Like the folding cane, these aids can go back into the pocket when not needed, plus they're usually handy for spot checking, rather than prolonged peering.

For the totally blind person, the long cane serves as an extension of the finger, probing the terrain ahead to detect drop-offs, rises, obstacles, and shoreline between sidewalk and grass. Mobility instructors teach students without travel vision the Hoover technique. An ophthalmologist by that name developed this method shortly after World War II. The user holds the cane at belt buckle level so that it extends several feet ahead. By swinging the cane in an arc as wide as the shoulders, the user taps the tip on the ground to the left as the right foot steps forward. The cane swings to the right to ensure clear sailing for the left foot as it moves forward. Never mind that you can't dance to the rhythm of the beat—this movement comes quickly with practice. Ideally, the cane length measures from breastbone to ground, allowing for reaction time to stop for obstacles or steps detected with the cane. Some people prefer canes to be even longer.

"I can't swing my cane back and forth through a mob of Christmas shoppers," objected Bob. "I'd feel awful if I tripped somebody."

Bob learned the cross-body technique. He grasps the cane farther down the shaft, shortening its reach. Carrying it diagonally in front of him, he could find obstacles but was unlikely to send someone flying. He discovered doorways by trailing the tip along the wall until he came to an opening.

Learning to use a cane properly might change your attitude from resistance to acceptance. Realizing that it can see you through a pinch if you are partially sighted or save your shins if you're totally blind, you won't project your negativism to the rest of the world. The white cane is universally accepted as a symbol that the bearer has impaired vision. The red tip, six to eight inches long, has no significance. Some mistakenly assume that the user is partially sighted. To my knowledge, it is a variation without symbolism—maybe somebody thought that plain white was too drab.

Some eye conditions, particularly retinitis pigmentosa, cause virtual night blindness. You might manage perfectly well during the day, yet tumble over curbs and obstacles at night. Should this be the case, you'd be smart to learn the Hoover technique if you venture out alone after sundown. Anyone using a cane after dark should cover it with Scotchlite®, a reflective tape easily picked up by headlights. You can buy Scotchlite from the American Foundation for the Blind or drop by a bike shop, since most sell it.

White Cane laws are on the books in every state, although they vary somewhat from one state to another. These statutes protect a blind person with a white cane or dog guide. But don't charge into heavy traffic against the light, counting on drivers to watch out for you because the law is on your side. Unfortunately, many motorists don't know the law or ignore it. When invoked, White Cane laws are usually after the fact, following an accident.

Extending your cane slightly before stepping off the curb will alert drivers. If you expect that a driver will turn in front of you, shaving it too close for comfort, hold up your free hand with the palm toward the car. This gesture draws attention to your attempt to cross.

When you're traveling on foot, wearing comfortable walking shoes can spare you agony. High heels or platform shoes can be stumbling blocks fastened to your feet. Besides, your footgear is liable to take a beating as you scuff against curbs and pad through puddles. I keep a pair of dress shoes stashed in my desk drawer. I wear walking shoes to and from work, which keeps my dress shoes looking reputable longer.

The good old days when you threw on a light coat to dash to and from the car are here no longer. Some of our mobility students dress as if they are still driving. When you have to walk a long distance or wait for a bus, it's miserable being wet or cold. Although your mother quit telling you years ago to bundle up for the weather, I shall keep doing so. I've seen too many folks half frozen because they weren't attired to face the elements. Bitter cold and wind can damage ears and hands. A knit hat that covers your ears usually allows sound to penetrate and is loose enough to push out of the way if you can't hear traffic. (Sounds do not filter through a hood as well.) Gloves, although not as warm as mittens, permit more freedom in manipulating a cane.

One totally blind student went out to empty the garbage in his shirtsleeves and became disoriented in the snow. Fortunately, a neighbor heard his calls for help before he became frostbitten or suffered serious injury.

Snow is the blind person's fog. It deadens and distorts sounds, conceals sidewalks, obscures landmarks, and forms dangerous barriers at street corners. Yet you can't hibernate like a bear, coming out only after the first thaw. Naturally, you'll avoid outdoor forays if you fear getting lost in the snow, but when you must venture out, flex your knees as you walk to maintain balance. You may not notice that sheet of ice ahead, so take it slowly. Don't walk where you are isolated, if possible, as you will most likely need more assistance in heavy snow because of tough going. When you aren't sure if you can find your own house, hang wind chimes on the porch as an audible signal or leave the porch light on if you can see it. If the chimes set your teeth on edge, take them down when you go in.

Those without travel vision should take Mother Nature seriously. A totally blind woman rode the bus to work hundreds of times. She became turned around on her two-block trek to the bus stop in early morning as she plowed through deep snow. She wandered aimlessly for two hours as the neighborhood slept. She finally roused a sleepy couple. Had she not been warmly dressed, her experience could have been a disaster. After that adventure, she takes a cab to the major bus stop when snow is deep.

Being unable to drive is one of the bitterest pills to swallow for those who have lost their sight. Although most people don't jump up and down over the prospect of riding the bus, it may be the only option. If you board the bus with cane in hand, the driver won't grumble when you ask him to call your stop. By sitting behind or across from the driver, you can gently remind him when you think you're approaching that point. Remember that he is busy piloting the coach through traffic, answering passengers' questions, maybe even making change. It's not impossible for him to forget your street. If he forgets, you forgive. Just be sure you know where you are when you get off. As an extra precaution, I often ask a nearby rider to watch for my stop.

When you're puzzled about the location of a bus stop, you can usually assume it's on the far side of the intersection. But you can request to be let off on the near side of an intersection so you don't have to double back. Most drivers are obliging.

Many towns and cities don't have the luxury of good public transportation. So that you won't wait for what seems to be forever, you can get printed bus schedules for the routes you frequent. Bus companies have information clerks who will tell you arrival times. When you call, they'll also tell you what bus to take if you're headed into an unfamiliar area.

A necessity for the brave spirits with hearts set on venturing into unknown territory is a street guide listing all streets alpha-betically and breaking down blocks according to addresses. They are common in larger cities and can be found in book stores and bus stations. Even if you can't read them yourself, street guides can help you to visualize the route you are taking.

Some public transit companies charge no fare for passengers using a white cane or dog guide. Others offer reduced fares or ask that the blind person carry an identification card to qualify for this concession. Since policies vary, you'll need to call your local bus company.

Unfortunately, buses don't go everywhere or run all the time. Transportation for the handicapped and senior citizens is available in many cities. Riders usually have to call a day ahead for arrangements. Because others rely upon the service, you aren't guaranteed an exact pickup time. There is a nominal charge for this door-to-door service. To find out if this form of transportation exists in your area, call the local bus company, look under "Transportation" in the phone book, or check with an agency for the blind or a community agency.

Taxicabs are another way of getting around. Although they are expensive, there may be no choice. If the cabdriver knows you are blind (the dispatcher will pass along the message), he will ring the doorbell or toot the horn to let you know he is there. He will also accompany you to the door of your destination if you ask.

A few blind people I know keep a car for someone else to drive. They pay their drivers, reasoning that friends might not wish to add extra miles to their automobiles or not have a car at their disposal. If you have owned a car, I don't have to dwell on the cost of maintenance and insurance for other drivers. A partially sighted friend has a sales job that requires trips around the state. She owns a car for these junkets. A blind couple enjoys the convenience of having a car when someone is able to drive it. One student who suddenly lost his sight had been a race car driver. To give up his personal car would have been an emotional upheaval—he kept it for family members to drive for themselves and for him.

Some states will issue a restricted drivers' license to applicants fourteen to sixteen years of age. Such licenses are granted to youngsters having parents who are blind when no one else in the household can drive. If you are thinking about your teenager getting in trouble behind the wheel, don't worry. Usually the young driver must be accompanied by a blind parent, or he cannot drive. Some states also issue motorcycle licenses to people having partial vision. For more information, inquire at your local secretary of state's office.

Many partially sighted people see well enough to ride a bike when traffic isn't heavy. A social worker who never learned to ride a two-wheeler as a kid pedals an adult tricycle to the office every day. Some people with enough vision can manage a moped. Totally blind folks can get exercise and go places on the rear seat of a tandem bike.

As you set out on your own, you'll have to ask information from sighted pedestrians occasionally. Don't faint if someone tells you, "It's over there," or, "The hardware store is just beyond the red sign near the corner." Hang on—you have the undivided but misdirected attention of a live body. Unless the bystander is incoherent or as confused as I am, I pursue the quest.

Suggesting that he face the same direction as you want to go eliminates the mix-ups of left and right for the most part. If he insists upon pointing, and you can't see where, extend your hand and ask him to point it toward your destination. Try not to snap at people when they offer useless information such as, "This way." It just embarrasses the helper. Like a detective, dig for specifics so you'll know the direction of "this way." If you can use visual cues, such as buildings or signs, explain that you can recognize them. That will make the pedestrian's description easier.

Although fifty-nine-year-old Sam could see well enough to stay on the sidewalk and follow white lines across an intersection, he agonized over the possibility of becoming lost. "What if I make a wrong turn? Or miss my bus stop, or lose count of streets? What if I just don't know where I am?"

It could happen. As long as you're not disoriented in the middle of a busy intersection or on a railroad track, you'll be safe. Should you become confused in the middle of a busy street, stay calm and stand still. Hold up your cane so drivers can see that you are blind, but don't move—a moving target is more likely to be hit. Chances are someone will stop to help you.

If you lose your way when there are no other pedestrians, you'll have to go into a building or even up to a house. When the rest of the world seemed to have vanished, I've been forced to flag down a motorist. (Of course, I just wanted directions, not a ride.) Don't think that you're the only person who ever becomes lost, either. How many times do drivers miss an exit from the expressway or take a wrong turn on a trip and travel miles out of their way?

Don has retinitis pigmentosa and, at forty-three, travels safely enough. He wondered if he should learn to travel like a totally blind person because his ophthalmologist told him that he would be likely to lose most of his sight. His instructor suggested to Don that he learn the Hoover technique to protect him at night when he couldn't see at all. Some professionals blindfold a student to teach this method. It often happens that induced total blindness is so threatening that the student can't concentrate. Besides, it's natural for people to depend on the sight they have as long as they have it. Although skill with a cane develops in training, it's like any other technique, fading without constant reinforcement. To know that there is a system on which totally blind people can rely is enough of a reassurance for Don.

When you are ready to travel alone, your ventures probably will create more anxiety for family members and friends than any other of your newfound freedoms. They may envision you plunging headlong down steps, dashing unaware into traffic, or becoming hopelessly lost. Parents of blind children express this fear, which can result in holding youngsters back just when they are most vibrant and resilient. Your loved ones may not be aware of the scientific approach to traveling with visual impairment and of the precautions you have spent hours in mastering. You can dissolve part of their worry by having them observe your training. They will work out their apprehension gradually, just as you did. Eventually, they will be relieved that they don't have to accompany you on every errand.

If your spirit is willing to get up and go and your body is able to follow suit, training in orientation and mobility can widen your world. Don't expect travel, even with residual vision, to be as carefree as it was when you were fully sighted. Just know that with proper instruction by someone who can gauge your physical stamina and psychological readiness, you can flee those four walls. You can take off when the whim strikes you, not waiting for somebody else to take you. Mobility instructors work with children in schools, visit adults in their homes, and are on the staffs of rehabilitation agencies for the blind. If you participate in a rehabilitation program, mobility will be an integral part of your curriculum.

"I feel like a liberated human," said Betty, forty-seven. "I haven't been out on my own for four years. Now that I'm confident in what I'm doing, and have plenty of practice—World, here I come!"

Chapter 20

SHOULD YOU GO TO THE DOGS?

W ell-meaning friends and associates, spotting a dog guide at work, jump to the conclusion that the animal is an answer for eighty-year-old Aunt Maude, who is blind and can't walk more than a few steps because of a badly mended broken hip. Or they insist that fifteen-year-old Dennis, in the midst of high school and adolescent tumult, suddenly would find himself if he had a dog. They somehow feel that if a dog wears a harness and the handle of that harness is placed in a blind person's hand, the pair will be happy and safe forever after.

Before making the decision about a dog guide for yourself, let's unveil some of the mysteries and correct some misconceptions. *Dog guide* is a generic term, referring to dogs specifically trained to lead. Each school takes pride in the name borne by its canine graduates: Leader Dogs, Seeing Eye Dogs, Guiding Eyes, and so on. If you don't know from where a dog came, you are safe in calling him a dog guide.

Dog guides will protect you. No school trains dogs to attack. Because these animals are in the public, petted and jostled by strangers, they must have a placid disposition. To expect a dog to attack upon command is foolish and dangerous. Training for attack or guard dogs is completely different. Dog guides that snap or bite ordinarily develop this trait through wrongful encouragement by their owners.

Dog guides don't know where you're going. That pooch is no more an automatic pilot than is a car. True, they may anticipate routes that they follow repeatedly. But what if you decide to go to the post office instead of the deli—do you let the dog dictate your destination? Because the dog walks faster than most people using a cane, your sense of orientation must be sharp. You issue commands such as "Forward," "Left," and "Right." The most patient dog will become disgusted with the owner who changes his mind by miscalling directions often. He'll just go ahead and do what he pleases, getting you hopelessly lost.

Dogs cannot tell when a light is red or green. Even the most highly trained dog guide, like all other pooches, is color-blind. He expects you to give the command "Forward" when parallel traffic is moving. Still, the dog will deliberately disobey, refusing to cross when oncoming traffic is near. He has been taught to exercise intelligence in time of danger. Also remember that he doesn't relish the idea of being run over by a Mack truck any more than you do.

"I bought a Bouvier puppy to raise so she could be trained to lead me," recalled Diane, a twenty-five-year-old college student recently blind from diabetes. "When I notified the school, they informed me that first of all, they generally don't accept the breed. They also said the trainers match up dogs with students, and even if my pup were trainable, her personality as a guide might not be compatible with mine."

Professional dog guide trainers spend at least three years in apprenticeship. Besides learning to handle their four-legged charges, they learn to size up a blind person's gait, life-style, and need for a dog. Someone living in a small town who doesn't walk more than six blocks requires a dog who is easy to handle, content without challenges. A peppier pooch would be the choice for someone who walks longer distances in heavy traffic. A man who is six feet four inches would be more comfortable with a large dog. A small dog is more suitable for the petite, five-foot tall woman.

Now you're wondering what a dog can do for you. Although I am mostly familiar with the Leader Dog School in Rochester, Michigan, other schools accomplish basically the same objectives.

A dog guide will do just that—guide a blind person along a sidewalk or shoulder of a road. It will stop at curbs and steps, awaiting a command to move forward. Besides discriminating between left and right, it will obey simple commands such as, "Find the door," "Find the car," "Find the elevator," and sometimes (but don't count on it) "Find the chair." (That's a command I don't give too often, since my dogs have never been choosy about whether the chair is occupied.)

A well-trained student and dog team is a picture of harmony. The dog walks at his owner's left. (A dog can be trained to walk on the right if the user's left arm or hand is impaired.) The pair weaves with confidence through crowds, crosses streets without veering, and locates doorways on target. It is truly a matter of fifty-fifty teamwork—the human knows where they are going, and issues commands and corrects the dog for mistakes. The dog, eager to please and enjoying his work, serves his owner with pride.

"Why should I consider a dog when I'm already quite skilled with a cane?" asked Bob, the man blinded in an industrial accident.

I reminded him that a dog guide is one means of mobility, not a panacea for the skinned shins and curbs he tripped over when not swinging his cane properly. Just as no human is perfect, the dog can make errors in judgement, such as brushing its master against a parking meter, forgetting to stop at a curb, or looking to a friend for petting instead of tending to business. Unless a dog works regularly and its master maintains training, it will become sloppy.

Some blind people decide against a dog for other reasons. Plenty of people, blind and sighted, don't like dogs. The animal is a responsibility, since feed costs the same as that for any large pet dog. It has to go out four times a day, should have regular exercise, and will require medical care occasionally. Because the dog is a reflection of the owner, it should be groomed daily. Unlike a cane, it can't be hung in a closet when its services aren't required. Or perhaps other family members need lots of time and attention that keeping a dog would interfere with, such as small children or infirm parents.

On the plus side, I find that walking with a dog demands far less concentration. I don't have to puzzle about circling an obstacle—I don't even touch that bike as my dog and I swerve around it. Some intersections give me the chills; the dog in hand provides an added sense of security. A dog excels in traveling on snow-covered sidewalks because he can rely upon trees, lamp posts, and parked cars to keep him on course. Hanging on to a four-legged companion, I'm less likely to tumble over snowdrifts or slip on ice.

A dog is a natural conversation starter. People approach to ask what the dog's name is, how long I've had him, or how much he weighs and eats. Sometimes I feel as though I'm nonexistent, taking the back seat to a canine. Dogs have an almost universal appeal and, recognizing that attraction, patience is needed in answering these inquiries.

My description of training of dog and student is based upon experience with Leader Dogs for the Blind. Although some dogs are donated, most have been bred especially for the work. Breeds most commonly used are the German shepherd, Labrador retriever, and golden retriever. Intelligence, stability, and good disposition are the main criteria for selection. Pooches don't have to be purebred—in fact, crossbreeds can become excellent guides. Canine candidates must be between one and two and one-half years of age, of either sex, and physically sound. Each dog undergoes a ten-day quarantine and thorough examination to rule out disease or congenital defects.

As each trainer picks out eight or ten dogs for his string, he looks for variety—big, small, outgoing, retiring, frisky, and slow. When he hands over the leash to a student in four months, he is acting as the matchmaker.

Dogs learn basic obedience: come, sit, down, and stay. They look upon the harness at first as an invitation for a walk. The recalcitrants view it as a nuisance and need a little coaxing. Sighted trainers teach the animals the tricks of the trade, from stopping at curbs to being mindful of traffic.

Some dogs never last through training. They can be rejected for being shy of traffic or unfriendly toward strangers or simply for not accepting responsibility. They may flunk because of being too tempted by other dogs and cats and lurking squirrels and birds.

But dogs obviously aren't robots. When they do slip up, the trainer verbally corrects with a sharp "No!" or "Phooey!" If the mistake is big, such as not stopping for steps or leading the trainer into an obstacle, a short, sharp jerk on the leash snaps the transgressor back to awareness.

"What can I expect when I get to the school?" asked Mary, totally blind and in her early twenties. "I'm a little apprehensive about getting my first dog."

Mary was a little taken aback to learn she would live in a dormitory for a three-and-a-half week training session, with visitors allowed only on Sunday afternoons. Arriving on a Sunday, she and other students would spend three days in a get-acquainted period—not a social whirl, but an opportunity for trainers to match students with dogs. During one early routine, a trainer takes the place of the dog. Students learn to give commands, follow the guiding harness, administer correction, and, most important, provide praise.

My first trainer stressed: "Remember, that dog isn't a machine. He's not going to work for you unless you tell him and show him that you appreciate what he's doing."

After each student finally is paired with a dog, the two spend an afternoon and evening getting to know one another. Many people have waited and debated a long time before making this move and somehow expect the animal's immediate allegiance. The dog has spent four months with his trainer, and will keep that person high on his list of favorites for the rest of the training period.

Students begin training with their dogs the next day. Routes are on school grounds and are short, with expectations small. After strolling a few square blocks, challenges become more complex. By the end of training, the team has worked through heavy town traffic, wandered through stores, and meandered along country roads. While each blind person is acquiring a new form of mobility, trainers maintain a watchful eye. Some even use bicycles or walkie-talkies to keep up with their charges.

"I haven't been this active in a long time," said Elmer, a fifty-seven-year-old man getting his first dog.

Elmer followed a rigorous regimen. His class was up at 6:30 AM to take their dogs to relief. Morning and afternoon working trips to town were regular. Lectures on care and feeding, common diseases, and problems that can pop up in handling consumed three evenings. Otherwise, students with enough pep were free to entertain themselves with games, TV, radio, and stereo in the lounge.

"I always thought that my dog and I would leave and operate like clockwork," said Ruth, the college professor with low vision. "Now I understand why trainers caution us about the adjustment period."

Like most other first-time dog recipients, Ruth hadn't counted on the transition that lasts from six months to a year. Although dogs are flexible, they take time to transfer affection from trainer to student. After living in a kennel four months, the dogs set up housekeeping in a dormitory, only to abandon it for a new home. Dog and trainer worked together thirty minutes twice a day; the new owner may have his dog in harness from morning till evening. The pooch is at the ready while the owner is at work. Family members and friends will be appraising the new dog. It even may have to adjust to other pets already in the home.

"What about my six-year-old cocker spaniel?" questioned John. He didn't want to give up the pet his children grew up with and he had such strong affection for.

I have known dog guides who fit in smoothly with other dogs, and even cats. Remember, though, dogs are imitative creatures. If the family dog sleeps on the couch, barks at every noise, and begs at the table, the well-mannered dog guide soon will follow suit.

Although the Leader Dog motto is: "Whither thou goest, I will go," don't take it literally. Some situations—baseball games, movies, etc.—are awkward with a dog. A few areas, such as within a hospital, should be out of bounds because of possible infection from dog hair or dander. But, dogs can ride on public transportation, even airplanes, and the blind passenger doesn't need an extra ticket for the dog at his feet. The dog can enter restaurants, although managers or owners occasionally may object because of public health rulings that prohibit animals. They usually acquiesce if the dog user calmly explains that the dog guide is an exception.

Despite the fact that most people like dogs, some folks have phobias or allergies, or simply dislike the animals. I recall a woman screaming in terror as I walked through the lobby of the hospital where I work. My embarrassment was secondary to her horror. As a matter of courtesy, I ask friends I plan to visit for the first time if they mind the dog's coming. Regardless of friends' fondness for dogs, I keep my companion under control at all times. Even he can be a pest by sniffing food or constantly seeking attention.

Ron is a forty-one-year-old diabetic whose vision is waning; his sight still allows him to travel fairly well. He wondered if he should apply for a dog. Some schools accept students having travel vision while others do not. They may leave the decision to the prospective student. If the partially sighted student depends upon his own sight, he isn't giving the dog a chance to lead. The wise pooch quickly figures out that he isn't needed and will forget his training or not respond quickly enough when expected to work.

Many people wrongly think dog guides cost the student an exorbitant amount. Some schools charge $150 for the first dog, and fifty dollars each for subsequent dogs. Other schools have no charge. Some schools even pay travel expenses for students, although most leave this responsibility to the student. You can call or write specific schools for such information.

In trying to keep this treatment objective, I've left the bond between dog and owner to the last. Dog lovers need no elaboration. Unlike most family pets, the dog guide is with his owner almost twenty-four hours a day. The dog becomes as dependent upon his master as the master is upon the dog.

I met a woman who was indifferent, almost hostile toward dogs. She acquired a Leader Dog to experiment with this mode of travel. Within a month, she became inseparable from her golden retriever.

Tragically, a dog's life span is a fraction of that of a human. A working dog serves an average of eight years. A few owners retire their dogs with people generous enough to give it a few years of carefree pasturing. Other owners work their dogs until the last day of the animal's life. Dog guide schools probably issue more replacement dogs than first dogs. Returning students don't know it all—they may have fallen into sloppy handling habits. The new dog never really replaces the last; he is a successor with a different personality, gait, and manner of obeying commands. Although most students welcome the new dog because of the void left by losing the last, they can expect an adjustment period with the new dog, too.

When weighing the decision about getting a dog guide, assess your health. Not only will you participate in strenuous training, you owe it to the dog to work him regularly afterward. If you've been as active as a mushroom, try to squeeze in brisk walking either by yourself or with a companion before training. Most schools don't accept students under the age of sixteen. They generally discourage high school students because the dog is likely to become the school mascot instead of his owner's guide. Can you afford feed, veterinarian checkups, and occasional medicine? The investment of maintaining discipline and rewarding with praise can yield some blind people an efficient means of independent travel, plus years of loyalty and companionship. Like any weighty decision, you should consider it thoroughly before making that choice.

Chapter 21

ARE YOU LEFT OUT
WHEN IT COMES TO YOUR RIGHTS?

W hen I heard from my opthalmologist that I was going blind, I just didn't know where to turn. He didn't know what services were available in our area either." This is another quote that can't be ascribed to just one student. As I hear it repeated so often, I wonder by what stroke of luck or resourcefulness these people ever reached our agency.

How can you get off the merry-go-round that isn't very merry when you're depressed, desperate, and looking you know not where for help? I wish there were a simple, straight answer such as to look under "Blind" in the Yellow Pages. That usually won't work because you need the name of the specific agency you are seeking.

Over 700 agencies, schools, organizations, and services for the blind exist in the United States. Each state has a central department that works with clients who meet its criteria. This department may be part of a larger agency, but if you locate the state agency for the blind, you're likely to be steered in the right direction, regardless of your circumstances. To bewilder you even more, agencies for the blind fall under several categories: department of education, department of social services, bureau of vocational rehabilitation. You'd be hard put to track down Michigan's, because it's under the department of labor.

Remember—librarians are great sleuths. I'd put my money on

starting with one of them. If you aren't a Talking Book patron, call your closest public library to learn where to apply for Talking Book services. That's our second call — the Talking Book library. Start at the top by asking to speak with the head librarian. Tell that person that you are legally blind and need the name, telephone number, and address of the closest office of the state agency for the blind. You should strike gold on your third call. Be prepared to give a few facts so the counselor assisting you won't waste time, such as your name, age, degree of vision, onset of blindness, and other disabilities and particulars about the kind of help you're seeking. State agencies serve clients who have vocational goals or are striving toward them. Generally, these clients range in age from sixteen to folks sixty-five and over who may hope to become homemakers so another person in the household is free to work.

"We're looking for a support group for parents of children with retinitis pigmentosa," stated a caller.

"We've just discovered that our baby daughter is blind. We're frantic about what we should do for our child," said another.

And a third: "My father has multiple sclerosis and is nearly blind. Our family just can't manage his care anymore, but we don't know anything about nursing homes."

Such persons would not meet eligibility requirements for state agencies, but staff members have at their fingertips directories to help with the right resource. When seeking assistance from a state agency, remember, you don't have to be totally blind. Legal blindness means anyone with visual acuity of 20/200 or less with best of correction, or a field restriction of twenty degrees or less. People having a serious visual impairment but who are not legally blind (above 20/200 to 20/70 acuity) may be eligible for services from the state vocational rehabilitation department. This department is known by many names, also, and the state agency for the blind can put you in touch with the closest office.

The American Foundation for the Blind sells a complete directory listing most public and private agencies state by state. It briefly describes each organization's purpose, covering everything from camps for blind children to retirement homes for the elderly blind. Chances are you can locate what you want by starting on the local level.

After your intake interview with the state agency, you will need a medical and eye examination. The eye examination determines your legal blindness and helps determine your eligibility for further services. The ultimate goal is to return clients to employment or the status of homemaker. Staff members will call upon every resource for a person to attain this objective. Eye surgery, treatment, or low-vision aids to restore vision are always primary considerations.

The counselor may recommend rehabilitation at a state-operated or private center, where you could learn skills such as techniques of daily living, mobility, Braille, typing, use of recording equipment, basic home repairs, and crafts. Counseling is an integral part of such programs, focusing on vocational exploration and adjustment to blindness.

Some rehabilitation centers have dormitory facilities where clients stay from a few weeks to several months. Most participants go home on weekends. Other facilities are nonresidential, since clients come in daily for training and return home each evening.

For those who find attendance at a center impossible, rehabilitation teachers will make home visits. Because the teacher can visit only once a week or so, training takes more time.

Besides rehabilitation and efforts toward improving vision, state agencies can help a client prepare for work by sponsoring training programs such as auto mechanics, nurse's aide, or medical transcription. If a person's goal demands a degree, the state agency will often assist with college tuition and other expenses incurred in higher education.

"What about the rest of us who won't be working?" questioned Arda, sixty-nine. "Where do we go?"

Many agencies for the blind devote efforts toward other segments of the blind population: senior citizens, children, and people having other disabilities. Your state agency for the blind or Talking Book librarian can direct you to them. Some provide rehabilitation either in a center or client's home; others specialize in recreation or sheltered workshops, or act as community resource consultants. For help with retarded children and adults who are blind, and their families, write to the National Association for Retarded Citizens. Those concerned about people who are deaf-blind should contact the Helen Keller National Center for Deaf-Blind Youths and Adults.

Forty-one-year-old Tommy had worked since childhood, despite congenital cataracts. When the foundry that employed him closed, he couldn't find another job as an unskilled laborer because of his decreasing vision and no marketable skills. Having virtually no formal education, he wasn't aware that he could have applied for Social Security Disability Insurance (S.S.D.I.) as soon as he lost his job.

For many folks, the words Social Security ring of retirement and survivors' pensions, but the agency plays another role: People who cannot continue working because of a serious disability (legal blindness is considered such), and who have contributed to Social Security for the required number of quarters, are eligible to receive S.S.D.I. checks. The amount is based on the length of time they contributed, previous earnings, and number of dependent children who qualify for coverage. S.S.D.I. checks will not begin until six months after you have stopped working and are contingent on your blindness being expected to last twelve months or more. As in Tommy's case, payment is retroactive for a year if application is not immediately made upon loss of sight.

To outline requirements would be pointless, because regulations change constantly and the formula for computing earnings is complicated. If you have paid into Social Security or are the survivor of a spouse who contributed (nine out of ten employees do), you owe it to yourself to investigate your eligibility. You can call your closest Social Security office for more details or go in person. When you visit, take with you necessary documents such as Social Security card or copy of the number, birth or baptismal certificate, marriage certificate, children's birth certificates and Social Security numbers, and W2 forms for the last two years of employment (or federal income tax returns for the last two years if you were self-employed). Add a list of names, addresses, and telephone numbers of those who have treated you for your disability.

Remember that when applying for S.S.D.I., your current income is of no consequence — J. Paul Getty could collect if he met the criteria. But legal blindness is likely to net you more than a claim based on another disability such as high blood pressure or low back pain. Just be sure that blindness is the basis of your claim.

Your application for S.S.D.I. may be denied, or the amount granted may look unfair to you. You can ask the Social Security Administration to reconsider. If you are still unhappy about the decision, request a hearing by an administrative law judge. Your appeal can go before a review council and as high as a federal court. The Social Security Administration will not charge you for these hearings. If you hire someone to represent you, his fees must fall within Social Security guidelines.

You may be able to work only part-time because of your sight loss but hesitate to do even that for fear of losing your S.S.D.I. Blind S.S.D.I. recipients can earn an annual exempt income, the ceiling for which rises every year. At this time it is almost $5,000 annually.

Emile, forty-nine, worried about jeopardizing his family's financial future by returning to work full-time and losing S.S.D.I. Suppose he discovered that he no longer could perform his duties? I reminded him that he could continue receiving S.S.D.I. checks for the first nine months of employment, although earning a full paycheck. When he had proved himself at the end of this probationary period, his S.S.D.I. checks would stop. Should he find out later that he couldn't meet job demands, he could return to S.S.D.I. without delay.

Blind persons receiving S.S.D.I. also can apply for Medicare, another word associated with retirees. Medicare coverage usually begins two years after the first S.S.D.I. check. Patients requiring kidney dialysis or kidney transplants are covered immediately. Medicare offers two plans that partially pay for hospitalization and medical care. You can apply for either or both. Premiums will be deducted from your monthly S.S.D.I. check. Medicare doesn't begin automatically—ask and ye shall receive, when you're eligible.

Again, regulations are so complex that it would take another book to tell what Medicare covers. Call your local Social Security office about specific inquiries. Or, you may be lucky enough to find someone knowledgeable in your hospital's patient billing department or in your doctor's office, where people specialize in Medicare coverage. Your Talking Book librarian can send you a disc recording on Social Security, Supplemental Security Income, and Medicare. A new disc is issued each year for updates.

Naturally, some people fall through the cracks because they never paid into Social Security, or haven't worked enough quarters. Supplemental Security Income (S.S.I.) is meant for the needy, elderly, disabled, and blind in this category. Your present income and assets will determine the amount of S.S.I. checks. Don't worry— you don't have to sell your house or car to qualify. Such factors as checking and savings accounts, pensions, or dividends do count. Sometimes blind children are eligible for S.S.I., depending upon their parent's income.

Apply at your local Social Security office. Although the Social Security Administration administers this form of assistance, funds come from general revenue. Again you are more likely to receive larger checks if you base your application on legal blindness.

You also can work while receiving S.S.I. benefits. Checks would continue if your job is low paying. It's another point to check when you apply.

If you qualify for S.S.I., you are likely to receive coverage from your state Medicaid program. Take your questions about Medicaid to the Social Service office nearest you. Provided that you are on a low income, you can also ask about your eligibility for food stamps. Some states make an additional contribution to blind recipients of S.S.I.

Ruby, sixty-three, is legally blind and a severe diabetic. She and her eighty-year-old husband feared giving up their home because of their poor health. Through their local Social Services department they were able to get assistance with housekeeping, transportation, and meal arrangements.

If your health is so fragile that you share their fears, contact your local Social Services department, public welfare, or public assistance department. The rationale is that it is far more economical to enable people to continue living in their own homes, even if outside help is necessary to keep body and soul together.

If you are sixty-five or older, your local or state agency for the aged may give you a hand in other matters such as transportation, nutrition, legal and financial counseling, and housing. They may assist in such affairs as letter writing for you. Seniors, regardless of sight, receive a form of respect for their years. They get discounts for everything from car washes to restaurant meals and prescription drugs. If you think you're missing out, call your local senior citizen organizations or agency for the aged. Don't stop there, though. Inquire about senior citizen discounts from salespersons and waitresses as you do your errands.

If you are looking for specific information about visually impaired older people, the Center for Independent Living in New York City has worked on programs to teach these folks to cope with a visual handicap. Besides training clients at the Center and in their own homes, they offer self-study courses in large print and on cassette for a small charge. The Minneapolis Society for the Blind offers a free pamphlet entitled "Caring for the Visually Impaired Older Person."

Another source of income sometimes overlooked is long-term disability insurance. This fringe benefit is paid by an employer to a private insurance company. Of course terms vary, but they generally cover an employee who has become permanently disabled, with the disability expected to last more than a year. This insurance usually includes disabilities not incurred on the job. It's a fringe benefit of which many workers are not aware. I have known several students who received a percentage of their former wages or salary until age sixty-five. Because you must make your claim within a specified time after leaving your job, time is of the essence. If you are uncertain, contact the benefits section or personnel office of your last employer, or your union steward.

If your blindness was caused by an accident, are you receiving fair treatment from the insurance company? One student was an innocent bystander during a party store holdup, where he lost most of his vision from a gunshot wound. He engaged an attorney to represent him; the attorney's fees were a percentage of the settlement. Had he not sought a lawyer, he probably would not have been awarded what was his due.

At thirty-two, Bill is a veteran whose eye disease wasn't detected until he was serving in the army. Although he has been granted a pension, he did not take advantage of rehabilitation training, job preparation, and the aids and appliances to which he is entitled. The Veterans Administration operates several rehabilitation centers for veterans, regardless of whether their blindness is service connected.

Besides rehabilitation training, you might be eligible for a pension from the Veterans Administration, even though your blindness is not service connected. Your present low income is one of the criteria for such a pension. In addition, should you be housebound, you may qualify for aid and attendants from the Veterans Administration. An attendant would assist you in dressing, eating, bathing, and housekeeping, if your physical condition warrants. If you served in the military at least one day during wartime (you didn't have to be in action), you can receive medical care from V.A. facilities.

There is an organization that is committed to the rights of blind veterans. You can contact the Blinded Veterans Association, which will check into your claim and send you a cassette copy of "Veterans' Benefits.".

The mere mention of income tax returns makes many folks edgy. Have you filed income taxes since you became legally blind? Legally blind taxpayers can take an extra exemption on federal returns. This exemption applies to blind spouses but not to blind children. You're not washed up completely if you didn't file for this claim. You can fill out an amended form, which more or less says that you made a mistake. With the federal government, you can go back three years to recoup your losses. Don't panic—an amended form won't bring the auditors banging on your door. You can pick up these forms from your local Internal Revenue office— folks there are obliging enough to help you fill them out.

Don't assume Uncle Sam will take your word about legal blindness. Back it up with a report or certificate of legal blindness from your ophthalmologist or optometrist that states the date of the onset of blindness. Provided that your condition is permanent, you need to send this statement only once, referring to your status in later years.

Also, don't assume that your tax preparer knows it all. He may not recognize your legal blindness, especially if you have high partial vision. Several students have been ready to chew out their tax preparers for not catching this exemption, but they themselves were at fault.

Most states also grant an extra exemption on state income tax returns for legal blindness. Your state treasury office will give you this information. Also, inquire if your state has a provision for blind property owners. In some cases (depending on the state and your total income from all sources), you are entitled to a rebate from the state based on the percentage of property taxes you paid when compared with your income.

If you were eligible but did not apply for the state income tax exemption or the rebate for property taxes for a blind property owner, ask about amendment forms for both instances and how far back they can be filed. Again you'll have to include a copy of your eye report.

Many utility companies provide discounts to handicapped or elderly consumers who live on a fixed income and are the head of a household. Contact the nearest office of your gas and electric company to see whether you qualify. Although you may have to go through yards of red tape to prove that you meet requirements, it could be worth it, since energy bills can take a big bite out of your budget. You may be steered to your local Social Services office to seek Energy Assistance.

Naturally, you want your vote counted when the next election rolls around. Absentee ballots are easiest for most blind voters. If you are a registered voter, you can call your local city hall several weeks before an election to request that an application be sent to you. Usually you have to apply for an absentee ballot for each election. Having the ballot in the privacy of your home, you can pore over it yourself, or ask someone to help you. If you show up at the voting polls in the flesh, you can take anyone of your choosing inside to assist you. Those who can operate a machine themselves won't screw up the works if they bring a sample ballot (one clipped from the newspaper) with them that they have previously marked to use as a guide. If you vote alone and require assistance, some election commissions insist that a member of both major parties accompany the blind voter into the booth. I've been curious about three people squeezing into such a tight space but never tried it.

Many states issue handicapped parking stickers to disabled drivers and disabled passengers. If you have the option, apply for a movable card or sticker to place in the windshield instead of a sticker for the license plate. Chances are you'll ride in more than one vehicle. Pick up an application from your secretary of state's office or wherever motor vehicles are registered. Often your doctor has to fill out part of the application.

Having your windshield sticker laminated will ensure its survival. Such a permit is handy when your driver drops you off near a building, leaving the car to show you inside. Your shopping companions will think you're terrific when they can park in the handicapped space and don't have to truck a half mile across the parking lot, loaded down with packages.

While you're at the secretary of state's office, you might inquire about a state I.D. card for blind persons. This identification is as acceptable as a driver's license; it bears your picture and the information that you are legally blind. Try cashing a check without such identification and you'll see the need. Usually your birth certificate and proof of legal blindness are the required documents. Not every state issues an I.D. card specifically for the blind. Some states provide nondrivers' identification that does not indicate legal blindness.

Betty is not a senior citizen, but is the legally blind head of a household consisting of herself and her teenage son. When she heard of a service intended for seniors that consisted of routine home maintenance and yard work, she called the organization. She discovered that she qualified for such aid as a handicapped homeowner on a fixed income. Now she pays minimal charges for such chores as painting, simple repairs, and grass cutting. Organizations granting these privileges are scattered and do not abide by standard regulations. If you think you might be eligible, contact private and public agencies for senior citizens to see whether this assistance is available and whether you would qualify.

Adequate housing is another primary concern, especially for the elderly and handicapped. Where and how to find it requires the doggedness of a detective. Although costs for many nursing homes are covered by Medicare, most older folks who are blind can manage quite well in a habitable apartment or other dwelling. Your state agency for the blind, local or state housing commission or housing authority, community referral agency, and word of mouth are starting points in the hunt. Many apartment complexes for seniors accept handicapped (including blind) tenants as well. In some cases, an applicant need not be sixty-five or older. Often these dwellings are subsidized, making them affordable for people with limited incomes.

Some people shy away from giving up their homes, even though their spouse died or their children have moved away. If you're in this dilemma, have you considered sharing your home? Before slamming the door on that thought, you might calculate what it costs to keep the home fires burning single-handedly. You might work out an arrangement with another senior or toss around the idea of dividing up expenses with someone who is working but can't make ends meet on his own. I met an engineering student who lived with an elderly man. The young man cared for the home and yard, took his friend on errands, cooked meals, and cleaned house. He paid minimal rent in return.

If that idea strikes a responsive chord, contact the housing office of local colleges. You'll have to do some screening, but should the arrangement turn sour, remember that you are still in the driver's seat. You own the house. There is an organization, the National Shared Resource Center, that matches senior citizen homeowners with other seniors or those wishing to share housing. They try to match up personality, life-styles, and other considerations. Or you might like to read the book *Living with Tenants: How to Share Your House with Renters for Profit and Security*, by Doreen Bierbrier.

The American Association for Retired Persons will keep you abreast of affairs affecting older folks: Social Security, housing, nutrition, recreation, health care, transportation. They have an active lobbying group in Washington to ensure that older persons aren't shunted aside by legislators. You have to be fifty-five or older to belong but do not need to be retired.

Lions Clubs throughout North America and abroad dedicate their efforts toward the concerns of the visually handicapped. They donate time and funds to support everything from prevention of blindness to Leader Dogs. Local Lions Clubs can help procure Braille watches, optical aids, and adaptive devices for those blind persons whose needs are not covered by public agencies. If you require assistance from this service group, you probably won't find the local chapter in the phone book. Their membership often includes self-employed businessmen, doctors, and dentists. If you still can't track down your local group by asking individuals, write to Lions International for the club closest to you.

As prices continue to zoom, you still have to eat. Many folks are finding that co-op buying is one way to cut food costs. Some food co-ops charge a small annual membership fee, while others don't. They vary in selection and type of food—some co-ops don't have facilities for keeping fresh meat, for instance. Many allow working members to pay for a percentage of their purchases by working several hours a month. A blind man I know paid his due by bagging groceries for other customers. For information about food and housing co-ops, call toll free *1-800-424-2481.*

Are you still befuddled by rights and privileges to which you are entitled? Are you afraid of being smothered or lost in the jungle that lies out there? Arm yourself before setting out to whack your way through. Call ahead to the office or agency you intend to visit so that you'll bring necessary papers. If you think you might become bewildered or tongue-tied by a staff member, or overwhelmed by forms to fill out, take along a trusted friend who is articulate. You're not surrendering your business to your companion, nor do you necessarily want him to do the talking for you, but he can serve as an interpreter and pitch in with the paperwork. Should you be caught in a legal entanglement and not be able to afford a lawyer, call your county bar association. Frequently members volunteer their services.

To locate advocates for the handicapped, welfare rights groups, and other special interest groups, you can contact the American Council of the Blind, National Federation of the Blind, Office for Civil Rights, and the Office for Handicapped Individuals. To find out whether an agency, service organization, or commercial enterprise has a toll-free number, call *1-800-555-1212.*

You could call your state agency for the blind for help on the local level, even though you are not one of its clients. These organizations specialize in enforcing a person's rights and entitlements. You'll save yourself and them time by consolidating your questions and problems. If possible, write them out so you don't lapse into a verbal volley—they might fit into categories such as public assistance, medical care, or housing. Often answers come most quickly to the questions stated most clearly.

Other allies in your camp are your state representative and state senator. By contacting the office of a politician, you may well find that his aides will immediately begin working on your dilemma. Two factors are on your side: Politicians do want to hear from and respond to their constituents, and bureaucrats don't like the idea of politicians breathing down their necks.

Don't take the first no as the final no. Sometimes your request garners a negative response because a staff member just doesn't understand changing regulations, especially those affecting the legally blind. Don't dismiss this human foible. If a staff person turns you down, he may be thinking that this brush-off will turn you off from pursuing him again. Although perseverance may not be one of your character traits, it's one you'll have to cultivate when on the trail of those rights due you. Naturally, nobody wants to ask for charity. In many cases, you have paid for assistance via taxes or F.I.C.A. withholding.

Sure, the squeaky wheel gets the oil. But don't just squeak—roar!

Chapter 22

YOUR WORK HISTORY, YOUR JOB FUTURE

N ow that I've lost my sight, does that mean I'll never work again? If I go back to a job, what can I do as a visually impaired person?"

You may have asked that question yourself. It's another query that's impossible to attribute to one student, since I hear it from so many. You won't find a straight yes or no in this chapter, or anywhere else you look. The answers hinge on many if's, and here are a few for starters.

Consider such factors as your age at the onset of blindness, the existence of illness or other disabilities, your previous experience and marketable skills, aids and devices that may compensate for your visual loss, job market . . . and pure luck in landing a position. Like many blind people receiving S.S.D.I. or other forms of income, you may face the risk of losing this financial security by returning to the work force.

Unfortunately, unemployment of the visually handicapped, like that of other disabled groups, presents a bleak picture. Some estimates place it at 70 percent to 75 percent among those of employable age from eighteen to sixty-five. But before you throw up your hands in dismay, let's look at the 25 percent to 30 percent who are gainfully employed. Don't count yourself out as one of the unemployed statistics until you scrutinize the segment that is working.

Your return to the work force might rest upon what you have

done in the past, for which you have been trained. You reap the choicest fruits from experience:

Eliot, the electrical engineer who became totally blind from diabetes at thirty, started his own small company. Now he's busier than he ever was with the larger firm.

Ben lost his sight from the same disease at the same age. Although his career as a dentist was over, he returned to graduate school and now holds a position in public health administration.

Pat lost some of her sight from retinitis pigmentosa while she was in her midfifties. She began teaching, imparting to her student nurses invaluable expertise garnered from twenty-five years of being a registered nurse herself.

At twenty-seven, Joanne finally became totally blind from retrolental fibroplasia. She combined her work as attorney for a large law firm with six months of rehabilitation training. Upon resuming her position full-time, she accepted responsibilities other than, research, which required too much time plowing through references.

Cindy was twenty-six when macular degeneration halted her work as filing clerk for a municipal water department. After being fitted with low-vision aids and a closed-circuit TV magnifier, she returned to her job.

Forty-four-year-old Bob lost his job as janitor for a public school system when his supervisor discovered that Bob had a visual impairment. Bob was reinstated when he convinced his supervisor that his work was thorough, due to his efforts to leave classrooms and restrooms spotless.

When Roberta, a multiple sclerosis victim, found her position as accountant for a small music school too taxing, she thought she would have to quit. She learned to budget her residual vision by relying upon a talking calculator, instead of one with a visual display.

John, in his midfifties, lost all his vision twenty years ago in an accident. He earns a living from a dying occupation: he shines and repairs shoes in a bustling downtown office building.

Warren, forty-seven, was a cabinetmaker. Although he was not totally blind from an accident, he couldn't convince his former employer that he was still master of his trade. Warren opened his own shop, eventually hiring five people to help handle his thriving business. His reputation for fine craftsmanship spread so quickly he had more orders than he could fill.

When contemplating your job future, consider your job past in all its ramifications. Maybe you can't pick up exactly where you were before you lost your vision. But can you capitalize on your assets from another angle? Obviously, a former taxi driver can't hit the road again. But could he dispatch cabs, knowing the city as well as he does?

When you worked, did you use your eyes to peruse printed instructions, meters, gauges, dials, or cathode ray screens? These skills shouldn't be chucked into the category of impossibles — there could be modifications using magnification, or auditory or tactile feedback.

Most of us don't or can't keep up with technological advances. A magnifier for a digital thermometer could enable someone to be a nurse's aide, or a light probe from Science for the Blind could help a blind person "see" which phone lines light up. These are only a couple out of thousands of such devices.

"There must be certain jobs for the blind," persisted Jo, a homemaker blinded in midlife. "Isn't there special work reserved for blind people?"

Jo learned there are no special jobs for the blind — they can be found working alongside sighted counterparts throughout the work force. They teach on levels from kindergarten through college; they're found among social workers and psychologists, in nursing homes and hospitals. They serve as advocates, lawyers, judges, politicians, typists, word processor operaters, computer programmers, and computer analysts. They operate answering services and sell anything from Amway products to stocks and insurance.

True, there are some specialized training programs to prepare blind persons for particular positions. Both the Internal Revenue Service and the Social Security Administration train the blind to answer inquiries over the phone or in personal consultations. Other job training sites teach small engine or transmission repair, medical and legal transcription, word processing, piano tuning, physical and occupational therapy, assembly line work, food services, and small-business organization. These programs are scattered around the country.

Maybe you're undecided, like many voters before an election. You can't come up with a logical link with your previous work or never have been employed. Your immediate concern is to narrow down the options. Be aware of what jobs are available. Through your state employment office you will find an occupational inventory listing thousands of jobs throughout the state. Aptitude tests can steer you in the right direction, even if they do nothing more than stop you from making a false move.

Strangely enough, your interests and aptitudes may not coincide. You may have dismissed agriculture as a possibility, yet find your scores show strength in this area. (Blind people have been successful in raising cattle, pigs, chickens, rabbits, and even fish bait.) You may never have sold even Girl Scout cookies, but the tests reveal you have the potential to run a small business. Many blind people operate vending stands.

"I'm going to be a musician," announced Toby, twenty. He lost all of his sight in a gunshot accident and chose not to return to his old job as manager of a fast-food franchise.

Sure, a few talented blind people have hit the top, such as Tom Sullivan, Stevie Wonder, Terri Gibbs, and George Shearing. But the number of aspiring vocalists and instrumentalists who have not been successful is staggering. In such a competitive profession, only a few survive, sighted or blind. To expect to earn a living in music is tempting fate and risking starvation, but perhaps that talent can be channeled into related fields such as teaching, choir directing, or music therapy.

When you gird yourself for the job hunt, your greatest ally will be your counselor from the state or private agency serving the blind. He can shortcut your research by providing information about qualifications, education adaptations, and devices. He can arrange aptitude tests and assist in finding readers for occupational inventories. He often works closely with a placement specialist on the staff who beats the bushes talking with prospective employers about possible positions for the legally blind.

Besides specific job information and tips, your counselor can help you assess your job readiness. Do you need rehabilitation training to learn communications skills? Can you master enough mobility savvy to get you to and from the job and safely around plant or office? Your family and friends might overlook your personal appearance, but a prospective employer will probably scrutinize you. If you can't afford decent outfits to start a job, perhaps the state agency can make a clothing allowance.

Don't overlook civil service exams. You can take them on the municipal, county, state, or federal level, and make provisions for using readers or get extra time to fill them out yourself.

On the federal civil service level is PACE: Professional Administrative Career Examination for the visually handicapped, available in Braille, large print, or cassette. Call the Federal Job Information Center for more details.

Your Talking Book library can supply you with two sources of information regarding employment. *Dialogue Publications* is published quarterly on disc and in Braille and large print. Besides articles of general interest for its blind readership, *Dialogue* features a section on careers, job opportunities, and education. The National Federation of the Blind publishes *J.O.B., Job Opportunities for the Blind,* monthly on cassette. For more information, call toll free *1-800-638-7518.*

If you are considering a small business, the Small Business Administration may grant you a loan if your state agency cannot lend you capital. To locate the local office, look under United States Government in your phone book.

Career-planning courses are popping up in adult education. Besides tips on job trends and where to look, they give students information about writing resumes and filling out applications, as well as handling interviews. These classes usually are designed for sighted students, but you can glean a lot from them.

"I'm applying for a job as short order cook at MacDonald's," announced Bruce, nineteen. "My vision is 20/200, certainly enough for me to do the work. Should I tell the manager ahead of time that I'm legally blind, or wait for him to find out after I prove myself?" It's impossible to predict an employer's reaction to such information, but Bruce's idea of proving himself before the news got out was probably sound. The manager might not have been open to hiring a legally blind short order cook because of preconceived notions about the disability. Bruce did get his job, but may never have had the chance to flip a hamburger had the manager known from the beginning.

At twenty-eight, Anne was totally blind and wanted to apply for a full-time teaching position at a university. Although she didn't make reference to her blindness on her resume, she did mention it in her telephone interview with the department head, who later told her he would have been startled to see her stroll into his office with her dog guide.

If a question on the application asks directly about physical handicaps, your soundest, safest recourse is the truth. However, you may, like Anne, choose not to mention your disability on a resume. Your best ammunition will be answers to inquiries about how you can capably handle the position despite lack of sight.

Some legally blind job seekers, sensing that an employer is reluctant to hire solely on the basis of visual impairment, threaten legal action. Many states have laws against job discrimination because of a handicap. Consider such a move as a last resort. You won't be on the top of your boss's popularity list, even if you mention legal action but don't pursue it. If you have questions about your rights, contact the Office for Civil Rights, the American Council of the Blind, or the National Federation of the Blind.

What about that first day on the job? It's a biggy in everyone's life, and sometimes scary. Should you not see well enough to orient yourself, it might be wise to work with a mobility instructor or an astute friend before signing on. You'll want to know about such necessities as how to locate the restroom and cafeteria, how to find your work area, and where the bus stop is. If you are partially sighted, it'll be another chance to size up specifics such as lighting in your work place and how low-vision aids can help. But don't dash out and buy every device you can think of—it'll take weeks, even months, before you actually settle into your work routine and can reasonably assess your needs for adaptive devices.

After you cross the bridge with your employer, don't think you're on easy street quite yet. Colleagues may harbor qualms, although they may not say much about it because the boss has already hired you. Recently I had a call from the director of a hospital department. Three of his six-member staff became alarmed when he announced he was hiring a blind employee. They confessed they were concerned about eating lunch with their new colleague and were afraid he would make unreasonable requests of them. I assured the department director his new employee would fill the position as well as anyone with sight, although a few accommodations might be necessary. His staff members eventually would become accustomed to their new colleague, just as the new kid on the block becomes part of the gang. These precautions may seen unnecessary and unpleasant to you, but unfortunately they are facts of life.

Some blind people, including those who have never worked, or have other disabilities, are not ready for competitive employment. Tom, at thirty-two, has been totally blind since birth. He never held a job, except for a brief stint as a door-to-door salesman. Although his original plan was to train for transmission repair, he discovered that his poor hand skills and short memory weren't enough to realize this hope. Tom entered a sheltered workshop that accepted contracts and subcontracts for the federal government and private industry. He could keep up with small packaging and simple assembly.

Sheltered workshops have a significant place in the lives of some blind people. When the choice is between competitive work and nothing, many folks opt for something. Tim, thirty, was totally blind from birth. Mental retardation complicates his disability, making competitive employment out of bounds forever. Tim wanted some reason to get up in the morning, somewhere to go, and the satisfaction of bringing home a paycheck each week. He participates in an activities workshop where he and other clients, some sighted, work part-time at tasks best suited to them. They spent the rest of the day in acquiring such skills as personal grooming, social graces, handling money, and learning communications. Instructors and managers of such enterprises are often legally blind, which is another job opportunity.

Unfortunately, there are not enough sheltered workshops and activities to fill the demand. They are usually in large cities, not within commuting distance for those living in rural areas or far-flung suburbs. Sometimes applicants have to wait a long time for an opening. Work can be sporadic, depending on how much is sent to the workshop.

When weighing your vocational future, a number of ifs are on the scales. If you lost your sight recently, have you picked up the pieces of your personal world? Have you pursued enough rehabilitation training so that you are as independent as possible? If you can't return to your previous work in any capacity, would you launch a new career? Although many people switch vocations in midlife, are you willing to go back to school or embark on technical training? Do you want to take a chunk out of your life to make such a change? Suppose the job for which you are ready doesn't open up in your locale. Would you rip up roots for yourself and family to relocate? Do you have the motivation and stamina to continue knocking on employers' doors until one opens, or will you back down after a few slam in your face?

Some people are chagrined *not* to be employed. I remember the words of Doctor Joseph N. Schaeffer, retired director of Detroit's Rehabilitation Institute. "All of us hold up the work ethic as the highest ideal. It's so much a part of our ingrained thinking that we look upon not working as a failure. It's an injustice to condemn those who don't bring home a regular paycheck because they aren't able."

He was so right. If for some reason you can't become employed, your life can be just as fruitful and productive. You have no reason to feel guilty or apologize for your status. You are neither a dropout nor a cop-out from society.

Many blind people who are not working serve as homemakers, freeing another family member to become the breadwinner. If that is your role, don't think your self-importance has diminished. In fact, you probably work harder than you did on the job; the big differences are that you don't bring home a paycheck every week and your hours aren't regular.

One student retired in his late forties. "I couldn't risk my family's financial welfare by giving up S.S.D.I. and my company's disability pension for a position that paid less. I've still found plenty of reasons, far beyond that desk I occupied, to get up in the morning. I'm careful not to let myself slip into a rut. Besides planning activities with my wife and children, I volunteer several days a week to get myself out of the house. I'm as fulfilled as I ever was in my twenty years of going to a regular job."

Now you have seen both sides of the coin. If you really want to work, don't resign yourself to being forever jobless. As a visually impaired jobseeker, your pursuit will be much harder than it was when you were sighted. If you feel you're not worth your salt because you aren't employed, take jobs you don't like, or part-time positions. Get going on building those marketable skills. Don't give up if you don't land one today or tomorrow, but don't let those tomorrows slide by without trying to find what you want.

Chapter 23

ARE SCHOOL DAYS
ON YOUR LIFE CALENDAR?

T wenty-year-old Tony fidgeted as I asked him about his short-lived college career. After a year in junior college, his near-failing grades helped put him on probation. Sure, he stumbled into many of the pitfalls common to freshmen: too much partying and too little studying, no structured study habits, and cutting class. Some of Tony's shortcomings added up to his not taking advantage of resources as a visually handicapped student. He thought his partial sight was enough to squeak by. When he couldn't complete reading assignments because of eye fatigue, he never sought live readers or recorded texts. He just gave up. If he couldn't finish a test within the allotted time, he didn't ask the instructor for extra time because he could neither read nor write as fast as sighted students. He dismissed the Special Needs Office on campus as just for those in wheelchairs and totally blind students.

Tony had more learning to do than just that in a classroom.

If you're considering high school or college, or are already there, don't forget such boosts as the office for disabled students, organizations that will record textbooks, and special techniques for taking notes, doing research, and handling blackboard work. Don't believe you can do it all by yourself. Education makes enough demands, and you'll need reserves to derive the most you can from your courses.

At forty, James is about to complete work on a bachelor's degree, having attended classes for ten years. When laid off from his job as a supermarket stock clerk, he decided to wrap up his degree and go on to graduate school. He didn't know, though, that his state agency for the blind would pay tuition, books, and reader service for him. It even would have covered necessary expensive equipment such as a cassette recorder and typewriter.

Check with your state agency for the blind to find out if you are eligible for such financial assistance. Requirements vary from state to state. You probably will have to go to school full-time and not ease into the academic whirlpool by taking a couple of classes per term. One criterion might be for you to have psychological testing to determine if you are college material. Because state budgets are becoming tighter, you might be requested to check into scholarships. Besides applying for financial aid and scholarships open to all students, legally blind students can apply to the American Foundation for the Blind, American Council of the Blind, and the National Federation of the Blind. Recordings for the Blind annually awards blind college seniors who have attained high scholastic achievements. Incidental expenses (excluding tuition) may not be paid by the state agency. You must investigate to see what financial help you can expect from any source.

After enrolling, one of your first contacts should be with the office for disabled students. These departments are known by many names: Educational Resources, Special Needs Office, Education Rehabilitation Department. They are springing up on campuses of colleges and universities. If academic institutions cut their budgets, these services may be among those to suffer. Your admissions office staff can tell you if such a resource exists at your college. Even before registering, call for an appointment. Stop by to introduce and acquaint yourself with the staff and facilities at your disposal. Personnel can often help you with registration— you won't miss standing in lines for hours. You might find collections of recorded textbooks from your college, or they can help you to locate books from other sources. Frequently they will round up readers, provide access to closed-circuit TV magnifiers, cassette recorders, Braille writers, and typewriters. They can assist with arrangements for taking exams. Some offices go so far as lining up typists for papers or tutors for classes. If you require orientation to the campus, check with the special needs office to see if anyone can show you those labyrinthian ways. Some colleges assign one counselor to work with blind and physically disabled students. If your college doesn't offer these services, you'll have information from this chapter to forge ahead on your own or to fill in the gaps of the office that serves you. If you are in high school, often this legwork is covered by the resource or itinerant teacher. On the other hand, you may have to shoulder these responsibilities yourself.

It won't take more than a few days for you to figure out that one of the biggest barriers looming on your academic horizon is the large volume of reading. Somehow you must plow through that 300-page sociology text and 400-page history book before the term ends and not succumb to the temptation of using them as doorstops.

"I can read for myself," maintained Sheri, nineteen. "I'll just stop for a few minutes when I'm tired." Sheri quickly discovered that rest breaks consumed more time than she anticipated. Despite being buried in her books for fatiguingly endless hours, she netted diminishing returns.

Recorded textbooks can be the solution for many of your reading assignments. Recordings for the Blind, Inc., is a private, voluntary organization with a national network of local units that is headquartered in New Jersey. Volunteers read for those in kindergarten up through Ph.D. candidates. Readers are often experts on the subject being recorded—engineers read engineering texts, math teachers record math texts, books on foreign languages are read by those who speak that language as their native tongue. R.F.B.'s central library houses over 60,000 master tapes. When a freshman in Hoboken requests a specific book on introductory chemistry, which had been previously read for a student in Los Angeles, the book is duplicated and whisked off to the Hoboken borrower. This organization's twenty-eight units are constantly adding to their collection. Register with Recordings for the Blind before you begin school. You do want your number in the computer, don't you? For faster service, make your requests to your closest R.F.B. unit. To find out where it is, call your Talking Book library.

When R.F.B. has not recorded a book that you need, you will be instructed to send two copies. They will pay for one if you include the sales slip. As a reader records, a monitor sits outside the recording booth following the text. The monitor is alert to any miscues by the reader. Books are read onto four-track cassettes at the slow speed. Readers announce page numbers and tone index sections or chapters. When your cassette player is in fast forward or reverse, you'll hear the beep as a signal of a break.

Another resource is from the National Library Service. It issues a listing in large print and Braille called "Volunteers Who Produce Books." Groups that record, transcribe into Braille, or duplicate into large print are listed according to state, plus those that specialize in mathematics, science, foreign languages, and music notation. Reproduction into large print is expensive—about ten cents a page. Bell and Howell Corporation and the Xerox Corporation are two firms that will duplicate in this medium.

The Braille Book Bank is a collection of materials transcribed by hand into Braille. You can borrow or buy copies.

Your Talking Book library is another possibility for recorded books. Suppose you're taking a literature course, and all of Shakespeare's plays are either on disc or cassette. Most of the other classics, many best-sellers, outstanding works in social science, political science, economics, and psychology have been recorded by the Library of Congress Talking Book program. You will receive your copy in a few days. In addition, many of these regional and subregional libraries have a battery of volunteer readers who will hustle up a recorded book for you if necessary. Remember, you're dealing with librarians, who can ferret out books that you might have trouble locating. They can also inform you about other local volunteer groups.

"Usually we don't know what books we'll be using until the first day of class," complained James. "When I'm banking on a recorded edition, it could take weeks to get it." James's protest is logical. Again assume a detective's role. The bookstore is a natural starter for clues. The staff has to order textbooks months in advance. Show up armed with your instructor's name, course title, and section number. Leave with the title, author, publisher, and date of edition. You probably can sneak by with a recorded edition that is older. If that ploy fails, contact the instructor, explaining why you require information weeks before class begins—who knows, you may impress him by evincing such interest.

You can't count on having all of your books recorded. Sometimes an instructor will change his mind at the beginning of a course, or rely on portions of several books. If you can cover it by reading yourself, good. All is not lost if you can't. People who are paid or voluntary can read directly to you or can record sections that you request. Your state agency may pay (usually minimum wages) for allotted numbers of hours of reading per week. When you have to gather your own assistants, you can go several routes. You can ask an instructor to announce at the beginning of his course that you are seeking volunteers from the class. You might run an ad in the campus paper, or post a notice on a centrally located bulletin board. When you'd like help at home, place an ad in the community newspaper.

As you work with volunteers or paid readers, remember their time and other commitments. Some folks cannot devote more than several hours a week. You'll need to set up a schedule for these sessions just as you did for classes. You should expect readers, paid or voluntary, to keep appointments. Your end of the bargain is to be ready with specific tasks for them to accomplish—don't let them twiddle their thumbs while you hunt for a syllabus or take off to borrow somebody's physics book. Your recording equipment should be ready to roll. If your readers don't work out because they'd rather chat than read, can't read aloud acceptably, or don't show up for appointments, you'll have to let them go, since your academic career hangs on covering that material.

You'll have an ace in the hole by lining up a few readers before classes start each term. You might call on family or friends to pitch in before the recorded books arrive, or until your regular reading schedule is afloat. By having this backup system, you elude the danger of falling behind from the start, a disaster for a blind student because it is so difficult to catch up. A blind student can find himself on the wrong side of an avalanche when assignments pile up and he doesn't have the means to forestall it himself.

True, some reading doesn't lend itself as well to listening. Provided that you can read print, budget your residual vision to those assignments which you can more easily comprehend by reading yourself, such as science, mathematics, and other subjects that demand quality instead of quantity reading. Use recorded books when hundreds of pages have been assigned, and remember that you have a variable speed control on your cassette player. If you are a Braille user, expect a volunteer group to spend months transcribing for you. Not many Braille readers choose this medium because of the time needed to prepare textbooks.

Now that we've tackled reading, let's get into the classroom, where you'll be spending many hours. Don't think that your memory is elastic enough to absorb all that you hear — somewhere along the way, you'll have to take notes. Bold Line® paper from the American Printing House for the Blind can facilitate notetaking for partially sighted students. You can buy it in pads punched for three-ring binders. Browsing through bookstores, you'll probably discover notebooks with heavily lined paper that may suffice. Notebooks of varying colors or those with sets of pages in different colors are a quick way of separating subjects. As mentioned previously, experiment with different pens and pencils to see what works best for you. As you write or print, take care to keep your notes as legible as you can so that you won't be trying to decipher hieroglyphics when exams roll around later. Should your speed writing suffer, type your notes as soon as possible after class.

Braille users will have to be fleet of hand with slate and stylus to keep pace with lectures. Either lightweight Braille paper or a heavy grade of bond paper, either of which can be punched for a three-ring binder, will save you from writer's cramp. Braille writers are too heavy to lug and their noise will do more than keep the entire class awake.

"I never learned to write with slate and stylus until high school," bemoaned Pat, eighteen, before she began college. "I was afraid I couldn't take notes fast enough." Pat is not alone in her plight. Many people aren't swift enough with print or Braille, or don't use either.

Even sighted students are popping up with recording devices in lecture halls, much to the consternation of some instructors. In fact, some teachers prohibit their lectures from being recorded, although most likely they will soften with an exception for a blind student. If you rely on a recorder, the G.E. Modified 4-Track cassette recorder from the American Printing House for the Blind is the best machine for the purpose. Don't lapse into daydreaming or literally fall asleep at the switch. If you attended the world literature class three hours a week, it's improbable that you were so enthralled that you want to listen to three hours of lectures again. (When recording a class, check your equipment — batteries give out or tape can jam.) Start by dictating the title of the course and the date. Be ready with your finger on the pause button when the instructor digresses to a monologue on yesterday's football game or the recent election — that information won't help you on the final. Some students do not record the whole class; they summarize major points by dictating them quietly into the machine. The mike is so sensitive that you can speak softly without disturbing others. The tone index button on your G.E. recorder is another method of underlining salient points — you emphasize by pressing this button while recording an entire lecture. Playing it back later, in fast forward, you locate them quickly by stopping at every beep. Try to use one cassette for each subject so that you won't have to whir through the biology lecture to get to abnormal psychology. Label your cassettes for immediate identification.

Should you go the cassette route for note taking, you might make future studying easier by transferring recorded nuggets into print or Braille at your leisure. If print or Braille is out for you, you can condense by dictating onto another cassette. Set up the lecture cassette on your player as you record on the G.E. Modified 4-track. Again organization is the secret, since you won't feel like fooling around with a mass of material on tape when it is time for exams.

Since your cassette recorder is one of the most valuable and heavily used of your workhorses, it deserves proper care and cleaning. If you neglect its maintenance, it won't explode or self-destruct, but it will require repairs more often and will perform poorly. You'll find easy-to-follow directions in the instruction manual.

A sighted friend who taught graduate psychology courses was dining with me one evening. She surprised me by asking, "One of my students is blind. How will I handle the midterm exam with him? It's coming up in three days."

"Why, Helen, that's his problem to bring to you," I said. "You have enough to contend with in preparing and proctoring the test.

He ought to give you several options as to the way that he'll take it."

Another word to the wise: Don't bounce up to the instructor's desk as the exam period begins, expecting him to resolve this quandary on the spot. Your bid should come a few days before. Remember that many instructors have never taught a blind student and haven't the vaguest idea of how you can take the exam. Here are a few suggestions. When you see well enough to read, do as the others do. As you know, duplicated copies can be fuzzy. Request the original. Since you don't read as fast as your classmates, you should be entitled to more time if you need it. If it's an essay test, you may require more time to write legibly. Another option is requesting access to a typewriter. On occasion, an instructor will allow a visually impaired student to dictate answers onto cassette. Should you be unable to read tests, you can suggest that you bring a reader to go over the exam with you in the instructor's office. As the reader marks your choices for an objective exam, don't feel compelled to respond immediately to every question. You are free to say that you'll return to that question later. Sometimes succeeding questions throw light on those that have stumped you. Occasionally an instructor will tell you that he will give you the test orally. Answering directly to the test giver can have good or bad consequences. You may become tongue-tied from nervousness, forgetting everything you learned, or you might be so inspired as to talk your way out of a corner. If the teacher insists, you haven't much choice. It's only fair play to request that you return to a question when you are temporarily stymied, or stall for a little time to think of a response before spitting it out. Going to your instructor with these options gives him the chance to decide which way is most expedient for him and you.

Many teachers are prolific blackboard writers. If you can scan the board with a telescopic aid as you sit in the front row, scratch your inhibitions. You may have to request this special seat, even if it throws a seating chart off kilter. When there is ample blackboard space, you can ask the instructor not to erase until after class so that you can take advantage of perusing at close range. If you can't read the board, don't flounder or lose out. Asking the instructor to repeat what he is writing as he wields the chalk is one way. They do forget—remember that part of their notoriety rests on being absentminded. Check with the student sitting next to you, copying as he dictates. If a complicated graph, diagram, or long list of important points appears, you can give a classmate two sheets of plain paper with a sheet of carbon between. Your friend makes a copy for himself while writing one for you. If you intend to read those notes, ask your classmate to copy with extra care, writing or printing large enough for you. If it's a drawing that isn't too complex, it can be reproduced later with a raised line drawing kit from American Foundation for the Blind. This kit consists of sheets of polythylene film, a rubber mat, and penlike stylus. Lines drawn on sheets are immediately feelable and followed easily visually. Sometimes the teacher has written on the board before a class starts. If it's a bombshell like, "There will be a quiz next Friday on Chapters Five through Nine," there will be a collective groan to clue you in. It's wise to check, though, so you don't miss a gem because you didn't know it was there.

Try as you will to elude them, eventually your college (and even high school) courses will confront you with research papers. Becoming familiar with references within the library is your responsibility, not that of your readers. You direct your assistants to the sources you need to consult, not expecting these people to know where to look for what. Many references, especially indices and abstracts, are in microscopic-sized type. If there's no closed-circuit TV magnifier in the library, a reader can plow through these references much faster than a partially sighted student. As you gather a bibliography for your paper, note call numbers from the card catalog and titles of periodicals with their volume and page numbers. With list in hand, approach the librarian to request that some of these references be assembled for you at a specific time. This method is far more efficient than prowling through the stacks or digging up one or two books at a time. When recording research material, prompt your reader to include complete identi-fication of sources — author, title, publisher, city, and date of publi-cation if it is a book. When reading a periodical, record its name, date, and page numbers — each page number as the reader moves along. You can separate each source with your tone indexer. When you incorporate quotes or cite sources, you'll have all of this information for footnoting and bibliography. You won't have to retrace your steps, which are all there on tape.

Besides *Dictionary for Large Print Users*, by Merriam-Webster and *20,000 Words*, your search for just the right word might end with Merriam-Webster's *Thesaurus for Large Print Users*, each priced at $27.50.

You'll reap your harvest of research as you write the paper. Most students work from an outline, filling in by pouring ideas into a rough draft. If you read your own typing, you might find triple-spacing the rough draft easier so you'll have plenty of room for additions, corrections, and deletions. Legal size paper eliminates changing pages so often. If you don't have a triple-space mechanism on your typewriter, set the line spacer at one and one-half and hit it twice. When in doubt about spelling, don't stop to check—use all capitals as a signal for later. All capitals will also draw your attention to a point to be confirmed or clarified in the final draft.

Brailling a rough draft is awkward because you can't make changes easily. It's also quite a trip between a Braille page and typewriter keys. You can jot main points or topic sentences into Braille to organize your thoughts, then record from these notations, expanding as you dictate. If you record the rough draft, include punctuation and paragraphing. You can polish it into final form by using cassette player and recorder simultaneously. Your final draft should be spoken slowly enough so that you can type from it comfortably. By attaching a foot pedal either to the G.E. recorder or cassette player, you have your own dictation equipment. After your masterpiece is complete, get someone to proofread it for you, since typos, spelling, and punctuation errors can slide by you but might rile your instructor.

Science courses can be a challenge to a visually impaired student. Some activities such as looking through a microscope, drawing, dissecting, and visual observation of experiments may well be out of the question for you. Picking the right lab partner is crucial. He should be willing and able to describe fully and to perform tasks that your vision prohibits. In some instances, enlarged drawings, raised line drawings, or crude models from clay will increase your comprehension. Your share of the teamwork might come in writing up projects and experiments. By talking with your lab instructor prior to the beginning of the course, you can explain your difficulty. He might choose a partner for you such as a science major or perhaps even a graduate assistant. Your visual limitation should not penalize you, nor should it serve as an excuse for dodging a requirement.

Blind high school students can rely upon the same techniques, although expectations are usually on a smaller scale. If you attend a high school as the only blind student, and have no resource or itinerant teacher, you might be responsible for getting recorded books, working out exams, etc. An itinerant teacher visits blind students about once a week, assisting with these projects. These teachers have a degree in special education for the visually handicapped. They act as a go-between for student and teachers in the event problems surface because of a pupil's lack of vision. The itinerant teacher may even teach Optacon or offer basic orientation so the student can master the school's layout.

Some high schools and elementary schools include resource rooms for visually handicapped students. The trend is to mainstream children into regular classes with sighted classmates. The teacher remains in the resource room, which serves as a homeroom. She teaches children skills they must have as visually handicapped students, such as Braille, typing, and arithmetic, and instructs in the use of low-vision aids. For other classes such as English, social science, or history, blind students join others in the same grade. Resource rooms are equipped with Braille writers, recording and playback equipment, low-vision aids, and typewriters.

Almost every state has a residential school for the blind covering first through twelfth grade. These schools generally enroll children with additional handicaps. However, any legally blind child is eligible to attend. Children live in dormitories during the week, going home on weekends if distance isn't too great. If a youngster is recently blind, his parents might send him to a residential school for a year or so to learn Braille, mobility, and personal living skills. A resource teacher in an elementary or high school can teach these skills. If you want further information about education for visually handicapped students from kindergarten through high school, contact your local school district.

Through the Hadley School for the Blind (see Chapter 18), you can take courses for high school or college credit. You can't earn a high school diploma by studying only through Hadley, nor can you earn a college degree solely through this school. You would supplement your academic program through Hadley's accredited curriculum. For instance, you can enroll in a foreign language or psychology course through Hadley. As you introduce the idea to your high school counselor or college registrar, he probably won't be aware of this school. As you spring it on him, have a Hadley Bulletin in hand that explains affiliation with college extension departments, grading, and credits.

You can also prepare for the General Educational Development (GED). Although you cannot take the GED exam through Hadley, you can prepare for the five areas of testing. You will take the exam locally in Braille, large print, cassette, or with a reader. For more information about the GED exams for visually impaired students, contact your State Education Department, Adult Services Department.

Regardless of the level at which you're studying—elementary school or Ph.D. program—do you have a place to study? Don't camp out on the dining room table—nobody wants your geography notes as a placemat. That leads to someone moving your equipment and books. Even if it's a card table in the furnace room, the study space should be *yours*, a place for your typewriter, recording equipment, closed-circuit TV magnifier, books, papers, Braille writer, and other study aids. If you rely upon your vision, naturally it should be well lit. You might have the luxury of a bookstand to prop heavy print books, saving your cramped neck muscles. Off the beaten path, you'll be free of the distractions of TV, radio, and phone.

If you're living on campus and share a dormitory room with one or more roommates, you might not be able to establish your study domain there. It's a good reason to vie for a private room if possible, since you'll have plenty of opportunity for socializing elsewhere. When studying around others, use an earphone on your recording and playback equipment. With some ingenuity, and the help of a Special Needs office or counselor, you might be lucky enough to find a seldom-used room such as one that holds rare books. If your hole-away-from-home is in or near the library, you've struck gold.

Remember that effective studying doesn't mean how much time you've put into learning: It's what you derive from the time you devote. Should you question your study habits, you can even enroll in college courses which will teach effective methods of taking notes, preparing for exams, reading, and research.

"I'm not going to school for a degree. I just might take a class occasionally for enrichment such as one on investments or current events," mused Ernie, sixty-four. "Even though I'm not striving for a passing grade, I still want to get the most out of that class." Ernie can use most of the methods described. He can request books from R.F.B. or ask that they be recorded. Voluntary groups from his Talking Book library or local area will be glad to record books—they don't insist that a person be on the trail of a diploma or degree.

Don't assume that learning is outside your scope because of your visual disability. Although blindness may block one channel of acquiring knowledge and information, you have four other pathways open for you. The approaches you take might be different, more time-consuming, and sometimes arduous. But the results are the same as those for your sighted counterparts. Armed with techniques and resources, rise to the challenge and joy of discovery.

Chapter 24

IS YOUR LEISURE YOUR PLEASURE?

No wonder Jack's a dull boy. You'd be a bore, too, if you never did anything. Before delving into what's fun for you or how to start or resume recreation, figure out how much free time you have. If it's a lot, you can't play all the time—that's like having dessert at every meal.

Forty-five-year-old Dora has travel vision, but poor health complicates her life. She and her mentally retarded twenty-five-year-old son live in a small apartment.

"After my son leaves for his activities shop in the morning, it takes only a few minutes to tidy up the place. The day drags, almost without an end in sight," she sighed. "I realize that I can't hold a job, but I still want to feel useful and fill my long, lonely hours."

Dora had never thought of volunteering. At first she tried to dismiss herself as being incapable of helping anyone else. Besides, blind people were receivers, not givers of help. I convinced her plenty of people needed her. She now serves by delivering hot meals to the homebound for the Meals on Wheels program. As a volunteer driver waits in the car, Dora drops off a tray and a few cheery words.

Your talents, interests, mobility, and general health will dictate where and what you can do. Many of our students have found the large metropolitan hospital at which our department is located a good starting place for contributing their services. Arthur, thirty-two, sees well enough to sit at the Information desk four hours weekly, answering questions and giving directions to patients and visitors. Three totally blind women meet weekly to sew gloves for burn patients to wear over their bandaged hands—no fancy stitches, just enough to keep the gloves intact. Tom, thirty, joins the group after he finishes his job packaging for the Central Supply Room.

Other students have gone far afield. Arlene, in her midforties, lives near the zoo. She spends one day a week guiding visitors. Her descriptions of animals and exhibits have been derived from brochures recorded for her. Before he found a job, twenty-four-year-old Michael was a tour guide for children at the local science center.

The list of volunteer opportunities is endless. Do you like children? Could you tutor kids having a hard time in school? If you are skilled in crafts, are you willing to teach youngsters or adults? If you have empathy for older folks, you would make many residents of nursing homes much happier by a friendly visit occasionally, or wheeling around the book or sundries cart. You may not be mobile enough for such work, but you can capitalize on your hobbies by being at places that interest you, whether you're stuffing envelopes at the historical museum or answering the phone and taking messages at the local public radio station.

"I'm pretty much confined to the house," objected Joe, fifty-five. "I can't find places to do things for other people."

I put Joe in touch with the Suicide Prevention Center. He was able to attend preparation classes. After that, the center connected callers to Joe's home phone during specified times when he was on call. This system might also work with the twenty-four-hour crisis hotlines that are so widespread. Agencies for the aged often sponsor a buddy system. A volunteer agrees to call each day one or more seniors who live alone. These daily checks ensure that an older person is well, and add a lift to that lonely person's routine.

Are you active in a church? Your input on planning and service committees, cooking, serving, or cleanup at a dinner would be welcome. You might also teach Sunday school classes for all ages. Sonja, forty-seven, teaches Bible classes to third and fourth graders. Another church member records lessons on cassettes, a month's worth at a time, so Sonja can prepare for each week's class.

Instead of complaining about politicians, join the campaign of your favorite candidate. There are never enough people to handle telephone canvassing, passing out literature, or doing routine office work.

Besides making inquiries to specific organizations to which you'd like to offer your services, call your local community agency for the number of a central volunteer bureau that acts as a clearing house in your area. Other leads are the United Way, American Cancer Society, Boy and Girl Scouts, Big Brother/Sisters, and the Y.M.C.A. and Y.W.C.A. Most hospitals and nursing homes have a volunteer director.

Your initial contact might not send the volunteer director into ecstasy. It can be the old story of never having met a blind person before. Don't let yourself be stymied, too. Find out what the organization does and pursue inventively the tasks you can accomplish with little or no vision. You and the director may have to do some rooting around, but certainly there is room for another mind and pair of hands.

Clubs directed toward service, hobbies, and recreation are good reasons for you to get out of the house, and give you something to talk about when you go home. Many blind men belong to Lions Clubs. Besides attending regular meetings, they plan programs and help in fund-raising campaigns, and even hold office. Other groups meet to practice foreign languages, play board games such as backgammon, chess, or Scrabble®, invest in the stock market, or watch old movies. Some blind people join organizations of the blind for recreation and political lobbying. Two such organizations have local chapters throughout the country: National Federation of the Blind and the American Council of the Blind. There are also many small unaffiliated groups across the nation. To see if one is located near you, call the nearest agency for the blind. To find a special interest group, contact the club editor of your local newspaper.

"I used to love watching birds," reminisced Alec, sixty-six. "I don't get much out of looking through the strongest binoculars, so I gave it up."

After a little encouragement, Alec joined the Audubon Society and a city-wide group that supports a local park. He revels in long hikes with Auduboners, vividly visualizing what other members describe. He pitches in with fervor during spring cleanups at the park. Nobody minds that he sometimes overlooks small scraps of paper.

The American Youth Hostels, somewhat misnamed because it includes members of all ages, sponsors outdoor sports and attendance at social and cultural events. There are over 4,500 hostels around the world providing good, low-cost temporary lodging. They welcome blind members.

The singles scene bustles with people seeking camaraderie. Often affiliated with churches or independent clubs, their calendars of events are crowded with anything from ski trips to symphonies. Parents Without Partners appeals to single parents of all ages. Local chapters sponsor events for members with and without their offspring.

"I don't like to be with old fogies," grumbled seventy-two-year-old George. "Besides, I don't see well enough to manage in a strange place."

George changed his tune when his daughter accompanied him to his church's weekly meeting for senior citizens. Although he didn't try his hand at Ping Pong or card games, he drank coffee and indulged in the nostalgia of his thirty-five years spent as a railroad engineer.

Although senior citizen groups frequently are connected with churches, they also can be part of the city recreation department or under the auspices of the local agency for the aged. Besides recreation such as cards, bowling, dancing, and crafts, they might periodically bus the group to a supermarket or shopping center. They visit museums and historical sites and take trips over weekends or longer. Because disabilities often beset older people, a blind member shouldn't feel out of place.

The American Association of Retired Persons is probably the largest national organization of its kind. Besides offering members tips on recreation and travel packages, it keeps them abreast of legislation affecting the elderly, planning for retirement, and insurance.

Some blind people yen to become active again in sports or to acquire an athletic skill. Maybe you can't hunt, but you can enjoy tramping through the woods with a friend out to bag game. There's no reason you can't fish, unless it's difficult for you to reach the spot. Some states don't charge blind people for fishing licenses. If you can't steer a single bike, tandem bike riding is an alternative — you can rent tandems in some parks, bike shops, and gas stations. Blind folks who like jogging team up with a companion if they can't see well enough to run alone. Some tracks, especially designed for blind runners, string a wire overhead. They maintain course by holding a ring suspended from the wire. One blind man trained his dog guide to jog with him. If water is your cup of tea, you can swim, paddle canoes, or row. You can water ski by having an observer in the boat signal you when necessary by tugging on the towline or blowing a whistle. A partially sighted woman successfully pilots a houseboat in a river which is familiar to her. Another partially sighted woman, a sailor at heart, handles a Sailfish® by herself. Blind people learn to snow ski with a guide who skis alongside, giving instructions and calling directions. You can ice skate or roller skate by lightly holding the arm of your companion if necessary.

Beeper baseball is an adapted game for blind players. (Partially sighted players must wear a blindfold to even things up.) A sighted pitcher throws grounders; bases equipped with buzzers provide immediate orientation. There is a basketball with a bell inside for shooting baskets, with the basket also equipped with a buzzer.

Leagues for blind bowlers have become popular. People who can't see to make a straight approach follow a three-foot high rail with the free hand. A marker indicates the foul line. Sighted teammates announce what pins remain standing and keep score. These leagues compete in state and national tournaments for blind bowlers.

Visually impaired golfers aren't that rare, either. A caddy usually accompanies a blind golfer. There are national tournaments for blind golfers.

Other sports in which blind people become proficient are horseback riding, wrestling, and jujitsu.

Several organizations direct efforts toward outdoor activities for the blind. Blind Outdoor Leisure Development (BOLD) sponsors skiing, downhill and cross country, and national competitions.

Health Sports, Beacon Lodge for the Blind, Christian Record Braille Foundation, and BOLD operate summer camps for blind adults, and will even provide guides. If you like to golf or bowl, contact the United States Golfer's Association or the American Blind Bowling Association. The United States Association of Blind Athletes can give you more leads on athletics.

If you're a fresh air fanatic but don't want to indulge in vigorous exercise, try your hand at tilling the soil. Gardening can supply many pleasurable hours. There are several recorded books on gardening for the blind. A column in *Dialogue*, a magazine for the blind published quarterly, offers gardening hints for blind folks with or without a green thumb. You can also borrow recorded books on raising indoor plants. *Better Homes and Gardens* is available in Braille.

"I feel so left out when friends talk about recent movies that they've seen," fretted Ann, fifty-two. "They don't think to invite me to come along."

Ann's friends foster a typical reaction. Because a blind person can't see what's happening on the screen, people assume this entertainment is out of the question. I suggested to Ann that she diplomatically tell her friends that she would enjoy films, especially if someone would tell her about changes of scene or the appearance of a new character.

If you derive any benefit from optical aids, take them to the movie, play, opera, or sporting event. You won't see all the action, but half a loaf is better than none. When a game you're attending is broadcast, you'll stay right in tune with the crowd by listening to your transistor radio. By using an earphone, you won't disturb other spectators. It'll be hard hearing when excitement runs high, but you'll be charged by the electric atmosphere—you can scarf down hotdogs and guzzle pop or beer with the rest of the gang.

Don't cross off museums, or hobby and home, auto, and boat shows from your list. Our local art museum has been cooperative when I called to request a touching tour of sculpture displays. They provided a curator to accompany my friend and me to different exhibits. A blind man I know is a car and boat enthusiast. He wouldn't miss the annual auto and boat shows—they're his best way of keeping up with new models. Most exhibitors are flattered when a visitor shows such obvious interest and will let him examine displays as much as he likes.

Have you thought of reviving hobbies? People with low vision can still enjoy photography. George Covington, himself legally blind, offers hints on how in his book, *Let Your Camera Do the Seeing: First Photography Manual for the Legally Blind*, which is available on cassette (RC17386). Are you a tinkerer? Many blind people, after giving up driving, still work on the car, saving money and gaining a sense of accomplishment. Others dabble in woodworking, metalworking, and clay modeling. Again recorded books come to the rescue with how-to manuals. *Popular Mechanics* is published in Braille. Besides books, there are tools such as rulers and tape measures with raised markings and even audible levels. These products are available from the American Foundation for the Blind.

As the computer craze sweeps the country, some blind folks work with home computers. They read and take classes to master computer intricacies. There are several audible outputs, which literally make the machine talk. An enlarged CRT screen for partially sighted people is now in the prototype stage.

After losing all of her vision at fifty-nine, Arda didn't discount the possibility of learning new crafts. Although she had never knitted before, she convinced a friend to teach her a few basic stitches. Once her needle began flying, the same friend recorded patterns. She labeled colors of yarn with Braille. Were she more facile with Braille, she could have requested Braille knitting and crochet pattern books. Now she and you can read the book *Knitting and Crochet for the Physically Handicapped and Elderly*, by Shelagh Hollingworth.

Elaine, also in her fifties, decided to master macrame. She attended an adult education class. As the teacher demonstrated, her assistant showed Elaine how to tie various knots.

Local high schools, colleges, churches, Y.M.C.A.'s, and Y.W.C.A.'s abound with adult education classes. This is another way of waking up your mind, and a route for meeting new people. You don't have to worry about passing or failing adult education courses because most are noncredit. At long last you can learn conversational Italian, taste wines from around the world, study parapsychology, or brush up on black history. If it's a crafts or cooking class that you can't follow visually, you can follow suit with Elaine and ask the teacher to appoint an assistant or another class member to demonstrate for you. Many courses do not require much reading. For those that do, check Chapter 23. Some classes meet once a week for discussion and quizzes; you can tune in on lectures on television.

Don't overlook discussion groups and lectures as another form of mental stimulation. They are frequently sponsored by colleges, churches, and libraries. You could take part in a Great Books group by keeping pace with the discussion by reading selections on Talking Book. If you think that announcements of such events slip by you, call the community relations department of colleges or libraries or the local newspaper, especially a community paper. Often there is no charge for these events. Music is a pastime often associated with blind people. Whether you play, sing, or listen, you can fully enjoy this entertainment. Sure it's awkward to memorize scores instead of sight reading, but if that is the only way of mastering a piece, there's no choice. The Music Section of the National Library Services has a big collection of large print and Braille music, as well as cassette instructions for playing instruments.

For those who are serious about learning Braille music, two books recently became available. *How to Read Braille Music* (1975), by Bettye Krolick, is a beginning book written in simple language, appropriate for blind children and adults who know literary Braille, and sighted teachers having no knowledge of Braille. *Primer of Braille Music* (1971), edited by Edward W. Jenkins, is a beginners book written for adult readers and is useful for blind adults who know literary Braille and sighted teachers who wish to know more about the Braille music code. Hadley School for the Blind offers a course to teach Braille music notation to people who are adept with Braille, and another course in music appreciation.

"I though I'd have to drop out of our church choir," recalled Oscar, sixty-six. "I participated for years, but reached the point where I could no longer read lyrics."

Oscar took action on my suggestion immediately. The choir director reads lyrics of new hymns onto cassette tape, followed by a vocal rendition with piano accompaniment. Oscar memorizes lyrics by replaying the tape as often as necessary, and the choir retains a member with a rich baritone voice. Oscar would be an asset to any vocal ensemble.

Ham radio is another outlet that can put you in touch with people around the world, even if you can't leave your house very often. Hadley School provides courses starting with preparation for the novice license through general and advanced class licenses. They will teach you to become sufficiently proficient in transmitting and receiving Morse code to meet FCC requirements. You can borrow books, recorded or brailled, to learn on your own. You may choose communications on a smaller scale with citizens band radio.

Another far-reaching contact is correspondence clubs. "Voicespondence" is one of the largest, in which sighted and blind members exchange cassette letters. These clubs match members according to age, mutual interests, and preferred locale of correspondent. Remember, you and your pen pal can send cassettes postage free with the words: FREE MATTER FOR THE BLIND.

You can uncover other sources of entertainment by phoning your city recreation department. Public transportation companies in large cities usually issue brochures listing free entertainment in the city. Newspapers and radio stations usually run a calendar of events. Sometimes a blind person and his guide pay reduced rates for entertainment—anything from a football game to a rock concert. Your local agency for the blind would be the place to inquire.

Stanley, thirty-three, lost his sight suddenly from illness. He sorely missed playing cards with the fellows. His first goal when starting Braille was to learn enough to read Braille cards. After a few weeks, he was able to rejoin the guys, holding his own in the games. Braille numbers and suit initials appear on diagonal corners of the cardboard or plastic cards. These Braille markings are imprinted on standard and pinochle decks so that sighted players can use them as well. Stanley wisely began with games requiring only a few cards, not wanting to slow down the game as he checked his hand. By holding his cards beneath the table, he is careful not to tip his hand while sizing it up. Other players call cards which they deal face up.

If your eyes light up at the mention of a card game, you're

probably eager to resume. You can buy jumbo cards, standard or pinochle, in drugstores, department stores, or discount houses. Numbers and suits are designated in nine-sixteenths-inch print. For those with extremely low vision, Low Vision® cards indicate numerals and suits with huge print instead of pips and pictures. For rapid identification of suits, spades are black, hearts red, diamonds green, and clubs blue.

Bingo, an ever-popular pastime, needn't be out of your picture if you're an addict. You can buy wooden Braille/print bingo cards with squares recessed so markers won't move. Print letters and numbers are one-half-inch high. If you can still use conventional cards, you'll probably have to reduce the number or ask a friend to help watch them. There are Braille call numbers should you take your turn at calling.

You can also purchase other games with good color contrast and Braille or other tactile markings. These include checkers, Chinese checkers, Scrabble®, Monopoly®, cribbage, backgammon, Mastermind®, dominoes, and Parcheesi®.

American Foundation for the Blind markets all the games, playing cards, and tools mentioned in this chapter.

Nor has the commercial market ignored audible games. In a toy store or department store you can find Simon®, Name That Tune®, and Einstein®. These electronic games challenge players to repeat a set of musical tones by pressing corresponding buttons in sequence, or identify a melody after hearing just a few notes.

When it's your turn to entertain, don't bow out. Reread Chapter 14, "No One's in the Kitchen with Dinah." Your former grand-scale dinner party might boil down to inviting a few friends for dessert and coffee. You might opt for a party tray from the deli instead of whipping up six different hors d'oeuvres. What scares many visually impaired people away from inviting in guests is the thought of carrying everything off singlehandedly. One of my traditional holiday celebrations is a trim-the-tree party. Friends like to be creative, even in someone else's home. By just providing refreshments, I benefit from their artistic bent.

Don't let too much free time become your millstone. There's more to life than TV soap operas, hours on the phone, and wishing for ways to break the monotony. Remain idle too long and you'll think you can hear the grass grow. Try volunteering, developing hobbies or skills, taking classes, and sports and games, if you are able. If just plain getting there stops you short, perhaps a friend would be glad for your company. Someone involved in the same activity might live near you. By constructively and pleasurably filling that time, you won't vegetate into a dull Jack or Jane—you'll be more alive to the world around you.

Chapter 25

WHEN TRAVEL IS YOUR TICKET

W hether it's to Baltimore or Bombay, a business con-
ference or a visit with cousin Conrad, a trip can be exciting and
maybe a bit scary. If alone, you might be fretting about more than
forgetting your toothbrush. You might envision yourself stranded
at a bus drop-off in Podunk or hopelessly adrift at the Los
Angeles International Airport as your plane takes off without you.
Remember—you're not alone in this big, bewildering world. There
are ways of preventing wanderlust from backfiring into panic.

First question is: How will you get there? Since money is on
everybody's mind, you can save some by applying for an ID card
from the American Foundation for the Blind, using your state ID
card for blind persons, or proof of legal blindness from an
opthalmologist, optometrist, or agency for the blind. Present it at
the ticket counter of many bus companies, including Greyhound,
which grant a two-for-one fare, and you and a sighted companion
can ride for the cost of one ticket. This money-saver won't work if
you travel alone (even with a dog guide) or if your partner is also
legally blind. The bus companies' rationale is that your traveling
companion will see that you get to the right place at the right
time. Write to the American Foundation for the Blind for an application for this ID—at present it costs five dollars and two passport
sized pictures. An eye doctor fills out part of the form, which also
covers classification of the partially sighted (20/200 to 20/70).

Amtrak also offers reduced fares to legally blind passengers who don't need to be accompanied. Tickets are reduced by 25 percent, and you're not tied to time restrictions such as holidays. Again, you present certification of blindness, as with the bus companies.

Don't look for a break with the airlines. Of course, you can go standby just like anyone else. Senior citizens are eligible for a discount with some airlines, buying a ticket a day before departure. But you'll save more nickels by planning ahead and taking advantage of Super Savers when you can.

As for getting yourself aboard bus, train, or plane, there are tricks to getting where you need to go when you have to get there. Allow enough time before departure, because such conveyances wait for no one.

Absurd as it sounds, hang onto your own ticket. Recently a blind man nearly spoiled his vacation because his mother had his ticket. She was at home while he was at the bus station. Be sure the ticket agent or luggage handler returns that valuable document to you. If you can't read vital information such as time of departure and arrival or flight numbers, write it in large print or Braille on an index card to be stapled to the ticket envelope.

Some bus stations and train depots can seem like desert islands or hostile hotbeds. To ensure a friendly soul to help you, call Travelers Aid a few days prior to your trip. They can provide routing information for long journeys so other members of the network can meet you en route.

The Protective Service Department of Travelers Aid works with children and handicapped passengers traveling alone. You can expect an assistant to help you find the ticket counter, help you aboard bus or train, locate restaurants, rest rooms, phone, or taxi. Although Travelers Aid offices are located in major cities, they can call upon volunteers to meet you at stops where a branch isn't located. Many offices are open twenty-four hours a day, but some close on weekends and in the evenings. If you notify them in advance, they'll see that someone is there to meet you, regardless of the time. Travelers Aid also serves at airports, frequently working with small airlines having limited personnel, or with major air carriers during busy seasons. This voluntary organization asks a donation from people requiring its service but never turns down anyone unable to contribute.

If you fly, rest assured big airlines will accommodate blind passengers. They, too, request advance notice. When you make a reservation, let the clerk or travel agent know you are blind and traveling alone. You can specifically request to be met at curbside or check-in counter. If you are diabetic, it's also the time to order a diabetic meal if food is included while you are in flight. (You can also order a kosher or vegetarian tray ahead of time.) Someone will show you to the gate and, if you want to head off the crushing crowd, you have the privilege of boarding before the other passengers.

Many airlines now offer seating assignments with reservations. You can be certain of sitting next to your companion without a last-minute shuffle. If you're flying with a dog guide, you should alert personnel. The bulkhead seat, first in the cabin, allows more floor space for the pooch. Remember, you don't have to buy an extra ticket for the dog, nor is he subjected to riding in the baggage compartment. You won't be seated next to the emergency exit, since it's unlikely that a blind passenger would lead the way out in an emergency landing. Should you be carrying a straight cane, the attendant probably will ask you for it during flight. Regulations prohibit such a cane held by a passenger while the plane is airborne; turbulent weather might turn it into a projectile. Some cane users prefer the collapsible variety when traveling by air.

Upon landing, another staffer will help you pick up baggage, or locate a taxi, limousine, or phone. If you are making a connecting flight with another airline, the carrier with which you originally booked will notify other airlines for assistance. Don't get rattled if somebody shows up with a wheelchair that you neither requested nor expected—wires do get crossed.

Once underway, sit back and relax. If traveling a long distance by bus, you'll be smart to pack your own lunch. Gobbling down a meal while watching the clock invites indigestion. Should you want to go to the diner or club car on a train, give the word to the conductor. When I'm in the mood for company, I ask him to look around for a friendly traveler to see if that person, too, would like company while dining. A flight attendant will teach you how to use the oxygen mask. Don't worry. Everybody else watches this demonstration at the beginning of every flight. Remind the attendant to point out the call button, light, and air vent overhead. If you want to go to the restroom, or need a blanket or a drink, hit the call button.

When you're traveling on your own, regardless of mode of transportation, slip-ups can happen. If you think you've been forgotten or overlooked, or find yourself uncertain of finding the counter, flag down another passenger or even the fellow sweeping the floor. Such a reminder as, "I'm to leave at 1:05 and it's 12:55," won't land you in the pest category. Even if you don't ordinarily carry a cane, you're better off with a collapsible cane up your sleeve or in your hand to serve as immediate identification when you need help. Frantically searching a terminal five minutes before departure is no time to prove your independence or to go exploring.

When packing for that bon voyage, common sense dictates that your luggage be labeled with your name and address inside and outside. If your bags would make a weightlifter stagger, think about luggage with built-in wheels or a collapsible luggage cart. Even if you leave the family jewels behind, you might be carrying such valuables as medication or low-vision aids. Slip them into a bag to carry with you. You ought to know the color and manufacturer of your baggage, since saying that you have a black suitcase isn't much to go on. If your bags look like a hundred others, slap on a decorative decal for easy spotting.

When you set up your temporary home in an unfamiliar hotel or motel, those four walls can seem like a solitary confinement cell unless you do something immediately about orientation should you require it. The bellhop will be likely to accompany you — con him into a rundown of the room and tip him extra for his effort. Clue him in on pointing out essentials, such as light switches, drapes or blinds (you don't want to be the local stripper by changing in front of an unshaded window), wastebasket, bathroom layout, closet, TV, and phone. Your impromptu orienter won't think of singling out blind-traps such as hooks on the bathroom wall or protruding closet racks, so prompt him to point them out. Most phones use zero for the desk. By dialing a room number, you can call other rooms. A telephone credit card saves money for long-distance calls because it is cheaper than calling collect or adding charges to your bill.

Once that bellhop leaves, don't imagine you've been abandoned. So you can't figure out the heating/air conditioning system — that's no reason to swelter or freeze. Or you've looked in the most likely places for towels and still can't locate them. Only a martyr would drip dry after a shower. Pick up the phone and tell the desk clerk that you are blind and want some help. In case your alarm clock was left behind, the desk will also give you a wake-up call in the morning.

Nor do you have to resign yourself to room service for meals with the TV newscaster as company. If venturing out unaccompanied ruins your appetite, call the desk to ask that someone come to show you to the dining room or coffee shop. If you are jittery about not getting back, request that an employee return later to walk you back to your room. If you can't see room numbers, you'll find that most are engraved or embossed. Without such tactile identification, make your own by slipping a rubber band around the doorknob. Should you blow it by trying to fit your key into the wrong lock, keep cool — nobody will shoot you for attempted breaking and entering if you explain why you goofed.

When illumination is high on your list, remember that hotels and motels are notoriously skimpy on lighting. Nobody will know the difference if you bring your own bulbs. They pack well in the cardboard sleeves in which they are sold.

Should your destination be to the home of relatives or friends, you'll not wrestle these hassles but may encounter a few others. Your host and hostess might be a bit edgy about your visit, especially if they haven't seen you since your sight loss. Again, being open with them from the beginning will make the transition smoother. Because they aren't around you constantly, you can't expect them immediately to accommodate your requirements, such as clearing the stairway or shutting doors. It's their home, so you must be constantly vigilant.

When you don't have travel vision, you'd be safer to use a cane in a strange home until you get the hang of the place. With your cane in a cross-body position, you protect yourself from bruised shins via the coffee table and preserve the prized antique lamp.

While you're visiting, it can happen that your host and hostess won't be around during mealtime—their routines continue, even though you are on vacation. Nor do you want them to feel tied down to you. You might suggest that someone show you the fixin's for your meal. It probably won't be an elaborate repast, but just enough to get you by. By having the vittles set out on the counter or knowing their location in the refrigerator, you won't feel like a thief in the night as you snoop through cupboards. You might also ask that your place be set. Don't forget a rundown on the stove or microwave if heating food is part of your meal preparation.

While on the road or in another locale for a while, you don't have to forgo Talking Books. First off, you can while away many miles by listening to your cassette player. Perhaps the driver of the car and other passengers will enjoy your book, too. If Talking Books set their teeth on edge, plug in an earphone or headphones. You can have Talking Books sent either by your local Talking Book library or by the library that serves the area where you are staying. You'd make arrangements by starting with your own library at home. If traveling outside North America, you would receive service from the National Library Service. You can also borrow Braille books while on the move. To save the cassette player battery, you can purchase an adapter that fits into the cigarette lighter outlet. But while off in your own world buried in a book, you owe it to the driver to carry on a conversation sporadically. Highways in straight stretches can become monotonous, even mesmerizing.

Those faraway places with strange-sounding names are not meant for sightseeing by only people with normal vision. It's easy to obtain tourist information before you arrive. Folks who lead bus and boat tours have a knack of being lively and descriptive of historic landmarks. In fact, it's an excellent way to become familiar with a city, although you have been there many times.

When Karen, totally blind and just out of college, went to Europe with a study group, she hadn't intended to leave her companions. When she couldn't find any takers for a bus trip through southern Spain, she booked the trip by herself. What a shock to discover that none of the other fifty-three passengers spoke English! In fact, Catalan was their native tongue, and Karen spoke nary a word. Fortunately, some who knew Spanish rallied to Karen's curiosity, vividly describing mountains, seacoast, and fruit orchards as they passed. They realized they became more aware of landscape as they put it into words. Even those who couldn't converse bridged the communication barrier by serving as guides during mealtimes and stopovers.

So heartened was she by this experience that Karen booked another trip to Europe on her own. Having had sight as a child, she visualized paintings described to her in galleries and museums. Guides waived restrictions so she could touch sculptures in the Louvre and Sistine Chapel. Karen maintains that her success in traveling alone is due to her being open with others, telling them without apology what she wants to see and where she would like to go.

Before visiting Washington, D.C., I contacted the local office of Carl Levin, one of our United States senators. His staff went all out to provide me with private, hands-on tours of the White House and Smithsonian Institution. While strolling through the White House, I skinnied under ropes to touch furniture and china. At the Space Museum a retired Air Force colonel explained a space capsule as I examined it. Another blind woman and I explored a seventeenth-century house reconstructed in the Museum of American History. Staffs of United States Congressmen are most obliging about making arrangements for constituents, and probably would make special arrangements for visually handicapped visitors to our nation's capital.

Because I am fond of horseback riding, I have spent vacations at a dude ranch in Montana at least a dozen times. Other guests seemed delighted when I asked for accounts of scenery as we rode through rugged mountains and rolling plains.

If the Great Outdoors calls you, you might like to amble around Oral Hull Park for the Blind near Sandy, Oregon, thirty miles from Portland. You can wander over nature trails, sniff your way through fragrant gardens, listen to and watch birds, and fish to your heart's content. In the lodge you can play piano or organ or browse through a library stocked with Braille and taped books.

Considering current motel and hotel rates, it's a bargain: $3.50 per person for overnight accommodations. This facility can house forty-eight guests at a time.

If you're a gambler by nature, some casinos in Atlantic City and Las Vegas operate blackjack tables at which both cards are dealt face up. If necessary, ask the dealer to call your cards and his as he deals. Reports are that there are Braille slot machines in Atlantic City. Clanging bells and clinking coins are enough for me.

George and Sue, a blind couple in their midfifties, went to Israel during the unrest of 1969. They contacted the national agency serving the blind through the American Foundation for Overseas Blind. An Israeli staff member called as soon as they arrived, offering arrangements for them to see sites of interest. On another trip abroad they booked a tour through a travel agency. By teaming up with a sighted husband and wife, they made a carefree tour of England. Their advice to blind members of a group is to be ready to leave on time, bags packed and outside the door.

You can book a trip through one of two nationwide travel agencies that specialize in tours for the handicapped, including visually impaired, slow walkers, hearing impaired, and wheelchair users. Evergreen will arrange trips inside and outside the United States. Wilkes makes arrangements mostly for England. They will procure guides and arrange for stop-and-touch tours if you like. Your family and friends are also welcome on such trips. Some travel agents maintain that they can book trips for the handicapped, especially regarding wheelchair accessibility. It's best to stick with agents who handle such requests routinely. One couple using wheelchairs became frustrated when they could barely maneuver along the companionway during a cruise.

Senior citizens rank high among well-traveled folks. Seniors— over sixty to be specific—might find an off-beat vacation through Elderhostel. This concept is a takeoff on youth hosteling with a slant toward mature people. Having affiliates with over 600 colleges and universities in North America and Europe, this organization offers week-long courses on anything from current affairs to stress management through yoga. You attend lectures or discussion groups only part of the day, allowing time to sample local color. Because participants usually stay in college dorms and dine on campus, rates are reasonable.

If the travel bug bites, it might be of some consolation to know that so many blind people travel alone or in groups with sighted people. I read about a seventy-one-year-old blind man who crossed the United States on the rear seat of a tandem bike. Many blind college students spend a year abroad as exchange students.

If your dog guide is joining you on your journey, you'll have to plan for him, too. If his feed is only available locally, start him gradually onto a diet of a national brand. Then you can buy dog food at your destination. A bathing cap is an easy-to-carry container for water en route. Don't feed or water your dog for several hours before departing. Should your trip be long, you will have to accommodate his relief breaks, too. (Good luck in finding grass near a terminal or airport.) Although dog guides will be welcome into public buildings almost everywhere in North America, you should carry the ID card from the school from which you graduated—it serves to soothe proprietors temporarily unnerved by a situation they have never faced before.

Trips to Mexico and Canada require you to show your dog's rabies vaccination certificate at the border. You'll need a health certificate from your veterinarian if you go to the Bahamas. When traveling abroad, check ahead about acceptance of a dog guide—Hawaii and England enforce a six-month quarantine, even on dog guides, because there is no rabies in either locale. If your trip takes you to places known to be flea infested, you can't avoid your dog's picking up those pests. He should be sprayed frequently while there or dipped just before coming home. Otherwise, those parasites will set up housekeeping in your home. When visiting areas that are warm, check with your veterinarian about starting your dog on heartworm medication prior to leaving, even if the season is cold where you live.

Whether you're traveling alone or with others, you'll encounter a spirit of camaraderie among fellow travelers and among those who call your destination their hometown. Sure, your routine will be disrupted, everything won't be where you expect it, but that's part of getting away. It can happen that you'll miss a bus or your luggage doesn't show up when you do. That can befall anybody.

But you will find that people are genuinely helpful, whether you are stepping off a bus 100 miles from home or getting off a plane in Bangkok. You can skirt the tight spots by planning ahead. When the unexpected arises, you rise to it. You won't be abandoned while the rest of the world rushes uncaringly by. Make your needs known. Become part of that world, because there's so much out there for you to see.

Chapter 26

HEALTH AND APPEARANCE

A STATEMENT OF YOU

S o you wouldn't be picked to pose for a vitamin commercial. Nor could you double as Robert Redford or Raquel Welch.
How you manage your physical well-being and appearance registers
your self-esteem. Nothing is more vital to you than health. Thus,
you owe it to yourself to take an active part in its maintenance.
Unless you are a bona fide hermit, others' eyes will rest upon you.
Anyone who is different, whether it's from having green hair,
walking on stilts, or being visually impaired, draws more-than-
usual attention. First impressions can be lasting. Let's be optimis-
tic and strive for the most effect with what you have.

Your relationship with your doctor is precious, sometimes sacred,
but remember, doctors aren't gods. You shouldn't be afraid to speak
up, to ask questions about your health or about resources taking
up where he leaves off. If you find that your doctor rushes you, or
does not address your inquiries, or talks to your companion instead of to you—take charge if you're able. Don't cower like the
forty-one-year-old blind woman who passively acquiesced when
her mother accompanied her into the examining room. When the
physician spoke, it was to Mama. Your companion should remain
in the reception room throughout your visit. Should your doctor

be defensive or uncommunicative, it's time to shop for another.

It's always a good idea to note questions before you visit. You can either become tongue-tied or forgetful. "Why didn't I show him that lump on my wrist," you mutter as you climb into the car. When unable to read the notes yourself, don't just meekly and mutely hand over the slip. Suggest that he go through those items with you to see if you have overlooked anything. It's your body at stake; you have a voice in its maintenance.

Of course, doctors have only a limited time to spend with you. The nurse should be familiar with your case and able to clarify directions for taking medications and treatment. You can bounce any concerns you have about the doctor off her, expecting her to channel them for you. If you still aren't satisfied, you won't hurt your doctor's feelings by seeking another physician, even if yours has treated you and your family for the past fifteen years.

Should you hurt yourself and not be able to determine the extent of the injury, it's time to put your Emergency Reserve List into effect (see Chapter 17). A first aid kit is a must. Don't expect your neighbor to dash to the drugstore to pick up burn ointment or gauze before attending to your wound. You can buy a kit with all the necessities from your pharmacy, or ask the nurse at your doctor's office to make one up for you. You shouldn't feel sheepish about having someone examine an injury—it's better to err in the direction of overtreatment. This precaution is especially true if you are a diabetic, because an open wound can become seriously infected and take months to heal.

Diabetes is a major cause of blindness, and people suffering from this disease will have other medical problems. You can learn more about this disease and such specifics as diet, foot care, and exercise from diabetic classes often offered at hospitals. You can also read *Diabetic Forecast*, a periodical on disc from the American Diabetes Association. To learn how to administer insulin independently, you and a health care provider should peruse the pamphlet, "Modifications on Insulin Techniques for the Visually Impaired and Blind Diabetic," by Alice Raftary. She discusses methods for a diabetic to measure and inject insulin. These techniques require the instruction of a nurse or physician.

Medic Alert is a nonprofit foundation that sells ID bracelets and pendants to people having a hidden medical condition such as diabetes, heart disease, or epilepsy. Were you to lose consciousness, such jewelry could save your life. You can call Medic Alert toll-free at *1-800-344-3226.*

Your city and county public health departments can offer direct health care services or give you leads on where to find what you need. You can expect to find vision and hearing screenings, health screenings for senior citizens, inoculations for children, visits by a public health nurse in some cases, nutrition counseling, and free or low-cost dental care. These departments also will provide environmental protection if, for example, your neighborhood is overrun with rats or the guy next door doesn't clean up after his five dogs. They even can help you obtain a birth certificate if you don't have one.

Another resource is an information and referral office found through United Way. Such an agency can answer such questions as where to borrow a hospital bed for your ninety-four-year-old grandfather, treatment for your alcoholic brother, counseling for you and your spouse, legal aid, and classes for diabetics and prospective parents. They are a gold mine of information on governmental and voluntary agencies that deal in health and human services. They also will refer you to profit-making enterprises when no other resources exist.

Smile and the world smiles with you. But you won't expose those pearly whites if they ache, are missing, or are stained. The condition of your mouth, gums, and teeth will affect your total well-being. Regular dental visits aren't high on anybody's list of pleasant pastimes, but they're essential for oral health. If you are on a fixed income and don't know which dentists can help, contact your city or county public health department, the information and referral service of the United Way, or your area dental society. You can dig up the phone number of the local dental society by calling any dentist's office. Like most other societies, there is no uniform name or listing for the phone book.

Applying toothpaste to brush doesn't have to result in a sticky mess. Go straight to the source by putting the tube into your mouth and nipping off the desired amount. If you do not have a tube to call your own, line up your finger besides the bristles as a guide to dab the toothpaste onto your finger first, then plop it on the brush.

Despite twice-a-day brushing, flossing, and regular cleaning at the dentist's office, your teeth or dentures can still be stained without your seeing or feeling the discoloration. Tobacco, tea, and iron pills are common culprits. Because commercial dentrifices for dental stain removal tend to be too abrasive (at least my dentist thinks so), brush once a week or so with baking soda. Commercial cleaners ought to whiten dentures.

Since you can't reflect on your image in a full-length mirror as completely as you would like, you may need to solicit an honest appraisal from someone who can give you a yes or no to a few direct questions. How do your posture and gait measure up? Are you a round-shouldered, head-drooping slouch with a protruding tummy? Do you walk with your toes pointed out like a pigeon or shuffle along as if you were treading on eggs, afraid that you will plunge over a precipice any moment?

Another category of hard-to-break habits, bordering on impossibles, is mannerisms—behavioral quirks developed more often by people who are congenitally blind. Were these folks able to look around, they'd realize that the rest of the world, generally speaking, doesn't rock, poke fingers into their eyes, flick fingers in front of their eyes, or loll the head from side to side. Theory holds that blind infants and children adopt such idiosyncracies to compensate for lack of visual stimulation. Whatever the reason, such behavior is a put-off to other people who won't be drawn to you if you're the only one at MacDonald's rocking as you eat, or if you sit with your head drooped on your chest while other fans watch the game with animation at the stadium.

Even though it's so hard to identify such habits in your general bearing, others may feel initially reluctant to bring them up, fearing your injured feelings. Should you really want to shake such habits, press for not only what's wrong but also how to make it right. How can I correct my gait? At what level should I hold my head? If people don't rock, what are acceptable ways of shifting positions? Attack one imperfection at a time so you don't become overwhelmed or discouraged. Since they may be so ingrained that you are not conscious of them, you may require reminders of your lapses. Suggest an inconspicuous signal such as a gentle touch on the arm or clearing of the throat.

While we're talking about body awareness, blind people certainly aren't alone in the battle of the bulge. Perhaps you've piled on extra pounds since your sight loss. Maybe you haven't practiced girth control because you feel entitled to eat, to compensate for frustration and anxiety. Besides, you might not be as active as you once were. Your body is so familiar to you that you don't notice its expansion. One congenitally blind student suspected (but wasn't sure) that he was overweight. He couldn't compare himself with others and finally drummed up enough courage to ask a staff member, who confirmed his suspicion.

I promise that this weighty issue won't drag on into a diatribe. Books on diet and nutrition are frequently best-sellers. You can read many of them as Talking Books. You can join Weight Watchers or Overeaters Anonymous, or participate in weight-loss clinics just like anybody else. Should you not wish to share your gains and losses by having someone read the scale, you can buy one, either tactile or talking, from the American Foundation for the Blind or Independent Living Aids. It's far cheaper to fashion your own by removing the glass cover from a conventional scale. Put a dot of Hi Marks at your present weight, another at your desired goal. It won't be accurate to the ounce, but should be good enough. To keep tabs on your dimensions, measure waist and hips with string cut exactly to fit. String doesn't lie—if you've expanded or decreased these regions, you will know.

Are you about as active as a pet rock since your vision decreased? Some blind people are afraid to move their bodies through space because they fear impending collisions. If your get-up-and-go got up and went, could it be that the less you do, the less energy and zip you have to do it? Forty-nine-year-old Joe protested that even walking wasn't enjoyable because of stress caused by mobility. Martha, sixty-three, would like to paddle around in senior-citizen swim classes but couldn't get to the pool. I suggested to Joe that he collar his seven-year-old daughter for an after-dinner stroll. It's healthier for her than TV. After a little prodding, Martha called the recreation center. To her delight, she found that a neighbor with a car was in the same class.

If you take swimming or exercise lessons at the Y., local high school, or health club, and are concerned about being unable to follow the action, call the instructor ahead of time. With time to think about it, that teacher may be more cooperative. (Some health clubs have refused membership to a totally blind applicant because they fear possible injury and their own liability.) If you prefer huffing and puffing along with Richard Simmons on TV, ask someone to at least explain or manipulate your body through the twists and bends.

Some blind folks use an exercise bike or a Rebounder, which is a miniature trampolene. You can read Talking Books that describe fitness routines or buy records with exercises set to music. Maureen Young, a blind woman who is an authority on exercise, has recorded a sixty-minute two-track cassette tape especially designed for blind persons.

A physical therapist friend warns that flab won't firm up in a week—count on three or four vigorous twenty-minute sessions a week over a few months before you see results. If you carry out your regime at home, give yourself more than elbow room. You don't want to zing head, arms, or hands during your gyrations, nor hold back for fear you will. Should your health be questionable, such as with diabetes or a bad heart, common sense dictates that you consult your doctor before starting a diet or exercise program. But poor health shouldn't keep you out of the running. There are armchair exercises for people who are quite restricted.

Since you can't visually monitor yourself, are you as fastidious as you should be about personal hygiene? Do you let your hair become lackluster and in need of shampooing, your nails looking like you've been digging potatoes? If you can't tell by touch or odor that you should wash your hair, ask somebody—you'll quickly figure out frequency of shampooing. Scrubbing daily with a nail-brush and cleaning with a nail file should take care of that business. Because you depend so much on your hands now, you probably want short nails. A clipper works well. When smoothing rough edges, move the emery board only in one direction.

A podiatrist tells me that toenails need not be trimmed straight across, and that you should round the corners because their sharp edges will cut into toes and snag hose. Use a clipper made for that purpose. If you are diabetic, your feet are especially vulnerable, and you might want a podiatrist to do that for you. If you can't get to one, entrust that chore to someone responsible, not your nine-year-old youngster. He adds that diabetics should never rely on over-the-counter preparations for removing corns or ingrown toenails because these acids can cause infection. He recalls a diabetic patient who dropped a bottle of corn remover on her foot; eventually she had her leg amputated as a result. Even though you consider these matters minor, take them to a specialist.

How you wear your hair is almost as important as its cleanliness. Most blind men and women find the wash-and-wear styles easiest to maintain after leaving barber or beautician. But don't fall into the trap that caught one man who insisted on a crewcut—look Ma, no combing. Opposite was the man who kept his hair at shoulder-length long after the flowing mane was a fad of the past. The blind woman who crimped her curls in a 1940s vintage was equally outdated. If you're in doubt about your hair, ask your barber or beautician if your crowning glory is up-to-date. Should you make a change, that expert can show you how to comb and arrange your locks.

Having the same person work on your hair helps immensely. If you have to economize, a barber college or beauty school charges far less, but you won't have the same operator, of course. If you are housebound, a call to a nearby establishment probably will bring somebody to your home. Some barbers and beauticians moonlight this way.

My unscientific survey on shaving reveals that blind men preferred electric to safety razors two to one. Whichever implement you use, follow with your free hand a pattern all over your face and throat. You won't whack a patch out of your sideburns if you rely on a part of your ear as a checkpoint. Which part depends on the length of your sideburns. Covering your moustache with a free hand ensures its remaining intact. Your Adam's apple is less likely to be sliced if you swallow while shaving your throat—it won't stick out as much. Word from the bearded who are blind is that other hands than theirs do the trimming.

But don't think that you have to pitch your safety razor, especially if you're one of those who insist that it gives a closer shave. You have been relying on that instrument all your shaving life.

Just be sure to change blades often enough. One survey respondent said that he shaves in the tub, and another likes a steamy shower.

Just in the nick of time come tips from dermatologists and barber college instructors for an unscathed shave. Don't bounce out of bed and rush for the razor. Body fluids make the face puffy and more prone to nick, so wait about ten minutes. Heat helps. It softens the skin, making facial hair more accessible to blade or electric shaver. (Common sense tells you to dry vigorously before working with an electric razor.) Let yourself get into a good lather with shaving cream or soap, allowing it to remain two minutes before applying the razor. This treatment softens whiskers. If you nick yourself, try to examine your face by touch for the tender area so you can avoid it for the next few days, giving it time to heal.

Some black men and those of Mediterranean descent suffer an unpronounceable skin condition in which facial hair doubles back on itself. Shaving with an electric or safety razor literally drags or tugs at the beard, causing irritation. According to reports, depilatory creams or powders used by women to remove hair from their legs will also remove a man's beard. Many men haven't tried this method because it doesn't seem macho. If you try this trick, follow directions for skin testing on the package. Another remedy for the sensitive skin syndrome is to rub in a thin film of skin cream before applying shaving cream.

Ladies who shave under their arms and legs follow basically the same technique and lead with the free hand. If you use a safety razor, lather up well and don't be heavy-handed on your shinbones. You will know if you have removed all the hair by feeling your skin after you have rinsed. Like the gents who favor safety razors, change blades often.

Some deodorants, especially roll-ons, leave a visible residue when they dry, whereas sprays do not. If you swear by roll-ons, dust off with a tissue after it has dried and before you put on a sleeveless garment.

If you are among the many women who think that Mother Nature has shortchanged them, you can make up for the slight with makeup. You may have hung back, afraid that you would turn out like a clown instead of being enhanced with a natural glow. People with residual vision might find lighted magnifying mirrors helpful—they are commercially available. When you can't see where you're aiming, sound counsel, a steady hand, and plenty of practice will ensure that you put on a pretty face.

Begin with an expert: another woman familiar with cosmetics who knows how to use them tastefully. She might be a saleswoman at a department store cosmetic counter, a home demonstrator of cosmetics, or a friend. Lighter shades are less likely to streak, but don't end up looking like a ghost.

These hints are general guidelines. What shades, kinds, and how much to apply will vary with each woman. Before starting, wash your face with soap and water, or use a cleansing cream. Layering was never in. Organize your cosmetics and return caps as soon as you are through.

Let's begin with lipstick. Before deciding where to go with that tube, part your lips, pull them taut, and trace them with your index finger. You can start in the center of your top lip, moving the tube left, returning and tracing right. From the center of your lower lip, repeat the procedure. Other people prefer beginning at the right, working in one stroke across to the left. Press your lips together, then blot gently with a tissue. Trouble spots are the corners of your mouth, cleft above your upper lip, and front teeth—dab at those with a tissue to be sure. If you are a bit shaky, put your elbow on the table, resting your chin on your fist.

Pam, thirty-one, is a rehabilitation teacher. Her partial sight isn't enough of a help in applying her own makeup, but she achieves a well-turned-out look and teaches her clients methods she has developed. To apply foundation, she suggests lotion because it is less likely to streak. You'll need advice as to how much, in either dots, dabs, or fingerfuls. Place them on each cheek, middle of your forehead, nose, jawlines, and chin. With slight pressure from your middle and ring fingers, blend to cover your face and throat completely. A light once-over with a tissue, particularly in the crevices beside your nose, will take care of any excess.

Admittedly, blush is even trickier. But even totally blind women can achieve that fresh, pink-cheeked look without seeming to be painted. To induce more prominent cheekbones, grin widely. If you use a brush, tap it on the side of the container first. To know where you are going, press the back of the middle finger knuckle against your face, just below your eye. Spread your middle and index fingers so that they form a triangle pointed toward your hairline, that area to be covered with blush. Apply with upward strokes, gently smoothing it in so that you avoid a pronounced line.

For the finishing touch of powder, try a soft-bristled brush. Again you can remove excess by tapping it on the side of the container. You may need several dips as you lightly dust your face. Use a feathery sweep of a tissue over your face to eliminate excess.

Although two shades of eyeshadow are in, you'll probably be out of luck trying it yourself. Cream or liquid is more streak resistant. While holding your lid down with the index finger of your free hand, apply the eyeshadow with the index finger of your dominant hand. Your finger offers more control than an applicator. You will probably require several dabs. A wet washcloth touched lightly to brows, corners of your eyes, and cheeks below will take care of spatters; then wipe off your applicator finger. If you wear thick glasses or use low-vision aids, they will magnify your eyes — you may opt not to use eye makeup at all.

Ladies, there are a few chores best left to others. They are just not worth the risk or effort if you can't see what you are doing. Plucking eyebrows, polishing nails, and applying mascara or eyeliner are among them. You can buy nail buff cream (applied with the fingers) and a buffer that will shine up your nails.

Your assistant in these cosmetic ventures is probably going at it for the first time, too. You can help her to help you by suggesting that both of you work out methods of measuring exact amounts — dipping the finger into the container for several dots, a full plunge for a dab. She may direct you to count the number of strokes. Encourage her to feel free enough to tell you to start afresh when you're learning. She should realize that your choice of shades ought to be close to your skin tones. For instance, a black woman has to be careful about cosmetics that are too yellow, brown, or rosy in hue for her complexion. No matter how skillfully applied, they will leave a mask-like effect. Even if you don't show your face to the light of day during the summer, a few stray sun rays can darken your skin, whether you are black or white. You might have to plan for summer and winter cosmetics, regardless of your race.

After your learning sessions, you can feel confident about applying makeup. Before you work this art down to a science, though, you'll feel more secure with someone's stamp of approval.

Without a doubt, one of the most sensitive areas for men and women is the appearance of eyes. Although poets tout them as windows of the soul and songwriters revel in their expressiveness, eyes that are discolored, disfigured, or misshapen can have a negative effect on others. Should you be aware of such a condition, your consciousness of it can affect your psyche. It is such a delicate topic that your family and best friend might hesitate to broach it with you. If questioned, they may brush it off with, "Never mind—we love you anyway—your shrunken eye doesn't bother us at all."

With a vast array of dark glasses on the market, you can camouflage for a few dollars. Gradient tinted glasses are dark at the top, becoming lighter near the bottom. Glasses with colored lenses are harder to match with an outfit. You are safer with those tinted black or brown.

You can carry the cosmetics of your eyes a big step further. An ocularist specializes in making and fitting artificial devices to be worn inside or around the eye. An artificial eye replaces one that has been removed. A cosmetic shell fits over an existing eye that is unsightly or an eye that has been eviscerated, the contents having been surgically removed. These devices are painted to look exactly like your other eye—only you and your ocularist will know. Nor do you have to sacrifice residual vision for the sake of appearance. Cosmetic shells and hard and soft contact lenses can restore normal appearance without obscuring sight.

Although the cost of such treatment is high, Medicare will cover it, as will Medicaid in some cases. Many private health insurance policies cover most of the expense. If your ophthalmologist or optometrist can't steer you to an ocularist, contact the American Society of Ocularists for the name of someone who can make a referral in your locale.

Good grooming doesn't stop with your face and hair. What clothes you wear is also important. Even if you stay home all day, remaining in robe and slippers doesn't do much for your morale, not to mention the spirits of others who see you in nightclothes at high noon. When you do don slippers, make sure they are sturdy. You can seriously injure your feet by stepping on the kids' jacks or the dog's bone.

Are your clothes in keeping with your age, status, and the times? One blind man continued to wear a collection of flowered shirts he bought ten years ago. Although still in good condition, these shirts were holdovers from a craze long since past. A thirty-year-old blind woman lived with her parents and dressed like her sixty-eight-year-old mother. Another blind woman bought only polyesters, because of easy care. She looked truly out of season in her summer white slacks in subfreezing weather. A blind college student showed up for classes in clashing colors. Instead of being counterculture casual, his garb was hideous. You might reread chapters 11 and 12.

When buying clothes, you'd be smart to stay away from high fashion and stick with classic styles, unless you have the money to update your wardrobe and the wherewithal to know when to stash the outdates until the cycle rolls around again. If you put on last year's ins when everyone else is out of them, you'll look like you stepped out of the flapper era or worse.

Striving for the classic look isn't as exciting but is safer. Yet even it alters. Ties, belts, lapels, and trouser legs become wider and narrower, and hems go up and down.

Paul is a totally blind judge whose grooming is immaculate and clothes are in good taste. When investing in a new suit, he returns to the same salesman who is familiar with his likes and dislikes. Paul buys several ties at the same time to complement the suit. He stays with solid shirts and socks. He advises a blind man purchasing clothes to tell the salesman the kind of work he does, or for what occasion he needs them. A judge will dress differently from a used car salesman.

A woman buying clothes would do well to buy coordinates sold by the same manufacturer. She can mix and match later.

If you had vision as Joanne did, insist as she does now on accommodation to the style and color preferences you developed when you could see. It's not unreasonable to ask if colors are bright or subdued, lines vertical or horizontal, plaids or checks large or small. If you have never seen, you have to memorize go-together colors and how colors can accent or complement your size and skin tones. For instance, if you are overweight, you'd avoid horizontal stripes and large patterns. Tall, thin people look even more elongated in vertical lines. While you're memorizing what goes with what, it's simple to remember that patterns don't mix—a print blouse with a plaid skirt would generate a few gasps.

Upon losing much of her vision from macular degeneration, Alice began wearing dull colors, afraid she might put together some clock-stoppers. Then a friend suggested to Alice that she visit a color specialist. This expert's evaluation took about an hour and a half as she matched a spectrum of colors to Alice's skin tones on different parts of her body, eyes, and hair. Alice left with a chart of shades that best accentuated her coloring and advice on how to brighten her dull wardrobe with accessories. You can find color specialists through a good clothing shop or the fashion editor of your newspaper. The assessment costs from fifty dollars to seventy-five dollars.

Even if your finances are limited and you shop at a thrift or discount store, don't be buffaloed by bargains on clothing that is outdated or out of sync for your age. If you are young and suspect that your parents steer you toward clothes like their own, ask a friend your own age to go with you, or depend upon a forthright salesperson who works in a department geared toward your age group.

Dog guide users and folks who have pets that jump on them or nest in their lap have another consideration: hair. Walk with a yellow Labrador retriever while you're wearing black wool slacks and those trousers will look like angora in two minutes. Your choice of color and fabric might be shaded by the degree to which pet hair shows. A complete brush-off several times a day also helps. Antistatic sprays somewhat repel hair but are not totally satisfactory. One of the most reliable methods of removing hair is masking tape, wrapped several times around your hand with the sticky side out.

Put your best foot forward and polish your shoes. You're fooling yourself if you think you're dressed to the nines when your size nines are shabby. Paste wax shines better than liquid and also covers scuffs more thoroughly. If you are a fussbudget about footgear, Meltonian and Tana shoe polishes contain dye and are meant for leather—they do the best job of covering scuff marks and leaving a high shine. You can buy these brands at a shoe store in any color from fire engine red to moss green. For in-betweens, neutral polish or Amway's shoe spray towelettes will add a gloss. To protect your hands from polish, try tear-off plastic gloves or thin rubber gloves from a drugstore or paint department. You won't need sterile gloves, which are far more expensive. To clean man-made materials such as vinyl, a damp cloth will do. Should they become scuffed, it's all over—relegate them to the grubbies for digging in the garden or strolls where you won't meet anybody else. You can remove salt stains from leather and man-made shoes and boots with equal parts of vinegar and water.

It's helpful to have someone inspect your clothes and shoes occasionally to weed out the out-of-date or ill fitting. You may not realize when shoes become scuffed beyond saving or clothes frayed, faded, baggy, or snagged.

Are you sure you have all your buttons? When they pop, or it seems a seam has split, you can repair them yourself. There is a wide variety of needle threaders and sewing aids marketed by the American Foundation for the Blind and Independent Living Aids. You can also find self-threading needles at notions counters. Some totally blind people have become proficient with sewing machines. For concise tips, read Alice Raftary's *Easy Adaptations for the Blind and Visually Impaired Seamstress*, a leaflet. You might also want to check out her booklet, *Crafts by Touch*. Should you con somebody else into making those stitches in time, at least supply a well-stocked sewing box. It isn't fair to expect your helper to come running in with lavender thread and a package of hooks and eyes.

You can't maintain your vigil on health and appearance alone. At the risk of wearing you out on the subject, I'll remind you that nobody, even with better-than-normal vision, is completely self-sufficient. When you can't monitor what's right, what's wrong, and how to right what's wrong, you will need help. Such counsel isn't easy to come by. Even your spouse or best friend may hold back from telling you that you grimace instead of frown, that your hair is unkempt, and that your clothes are soiled or mismatched. Your ophthalmologist or loved ones may not mention your unsightly eye. Family and friends may take the attitude, "We love you as you are," or, even worse, "You're blind so we can't expect any more from you." You have to take the assertive approach, pressing for honest appraisals, reassuring the person that the only way you can correct is to know what's amiss.

Your solicitation of assessment can initially cause discomfort and even embarrassment. When our hospital president picked me up for the awards dinner we were attending, I blurted out, "Do I look all right?" A bit taken aback, he murmured something about his wife being in the car. Perhaps she could assist. I quickly explained that I wasn't fishing for compliments, that I needed to know if there was a smudge of eyeshadow on my nose, dog hair on my dress, or a run in my hose. Now was the time to remedy such a situation, before stepping out the door. Understandingly he tugged at a price tag on my sleeve.

Those who point out flaws have no license for cruelty in their candor. To stop dinner table conversation with a remark, "You hair looks like you've been through a wind tunnel," or, "You're the only one at this dinner dance in a floor-length dress," isn't helpful— it's humiliating. You deserve tact and discretion as does anyone else. Not only should your informer let you know what's awry, he should be willing to suggest what to do about it or at least give you a goal toward which to strive.

Regardless of how you feel about it, other people will look at you more because of your visual impairment. Anonymity is one of the hidden losses incurred when your vision deteriorates. You may not be as conspicuous as Lady Godiva astride a snow blower or a skunk at a lawn social, but you will have your share of attention. Managing the inner and outer you as well as possible takes extra effort and time, as well as the resources of others. But its achievement says more powerfully than words, "I'm just as normal as the rest of you." Hold your head up with pride!

Chapter 27

CARING FOR CHILDREN ISN'T KID STUFF

W hether a babe in arms or a young adult about to flee from the nest, kids can be the joy of your life—you could hug them to pieces. At times, they will be the bane of your existence—you could pull out the hair that they have turned gray or hang them by the thumbs. Once here, they are for keeps. As their temporary keeper, you may be a blind parent with sighted children or a sighted parent with a blind child. This two-sided coin would require a book to treat each topic fairly. All we can do is to toss both subjects around, hoping that the spin-offs will send you in the right direction.

Parenting isn't all instinct. It's a whopper of a responsibility that demands maturity and practice, just like playing the violin. The results won't be rich tones and sweet melodies unless you know how to draw the bow over the strings. Many blind parents with whom I spoke enrolled in infant-care classes before the blessed event. You can find them through the Lamaze Society, city and county public health departments, American Red Cross, United Way, your doctor, or local hospitals. Should you have uncertainties after the baby is born, you can contact the city or county public health departments to request that a public health nurse come to work with you on techniques.

In classes you will hear lectures on nutrition, infant development, and common childhood diseases. These groups also get down to the nitty gritties: diapering, feeding, bathing, and dressing. Plant yourself close enough to see what's going on. If the instructor says, "This is a football hold for carrying a newborn," and you don't know whether she's supporting the baby in one arm or tackling the unfortunate demonstrator, get your hands on the subject. Don't hesitate to ask the instructor if she can drum up modifications. "How can I find the baby's mouth when I'm giving a bottle?" "Is there a way I can tell when he's asleep?" (A baby is sound asleep when its arm is completely relaxed, dropping from your fingers.)

The La Leche League encourages breast-feeding, which is a boon for blind mothers. You don't have to pack food for him when you're going on a picnic or bang around in an unfamiliar kitchen.

People who want to prepare even further can read a wealth of information in Braille and recorded form—yes, Doctor Spock and all the rest. These books cover childbirth, infant care, and child development from infancy through adolescence. Your Talking Book librarian will be able to advise you about which books are available.

One first-time father made no presumptions about diapers: He treated them as if they were always full. He preferred a changing table, where the baby stays put. A blind father who didn't own such a convenience used the floor. Separating the baby's ankles with one finger, he lifted them to elevate the baby's hips, pulling the diaper toward him and well away from kicking feet. Out of reach of grabbing hands were the pins, stuck into a bar of soap at the baby's feet.

Count on feeding as a messy affair, regardless of precautions. When giving a bottle, hold it near the neck with your index finger extended beyond the nipple. Your finger will locate the baby's cheek—then bingo, there is the mouth. You can also locate the baby's mouth with the thumb or index finger of your free hand. (Remember that when you reach for a baby, keep your fingers curved so that you won't inadvertently give him a poke in the eye.) You can feed some baby foods by enlarging the hole in a nipple and using a bottle. Karen, totally blind, fed her infant by wrapping her in a receiving blanket to restrain flailing hands. Karen cradled the baby's head in the crook of one arm, locating the corner of the baby's mouth with the index finger of the same hand. She grasped the spoon near the bowl with the other hand, allowing for better control. When the baby began protesting this bundle-feed method, Karen sat her in an infant seat well back on the counter, confining spills to washable surfaces. Other blind parents locate the lower lip with the thumb, placing index and middle fingers under the chin. They keep track of the baby's moving head while wielding the spoon with the other hand.

Food flies far when the tyke begins feeding itself. One mother's solution was to place wide swaths of newspaper in front and at the sides of the high chair.

Although you won't throw the baby out with the bathwater, you'll find that this little creature is slippery. One of the best methods for holding a baby in his bathtub is to cover your hand with a washcloth for a better grip. You can also make a simple mitt out of terrycloth for a slip-free hold.

Even though infants are resilient, they can get sick quickly or injured in an instant. Digital thermometers are usually easier for reading with partial vision. Totally blind folks can use a talking thermometer available from the American Foundation for the Blind. (It has interchangeable probes that enable you to use it for indoor and outdoor temperatures and even for cooking.) Of course, sensitive hands can perceive a fever, but if you can't see, you won't be able to notice some skin rashes. Someone should check the baby regularly for diaper rash. Liquid medicines are more likely to get where they're going when administered in a bottle. You can put it in a glass when the baby is old enough to drink from one. When the child is older, you can ask your doctor or pharmacist for tablets whenever possible. American Foundation for the Blind also markets a device to measure one or two teaspoons of liquid. Another option is to pour the medicine into a jar and dip it out with a measuring spoon. The Emergency Reserve List and a first aid kit are literally your child's potential lifesavers.

Newborns are easiest to care for because, although fragile, they are immobile. When that kiddy starts crawling and walking, hazards increase. Child-proof locks on kitchen cupboards and removing breakables are tricks of parents' trade, especially helpful for those who don't see well. One mother recalls that she put her lively little one into a playpen, swing, or crib whenever she couldn't be close enough to keep tabs. These were such times as doing laundry in the basement, answering the doorbell, and especially while cleaning, when she didn't want to risk running over the infant with a vacuum cleaner. Bells on fingers and toes are a bit farfetched, but one pinned to the back of the baby's clothes isn't. That jingle is a constant audible signal. (Clever tykes figure out how to take them off shoes in a few days.) That little bundle of joy will learn fast how far to go to get out of a limited range of vision, so be wary.

Paula is a partially sighted mother who is color-blind. She pins her two-year-old's outfits together before dropping them into the hamper and folds them together before putting them into the drawer. She buys only white socks. Paula imparts her organization to her toddler. Although Katie doesn't always remember the purpose of the toy box, Paula shows it to her each time she returns a toy to its place. Even with her usable sight, this mom treads lightly.

Footloose and fancy free is dangerous for a toddler, but holding him by the hand restricts him and you. A backpack for a baby is ideal. When the youngster is too big to tote but too little to trust unsupervised, try a harness made for children. It allows the little one freedom, but the parent can reel him in when necessary.

When that child is old enough to play outside, you'll have to insist on a report-in system to preserve your peace of mind. Kids will test you, as did three-year-old Debbie, who sat placidly in the middle of the lawn while her mother called frantically. That's where a neighbor found the little girl. Some blind parents work out trades. A sighted friend oversees outdoor play while the blind parent baby-sits during the evening. You might consider teaming up with another parent for trips to the park or beach or, as one mother did, enlisting a baby-sitter when her youngster went swimming.

Kids learn early that one or both parents don't see well or at all. Twenty-month-old Marci guides her dad around the plastic blocks scattered on the living room floor, even though she doesn't understand why. Children will accommodate and accept, sometimes better than adults. If your vision loss occurs when your child is able to understand, you owe him honesty and reassurance that you will continue loving and caring for him, although your ways of providing may be somewhat different.

One mother confessed she felt comfortable around her own children, but sensed uneasiness around their peers. She couldn't recognize her youngsters' friends when they came into the living room while she was in the kitchen. "Sit 'em down and give 'em a this-is-the-way-it-is talk," I counseled. "Start off by asking them to call out their names when they come in." A few weeks later she reported that the hordes of kids were again swarming in the house. She had answered a barrage of questions beforehand. The youngsters, seeing her operate with confidence in the home front, relaxed and didn't seem to notice any differences. When they forgot to call out their names, she felt free enough to call, "Who is it?"

Many parents introduce the reading habit to children early. Braille users can rely on Twin Vision books with Braille on one side of the page, print and pictures on the other. You can borrow them from your Braille lending library. You and your youngsters can listen to a variety of children's literature on Talking Books. When the child is old enough to read himself, he can follow the recorded edition.

As your child enters school, you will reinforce yourself as a parent by taking an active part in parent-teacher organizations and other groups connected with the school. Your visibility and involvement register as unspoken symbols of your lively interest in your child's welfare.

Sure, you'll find yourself in some dilemmas regarding your child and school. One mother was wringing her hands because her seven-year-old's teacher sent a steady stream of notes home. The print was so faint she couldn't read it. She resolved that problem by requesting that the teacher call her instead. A bit unusual, but the solution has worked ever since. Another mother regretted that she couldn't help her daughter with homework, nor could she appreciate papers that she brought home. But she did stay tuned in by asking for descriptions and results of the child's activities, and compensated by praising what she could perceive.

I recall a totally blind couple who had a large family. By the time the oldest daughter was eight or nine, she was literally mothering younger children. The hazard exists with no hard and fast rules to avoid it: Sighted children can be drawn into growing up too quickly. The convenience of another pair of eyes is alluring—serving as a guide, picking out items at the supermarket before they can read, coming in from play to find the paprika. You can't afford to let your place-for-everything system slip into shambles or allow your support system to crumble just because George will do it. Of course, kids need increasing responsibility as they grow older, but laying it on too heavy too young can be a staggering burden.

Many parents now consider themselves to be chauffeurs until the day their teenager earns that mixed blessing, the driver's license. When neither parent drives, they will have to drum up alternatives for themselves and the kids. Exchanging baby-sitting services for car pooling is an option; hiring a driver or using public transportation are others. One blind couple paid their teenagers the same rate given to their hired drivers, providing a means for the teens to earn extra money. They never wheedled their youngsters into staying home from the basketball game because of an errand to run or friends to visit.

Being parents of a legally blind child is a whole new ball game. You were probably overwhelmed, shocked, and panicky. You probably held a box seat ticket to a guilt trip when you made this discovery. "How could I bring a blind child into this world?" You may have denied the impairment, trusting that medicine would miraculously effect a cure or that glasses would fully restore sight. Some people never cash in that ticket; their reaction may take the form of overprotection or rejection, stifling or branding that baby for a lifetime.

Lila is an occupational therapist who specializes in working with parents of visually impaired children. She advises moms and dads to treat the youngster, regardless of visual acuity, with the expectation of normal child development.

Since most of her little charges have some sight, Lila suggests capitalizing on it: using color contrasts such as light toys on a dark rug, mechanical cars with flashing lights, or balls, beads, and blocks of varying bright colors. You can best help the ophthalmologist determine the extent of vision by jotting down what the child sees under various circumstances. Can he pick out a red toy on a red tablecloth? In what kind of lighting does he function best? When does he have the hardest time seeing? Although you encourage a partially sighted child to look and give him plenty of chances for close-ups, he needs reassurance that it's okay if he can't see what you point out to him, that it is nothing to be ashamed of, nor is it cause for bluffing.

Don't stop with visual stimulation for a partially sighted infant. Just as for one who is totally blind, sound and touch are vital. Give him objects of differing shapes and textures, explaining their variation. They may be as obviously opposite as rough and smooth, round and square, soft and hard. Speak to your child as you enter a room. When he is learning to crawl, turn on the radio for orientation and move the blind-traps out of the way. As he takes those first teetering steps, he'll be holding on to furniture just like any other teeterer. That isn't the time to switch the sofa from one wall to another.

All little kids explore their immediate environment with hands and mouths but learn early that this is a don't-touch world. "Put down that knickknack. Aunt Millie would be upset if you broke it." Why not hold that cut crystal swan in your hands so that the two-year-old can examine it thoroughly, and then move it out of his reach? "We're not buying that toy fire engine, so put it back and keep your hands off the other toys." Why not give him an opportunity to handle a few toys? You can make it clear that to hold and to have are two different things. It isn't a license for your kid to whip like a whirlwind through a china shop or lamp department, or poke fingers through a mynah bird's cage. He'll have to understand that some no's are absolute.

A thirty-nine-year-old woman, blind from birth, recalls sadly that her parents held up for her the impossible expectations that she act like everybody else in every respect. As a child, she never felt free to examine objects with her hands. It took years of psychoanalysis as an adult for her to overcome this imposed inhibition.

I vividly remember that, as a five-year-old, I found a fledgling robin on the ground in its first attempts to fly. Scooping the fluttering bird into my hands, I crowed about my catch to my mother and brother, who was seven at the time. His reaction was enraged tears because the bird, bearing the scent of humans,

probably wouldn't be accepted back into the nest. I do
mother's remark soothed my brother, but I never forgo
bird must die so that your sister knows what a bird look:
the bird must die."

Sighted children learn so much about their world almo
lessly through scanning. As parents of a blind youngster, y
constantly be on the watch, bringing this world within his
visual field or reach. For those objects which are beyonc
sense, you'll have to supplement with verbal explanatior.
him for walks, pointing out trees, fire hydrants, interser
parked cars, moving traffic, and traffic signals. Expose h.
public events for the sake of being among people and for enric
experiences. Never mind that you don't give a hoot about i
animals — shepherd him through the livestock exhibit at the .
allowing him to be close enough to see or touch pigs, cat
horses, and sheep. (Stuffed animals or statues just aren't the sam
If you're always in a hurry when you shop, leave the list at hon
and set off with the intention of exploring. Abandon your inhib.
tions but go armed with imagination. The fruit market, camping
and sports department, small auto garage, toy store, fire department,
electronics shop, storehouse for parade floats, and furniture departments are just a few possibilities. Remember that seeing with
limited vision or touching is fragmentary, so you don't want to
overload him by showing everything. You can always enlarge
upon and draw comparisons with what the youngster has experienced and what he can't. "This camping tent is made out of nylon,
the same fabric as your Windbreaker®. It will hold four people.
But a circus tent is made from the same material but could fit over
a whole block." "That calf you petted is only a few days old. When
she grows to be a cow, she'll be as tall as the pony you rode."

Don't delude yourself into thinking that once is enough. If you
saw a squash or a tennis racquet on only one occasion when you
were four, would you remember what they look like the rest of
your life?

Mannerisms received a mention in Chapter 26. Early childhood
is the time to nip them in the bud. Don't pelt that kid with a string
of negatives — give him some alternatives. "It's fine to rock on
your rocking horse but that's the only place kids do rock." If he

starts sticking his fingers into his eyes, put a toy into his hands to preoccupy him. Tell him he looks so much better when he holds his head up. When he lapses back into these habits, a gentle tap on the shoulder probably won't be resented, but nagging will. At three, he won't understand that these behaviors will set him apart; at thirty, it might be too late because they can be close to impossible to break.

Legally blind youngsters need to learn early some of the techniques of living with a visual impairment. The put-it-back-where-it-belongs lesson is a good starter. You could begin with toys, shoes, and coat. Say, "These corduroy pants are red and go on the same hanger with your red plaid shirt." "Your socks belong in the top drawer on the far right." "You won't spill your milk if you curl your fingers like this before reaching for the glass." Kids catch on quickly. You'll know when you've hit the saturation point and need to lay off a while. Instilling habits of organization will save wasted time and utter frustration later. By the time the child reaches adolescence, the typical teenager's clothes-strewn room won't be a danger. If he's blind and has to hunt for the blue tennis shoes in that jungle, he's got problems that should have been allayed.

Acceptable eating habits are another area that requires long, slow teaching. Sunday dinner when Grandma and Grandpa are guests of honor isn't the time to begin. All children start out sloppy. They eat with their hands, stuff their mouths, and chew with the mouths open. A child could become embarrassed or even petulant if you are constantly reminding him not to put his face too close to the plate, or to eat meatloaf with a fork, not fingers.

It may mean some private practice sessions. "I want to show you, Betsy, how to eat without getting too close to your food." Or, "Let's practice cutting meat this evening—you and I will have dinner before the rest of the family so we can practice using knife and fork on the hamburger patty." In such a relaxed atmosphere, children won't be so sensitive and will respond to the special attention.

One mother's cop-out was, "I don't have a degree in special education. Denny will be taught the right way to do things in school." You might have to recharge your patience batteries, plan strategy to minimize visual cues, and maximize locating food with utensils, resigning yourself to messes and misses. But you don't need intensive training to show your kid how to make a sandwich, sew on a button, or clean dust from the corners of the bedroom floor. Sure, it's easier and faster to do things yourself for any child. Look down the road—that thirty-six-year-old woman who didn't know how to wash dishes or the fifty-five-year-old man with deplorable eating manners could trace such shortcomings back to failure to learn early.

Five-year-old Mike likes to hole up in his room with radio, cassette recorder, and stereo. He can rattle off recording artists and current hits as well as any disc jockey. Although he can't put his finger on it, Mike suffers from the isolation of blindness like many of his grown-up counterparts. Don't kid yourself. Other kids can and will be cruel. But you can't run interference for your youngster, nor can you be his playmate. They may poke fun at yours because he wears thick glasses or can't catch a baseball. Fortunately, children·have short memories. The teased and the teasers will probably forget today's taunt by tomorrow.

The preschool age is the best time for your youngster to start playing with sighted children. At three and four, they are all as coordinated as so many elephants on roller skates, and not so likely to notice your child's visual limitation.

The mother down the block might have a qualm or two. You can set her mind at ease by offering a few reassuring words; that Susie or Jimmie is able to make mud pies or gobble down birthday cake without seeing as well as her youngsters do.

Once a blind child starts school, the same misconceptions will probably arise, directed by chums and even teachers. (The teacher doesn't always know best.) A school math teacher thought that a boy with low vision just couldn't concentrate. He put the fifth-grader in an office with newspapers on the windows to block out distractions.

The long-range solution is exposure, especially for classmates. Familiarity brings tolerance and acceptance. It is even more trying for a visually handicapped student to change schools often. Other students will grow accustomed to your child carrying a cane, holding a book up close, using a Braille writer, or needing to sit in the front row to see the blackboard.

Eugene and Wanda have three daughters who have partial vision. "We made plenty of blunders with the first, improved with the second, and worked it down to a science with the third," Wanda can now say with a laugh. "The hardest part was accepting the handicap. Every parent hopes desperately for a normal child. But once you come to terms with an impairment, you can work with the child to make the most of what's there."

Wanda advises other parents to encourage children to participate in school activities. It may take prompting on your part. Such activities could be the first-grade play, swim team, field trips, and Valentine's parties.

Tom, thirteen, put the plight of partially sighted children most poignantly when he confided to a psychologist, "I wish I were totally blind. Then people wouldn't expect me to see more than I'm able." Tom wasn't being paranoid. Teachers, classmates, friends, relatives, and sometimes even parents can't deal with the limbo of partial sight. They make a game of it or challenge the youngster by testing. "Can you spot that brown cow in the pasture?" asked a fourth-grade teacher. Nine-year-old Donna, wanting to be like the other kids on the field trip (or at least not the class dummy), insisted she could. When the teacher maintained that Donna saw the cow, her mother countered, "You gave her the answer in your question: brown cow. Next time tell her there's a brown cow in the pasture—and ask if she'd like to get close enough to touch the animal."

A child who sees somewhat sometimes won't have the insight to explain that he didn't snub a friend in the hall—the lighting was bad. He tripped over the tricycle on the sidewalk because it was out of his visual field but could play the video games because he stood right in front of them.

It's hard to pinpoint the right time to introduce low-vision aids to a youngster. With magnification comes limitation. Maturity and patience guide the user to maximum advantages. Motivation is the key, since it may be that your child would consent to using a monocular to watch the school basketball game, or that a simple handheld magnifier would make *Teen* magazine more pleasurable. Conflicting with a youngster's desire to see better is peer consciousness. "I'll look funny with that thing held up to my eye in the school gym." Many children are being encouraged to have low-vision evaluations by the fifth or sixth grade. Should yours be a renegade and reject devices, try again in a year or so.

In the meantime, you can employ good illumination for your child's benefit (see Chapter 6). Kids don't think of it, but they might better stay within the lines of a coloring book if they sat at the table near the window or a lamp rather than sprawling on the floor.

Even infants less than a year old wear glasses. A partially sighted man recounts the story of his ophthalmologist prescribing glasses for him when he was nine months old. "Everybody thought I'd pull them off and break them," he laughs. "Somehow I must have figured out I couldn't see without them."

Children grow toward independence gradually and naturally, but it may be harder for one who is visually impaired. You can sneak in these opportunities. When you and your six-year-old child go to the party store, ask what kind of candy bars are in the rack instead of handing out his choice. After hearing a rundown from the clerk, let the child make a decision, hand over the money, and take the change. Three years later when he goes with the neighborhood kids, it won't be a big deal.

Most kids eventually like to pick out their own clothes when shopping. When yours reaches that age and stage, create opportunities for independent shopping. Encourage your child to invite a sighted friend to join the shopping spree. Of course, the final approval is yours, but your youngster has had a word in the decision making, even if guided by a peer.

When you have other children who have normal vision, you need to be on guard about showering too much attention on the one. Sighted siblings may not shout discrimination in so many words, but they can keenly sense favoritism that might lead to resentment of their blind brother or sister. The double standard is a double-edged sword. Bobby is blind, so he shouldn't be expected to do his share of the chores. It may be unreasonable for Bobby to cut the grass or paint the garage, but he can clean his bedroom, do dishes, and carry out trash. Nor should blindness stand for an excuse for misbehavior. If you lay down the law for one, it must be for all. It doesn't give your kid license to be lippy and isn't the go-ahead when a tantrum is brewing.

Perhaps you consider yourself in control, well able to aid and abet your youngster in coping with visual impairment. You've put theory into practice; you've worked long and hard to help him make a niche in a seeing world. But have you mustered up so much mastery of these skills that you have rejected (and set the tone for your child's turning off) some of the practical tools of the trade? One father remembers that when his eighteen-year-old daughter returned from a summer rehabilitation program, she had her cane in hand. "You don't need a cane," he pronounced. "Why should you when you have us?" Fortunately, he came around to recognizing the folly of that statement. Now she wouldn't leave the house without a cane just as she wouldn't walk out the door without her purse.

The Braille-print battle is another that rages constantly. Some children can manage large print comfortably but find that when they leave school, little is available to them in this medium. Had they studied Braille from the first grade, they would have gained proficiency in several years. (Becoming facile with Braille usually takes longer than the time required for print.)

Veronica is seventeen and recently had a degenerative eye disease diagnosed. Frequent flare-ups caused further deterioration. Yet her parents insist that she continue with her junior year in high school with no provisions for her visual limitations. Ironically, she has no responsibilities at home because she doesn't see well. For whom does the show go on?

Should your eye condition be hereditary, such as retinitis pigmentosa, glaucoma, or diabetes, you might want to consider genetic counseling. Knowing the odds, you are better equipped to make an intelligent decision about family planning. One place to look for referrals is the local or state chapter of the March of Dimes.

If you want to read more about visually handicapped children, you can refer to the books *Teaching the Visually Handicapped Child* by Kenneth Hanninen, *Our Blind Children* by Berthold Lowenfeld, and *Visual Impairment in Children and Adolescents* by James Jon, Roger Freemon, and Eileen Scott.

You can bounce your joys, woes, and worries off other people in the same boat: parents of visually impaired children. Check with your local private or public agency for the blind to find out if such a support group exists. With others you can share experiences, learn about services, and exchange information about techniques. Should there be none, be enterprising and start a group. You'll probably have plenty of joiners.

Children! They are gifts for such a short time. How we love, nurture, and cultivate them will give rise to resounding echoes for the rest of their lives.

Chapter 28

INSIGHTS FOR THOSE WHO SEE

W hat should I say or do?" You may have voiced that question many times. Probably you didn't add something else which kicks around in your consciousness and is equally important: "I don't want to make a fool of myself." Some words to the would-be wise will settle some uncertainties when encountering someone who is blind. We'll work from general hints that apply across the board to specifics for those blind people who are special in your life.

Sometimes common sense and courtesy aren't enough. When in doubt, ask. "I'd be glad to help if you like, but I'm not sure of what to do." If that blind person accepts your offer, he is the expert and can explain the hows.

Exceptions to this rule are cases of imminent danger or embarrassment. If a blind pedestrian is about to step in front of an oncoming Mack truck or plunge down an open manhole, shout "Stop!" and call him by name if you know it. Even if you seize his arm unexpectedly, the why can come in a moment.

At the Montana ranch, a seventeen-year-old wrangler probably saved my life with quick thinking. After a three-hour ride, we were dismounting to rest near a stream. With one foot out of the stirrup, I froze as he called, "Margaret, stop. Get back on your horse and let me take the bridle." He calmly led the mare about twenty feet, then held her still as he explained, "Your mare stopped to graze two feet from the edge of a cliff. If you had piled off, a step backwards would have sent you down fifty feet onto the rocks below."

Your instant intervention could rescue a blind acquaintance's ego. You could prevent your friend from inadvertently sitting on somebody's lap or plopping a hand into a lemon chiffon pie on the table. But when there's time to plot strategy, let that blind person take the lead if you aren't sure.

Nobody relishes being reminded of past blunders. If a blind acquaintance calls you by name and five minutes later misses your identity, casually interject, "I'm John," and continue the conversation. Voices are easy to confuse, especially when there are many. You'll make blind people much more at ease by identifying yourself. If you're trying to get a blind person's attention and don't know his name, touch him lightly on the arm. It also helps to announce when you're leaving. You would feel foolish talking to thin air, too.

Should a blind person meet a mishap, bumping into a bookcase or upsetting a cup of hot·coffee, it's natural to show concern but discomfiting to dwell on it. A bit of humor can brush it off: "I realize my coffee's rank, but wasn't that a little extreme?"

Then there are the vagaries of partial vision. You're puzzled because you can't be sure what a person can see or not see. Vision can vary according to eye conditions, lighting, and physical or psychological well-being or just from day to day. Most people with limited sight appreciate someone pointing out a gorgeous display of flowers in a florist's window and the inquiry, "Can you see them from here or would you like to get closer?"

Nobody likes to be tested. Sibyl, twenty-seven, gets frankly irked when a few friends hold up fingers for a countdown or show her print of varying sizes to determine whether she can read it.

A few similar tips: A partially sighted person can use a cane or dog, too. These mobility aids are not restricted to the totally blind—that cane or dog is in hand for safety and identification.

When a waitress or salesperson directs questions to you instead of your blind companion, just shrug it off. When the waitress asks, "Does she want dessert?" just smile and say, "I don't know— ask her."

You don't have to watch your language around someone who is

blind. By avoiding words like *look* and *see*, you can box your-self into verbal corners. "Did you hear that TV movie last night?" "Did you read that—oops, I mean, did somebody read that article on the front page of the paper to you?" Blind people use those same words, which mean far more than perception. It's also OK to include the terms *blind, visually impaired,* or *partially sighted* instead of searching for euphemisms.

On the other hand, don't assume the sort of familiarity with a blind person you have just met that would permit you to inquire about the handicap. One psychologist believes people having a visible handicap such as blindness or paraplegia are open game for the curious. Dignity and privacy are precious. If your contact with a blind person develops into a relationship, the business of how long and what happened will surface naturally. After all, you wouldn't ask a bald stranger how long he's been bald or a woman beside you on the elevator how she acquired that facial scar.

Some traffic infractions that appear minor to you can cause a blind pedestrian anything from momentary panic to an accident. If you stop for a red light with your auto partially extended into the intersection, a blind pedestrian may think he has veered while crossing; and try to compensate by angling out into oncoming traffic. If you can't back up, at least roll down your window and call directions.

Right Turn on Red laws, effective in many states, are a privilege, not a right. Even if you are confident you have enough time and room to squeeze by someone with a cane or dog, remember, that person's safety is entirely in your hands.

Loud noises disorient blind people because they obliterate audi-tory cues. If you are operating a power mower, jackhammer, or floor scrubber, a blind passerby will bless you for the break of turning off that machine until he is safely past.

If a blind person calls upon you to read private documents, don't question what you read. If you are generous enough to offer to go through newspapers or magazines with him, let that person's tastes dictate what should be covered.

Everybody likes gifts, both giving and getting them. If a blind recipient cooks or keeps house, some commercially available labor-saving gadgets might be particularly helpful, such as an electric broom. Should you want to go grand scale, a microwave oven (with hands-on demonstration first) would be a prize. Quasar just came out with a model called Sound Wave® that announces each operation aloud. Sears sells The Talking Machine®, a clock radio with a voice output that can also be set by voice.

To tailor your gift more specifically to a blind person, check with your local agency for the blind to find a nearby outlet that carries commonly used items such as low-vision or Braille cards, games, puzzles, needle threaders, and rulers. Adapted kitchen aids, tools, timepieces, and talking calculators are other ideas. Be wary of low-vision aids — they almost have to be self-selected.

Many legally blind people want to continue reading. You can buy large print and recorded Bibles through religious bookstores. You can give a gift subscription for a large print, recorded, or Braille magazine. Call your closest Talking Book library for suggestions.

Why not give someone who is blind an at-your-service I.O.U.? You can specify when and for how long you are available. You can make a few suggestions: I'll help with your paperwork and get your filing system going. I'll take you shopping, to dinner, to the beauty shop or barber, or across town to visit a friend. I'll help you straighten up the house and prepare refreshments for entertaining. I'll sort through your clothes and do any mending. And so forth.

"What about those putdowns I've had when I slip up? I can't do everything right all the time." Sure, a blind person may rebuff your overtures of help regardless of how smoothly you make them. You might have caught someone on a bad day or run into a sour apple who is in a foul mood most of the time. That happens with people, and blind folks are people, first of all. Try again with that person another time, if you can. You still might be so turned off you can't approach that individual again, but don't cast out all blind people from your life.

If your purpose in reading this book is a particular person, how significant is that other in your life? Do the ties bind in blood and/or love? Or is your relationship student, patient, client, or someone in your work world? Now we'll get down to specifics.

Playing the odds, we'll start with the most likely: the senior citizen. Don't equate bad sight, especially when balanced by reasonably good health, with a one-way ticket to a nursing home. Nor do you have to begin building an addition to your own home. Listen. That parent may surprise you and just as soon continue living alone.

Strategy time. What does it take to ensure safe independence? Food—shopping for and preparation of; clothing—buying, washing or cleaning, identifying (if necessary); the roof overhead—house and yard maintenance; handling money, personal records, mail, bill paying; transportation.

By reviewing earlier chapters, you can help this older person resolve some problems, take on a few yourself, or pay for some services. Perhaps a staff member from a local agency for the blind can pitch in with some solutions by making home visits. Perhaps exchanging a too-large home for the camaraderie and convenience of a senior citizen apartment or finding a housemate are possible ways out.

Suppose now the other case: That senior citizen lives with you. If possible, give him a room of his own. Respect the need for privacy, time, and space. Remember the need to feel needed. Let Grandma peel spuds for supper. So what if she leaves bits of skin—they never did anybody in. Gramps might not get pots and pans spotless, but he does a passable job on the dishes. Scrub those utensils later if you like.

Two queens can't rule the kitchen, but one can make way for the other once in a while. Your mother-in-law might make the best spaghetti sauce this side of Italy or the most scrumptious Irish stew outside the Emerald Isle.

Man does not live by bread alone. That senior still requires recreation, wherever he lives. It's easy to tell Dad he'd feel better if he got off his duff and went to the Senior Citizen Center, but it's possibly a bigger plunge than that seventy-five-year-old with bad sight is willing to take by himself. Take it with him—you'll survive an afternoon of bingo or pinochle and a few lengthy reminiscences. After a few visits with you, he might surprise you and take the bus.

An oldster still may enjoy entertaining. If yours are the helping hands, tidying the house or fixing refreshments would be welcome. You can gracefully disappear when things are rolling smoothly.

Some older folks don't cotton to gadgets immediately, so don't force the issue. If an evaluation at a low-vision clinic is out because of expense or lack of motivation, consider a trip or two to an optical company.

If there is a flicker of enthusiasm for Talking Books, take a few minutes to listen with that loved one. Operating equipment and hearing instead of seeing a book might initially throw a senior for a loop. If you buy adapted games or playing cards, spend a little time practicing. Grandma will be more inclined to invite others to play when she's confident with these devices herself.

If you are caring for someone who has other disabilities besides blindness, your responsibility may tie you down. You deserve a breather. Some nursing homes will accept patients for temporary care such as a weekend or a week or two. Check your city or county public health department or the United Way. These short stays are usually covered by Medicare.

When blindness befalls your spouse, it's like a tidal wave that engulfs both of your lives. Reassurance that "We're in this together" provides the best life preserver, but it will take more than love and commitment to stay afloat.

If your spouse has to stop work, unemployment compensation, Social Security, long-term disability insurance, Supplemental Security Insurance, or General Assistance could cushion the fall.

Your spouse's loss of sight might mean giving up some previous responsibilities. Don't overlook his experience and input. If you must now handle record keeping and bill paying (and he formerly did), talk it out. It doesn't have to be a solitary chore. Don't forget trade-offs. If you now man the lawn mower and wield the paintbrush, can your spouse manage laundry and kitchen cleanup? If he finds appliances bewildering, a few how-to lessons and marking might be in order. It's not fair to expect somebody to fend for himself in strange territory, especially the kitchen. A little of your coaching can take many errors out of trials. Helping your partner be self-sufficient can bring peace of mind if you must leave for a while. At least you'll be sure he'll have food on the table and clothes on his back.

Child-rearing is a two-party system. The kids will pick up quickly enough on one parent's visual impairment. Be conscious of not pushing kids into the background while everyone is reeling from the shock of visual loss.

Rehabilitation training can mean leaving home during the day or for weeks at a time. Perhaps baby-sitting arrangements will be necessary. If the kids are too young to understand fully, they'll probably grasp that Mom or Dad went off to school but will be back to take care of them again.

Kids can feel guilty, too. They require reassurance, even when they cause accidents. "Yes, you forgot and left your trike on the sidewalk and Dad fell over it. When he learns how to use a cane, he won't fall over things like that. You didn't mean for him to fall, and I know you'll try hard to remember."

Before the onset of blindness, you and your partner were probably away from each other all day. Suddenly you're spending much more time together, and it could be wearing on both of you. Be watchful for the right time to pick up the threads of a former life. "Jack, you probably don't feel ready to swing those clubs yet, but wouldn't it be fun to be with the guys on the course? Besides, you can bend your elbow with the best of 'em at the nineteenth hole." "Liz, the gang at the office still want you to come to the Christmas party. You can catch up on three months' worth of gossip and bring the best macaroni salad in town."

Above all, keep those communication channels clear and open. With less visual feedback and chances to read written language, your partner will depend more on words and touch. You'll be offering more sorries than you ever dreamed possible about little stuff like leaving the bathroom door half open or a glass on the counter edge.

Until your lives hit an even keel again, you'll probably be carrying the heavier end. You, too, have feelings, moods of "I don't want to." While you are at peace with each other and the world, talk it out. You won't always feel like an after-dinner walk or a browse through the stereo store. You'll have times when you can't restack priorities or are out of energy. Your joint strategy might expand that support system to enlist others, to help with ordinary errands, or share your partner's special interests.

A third person, such as a staff member from an agency for the blind, or an empathetic counselor, can be a pillar of strength when the road gets rocky.

When our department holds Family Night for immediate relatives and friends of students, we hear such concerns as, "Sometimes I still feel self-conscious when my wife carries a cane while we're out somewhere." "I felt like a fool after I told my brother-in-law he was missing a luscious lady a block away." "I get tired of jumping every time Dad wants something." Participants swap solutions, realize that in some cases there are none, and share the feeling that others face the same highs and lows in their relationship.

It's never too early to start. When a blind social worker and his wife discovered their infant son was legally blind, they immediately sought professional help. (This father is well versed in blindness, having a mother and sister who are also blind.) No matter how bungling your attempts are to teach survival skills, expand that kid's world, and ingrain social amenities—try! If you insist you can't, then find somebody who can. Despite the odds you consider stacked against that youngster, gradually let go. Letting go is part of loving.

As a teacher, you may have a visually handicapped student among the sea of faces on the other side of the desk. Your first reaction might be that he will demand too much attention, rattle your routine, or disrupt class. By reading Chapter 23, you can discover techniques and resources for both of you. Forget that cliché "Teacher knows everything." If he is old enough, ask him if he has ideas about how you can best help him. If he is too young, consult the resource room teacher. Even if you're teaching an adult education course in aerobic dance or household repairs, that student might glean much more from your instruction if only you give him a chance for input.

When a blind hospital patient is under your care, your contacts will probably be fleeting. Announce yourself upon entering the room and leaving—rubber-soled shoes don't make much noise. Briefly inform the patient why you are there. If you come bearing food, some people will appreciate a rundown of what's on the tray. If the patient needs assistance, send somebody else if you can't stay.

A totally blind patient might like a quick orientation tour of the room, including bathroom and closet. A brief lesson on telephone dialing and operation of the TV might eliminate frustration.

Nursing home staffs care for many people with poor or no vision. When possible, wearing street clothes during the day perks up the patient's morale. You can help to restore pride in appearance by assisting with clothing identification. Many legally blind residents wouldn't sit on the sidelines during recreation if they had aids and games to enable them to participate.

Ah, and there are friends. Don't drop them just because they don't see as well. If the policy of "I'll be there when you need me" stood before, let it still stand. Don't dismiss the good times you had together as now out of the question. Ask your newly blind friend to go to the movies, take a spin on a rented tandem, or attend an antique show or rock concert. Remember, some spontaneity is missing because of the restrictions of transportation, so your friend's whimsical spirit is probably more willing than you think.

Despite your bond, it isn't ironclad. It's OK to say no when your friend makes a request you can't or don't want to fill. No and never aren't synonymous.

When a blind person walks into your work place as a colleague or employee under your supervision, expect that person's methods of getting the work done to be different from everyone else's. Give space and time to map out these approaches. Lay out the requirements for the job and then talk over the solutions. Should that worker need to be called to task because of poor performance or bad work habits, make your approach no different from that you take with any other employee.

Regardless of the niche assigned to that blind person in your life, think of him first as a human being and second as one who is visually impaired. You'll feel more self-confident armed with a few what-to-do's, but we all fall short and blow it no matter how well versed we are. After saying "I'm sorry," forgive yourself and forget it. If that blind person treads heavily on your feet or feelings, accept the apology and carry on.

When all is said and done, we have to face the fact that we are all human.

Chapter 29

YOUR VISUAL ACUITY
ISN'T YOUR FINAL SCORE

W hen I look at myself, I'm more than a pair of eyes that don't work right. I've come to grips with the feeling that they are part of me but not all of me. I won't be on top of this blindness all the time. But when my sight was perfect, I wasn't on top of everything 100 percent of the time either."

At thirty-two, Pam is losing her vision from glaucoma. Like every human ever born, she finds herself swimming upstream occasionally. The undertow she fights is blindness. The uncharted course she faces is the unknown: How will she keep herself afloat if she doesn't see clearly where she is going? She'll go down sometimes or get dashed on the rocks of despair. Little things will pull her under, such as losing the toothpaste cap or being unable to take her daughter to the park because she can't get there on her own. Whirlpools wait to be crossed, like earning a living and reentering the social mainstream. Neither is easy for a single parent who is legally blind. But Pam can buoy herself by her own efforts or reach out to others when she has to hold on.

According to the National Society to Prevent Blindness, Pam is among an estimated 500,000 legally blind Americans. Almost 47,000 join the ranks annually. Another 901,000 people have a serious visual impairment but do not fall within the definition of legal blindness. Among the leading causes of blindness are macular degeneration, diabetic retinopathy, glaucoma, and cataracts. Three out of four blind people have some measurable vision. More than half are over sixty-five. Approximately 20 percent are congenitally blind. Out of every 100,000 Americans, 225 are legally blind.

Don't let a string of statistics throw you; just know you're not alone. The most important number in your life is Number One: You.

How do you measure up to the Snellen Chart, that chart with the big E on top that hangs on the wall of your ophthalmologist's or optometrist's office? Its measurements boil down to numbers— figures recorded in your chart to guide experts. But only you can translate the meaning of those numbers into what you can and cannot see. Having no vision, you would score zero on even the most sophisticated tests.

Have you, like Pam, come to grips with that translation? Nobody chooses to be blind, but once it's there, do you at least acknowledge its presence? Have you quit denying that your sight is worse than it once was? Have you called a halt to bluffing with others? It's only when you accept sight loss as being real that you can start dealing with it on your own terms. Even if it ambushed you as an older person, you still deserve life in those years which remain.

I haven't touched upon the anatomy and physiology of the eye because this complex organ demands detailed explanation plus graphics to clarify. When something goes awry, diseases and disorders require even more description. One of the most concise treatments I have seen is in the book *The First Steps* by the staff of the Peninsula Center for the Blind. If you're looking for more depth, try Edith Kirk's *Vision Pathology in Education.*

Hope is a part of being human. Some of ours are real, a few false. Medical science has saved or restored sight in the past few years for thousands of people who would have suffered blindness five years ago. Technology makes its bid to compensate by extending residual vision or substituting with audible and tactile devices, but for over 500,000 people, the cure or solution isn't fully here yet.

We have to reckon with the now. If you have a visual impairment or are totally blind, have you found yourself in these pages, perhaps called by a different name in some of the anecdotes? Have some of the stresses and messes in your life been eliminated through hints and techniques? It's not a one-size-fits-all panacea. Some of the methods aren't applicable to you because you don't need them. For some problems you may have figured out better solutions. Take heart in knowing that there are other ways out in most instances. Yes, for some barriers there is no way around. I still can't tell you how to swat a fly or drive a car if you can't see what you're doing. When it's clear that you can't get around that stumbling block or one of those foggy situations when it would be simpler and faster for someone else to help you, then call upon that somebody.

Perhaps you read this book because a family member or friend is blind, or maybe you are a member of the health care, helping, or education professions or are a student. Just because I speak directly to the blind, don't feel left out by the use of the word *you*. You'll finish with a better understanding of what blindness entails and can teach others to dodge or overcome its pitfalls. I don't believe that you have to be blind to grasp these ramifications. You can't walk in another person's shoes, and there still isn't such a thing as a clone. Sometimes you just have to accept another's word just because he says it is so.

Views on blindness vary with those having the disability. Some people look at it as being totally debilitating. Others brush it off as a nuisance or inconvenience. I can't swallow either conviction. I see it as a serious, sometimes grave, disability that is surmountable most of the time. Its effects are not static, however. It will be different for each individual in how he feels and thinks at the moment or in what he is setting out to do.

Lorenz Graham, himself an established author, gave me heart to begin writing books. His wisdom was far more than encouragement to a shaky, uncertain novice. His words were a perceptive perspective that overshadows visual acuity, race, age, and station in life.

I met him only once. Yet our chance encounter was to change my outlook. That cross-country trip to California was meant only to revive a long-standing friendship with a doctor with whom I had worked and his family. I was hoping these dear friends could help me put together pieces of my broken heart, shattered by the loss of my father six weeks before.

It was a quiet evening. As we chatted in the living room after dinner, the doorbell rang, announcing Lorenz's arrival. It was soon apparent that this dynamic man, then in his early seventies, was a beloved friend of the family.

Lorenz and I fell quickly into conversation, rooted in the bond of writing. He had published a series of novels for teenagers, depicting the triumphs and perils of a black youth in a white world. The central character moved from the South to attend high school, college, and medical school in the North.

I listened with fascination as Lorenz, storyteller that he is, unfolded his own tale of defeats—publishers who rejected his manuscripts, editors who wanted to make radical changes in what he had written. I soared with him as he recounted the final victory, the long-sought prize of holding those bound volumes in his hands.

Cautiously I confided that I, too, wanted to write a book, but was afraid to begin. He urged me to start that book and take it a page at a time, just like taking life one day at a time. He cautioned me to expect and brace myself against turndowns and disagreements with editors and publishers, reminding me that we all experience disappointments. He warned me that the well of words would run dry, the page remaining maddeningly blank. "That's part of being alive—we're bound to hit that wall of frustration and restlessness. But never lose sight of your goal, whatever it is. For you will someday hold your goal in your hands."

I wanted to know more. "Lorenz, tell me how you got where you were going. How do you know so much about the black culture? Are you black?"

Silence. For a horrifying moment I thought I had offended this gentle man. His answer was to drive us both into the secret recesses of our own mind. "Yes, Margaret, are you blind?"

Stunned by the impact of his words, I was slow to comprehend. Without trace of a dialect, Lorenz's voice did not reveal his race. My Leader Dog was romping in the yard with the family dog. Sitting across from him, I must have maintained eye contact frequently enough during the last half hour, giving no clue to my blindness.

It was Lorenz who made the first move. Crossing the room to sit beside me, he embraced me, speaking words that I shall never forget, "May it always be this way for both of us."

I leave you with a wish, only a little different from the words of that wise old man, "May it always be this way for all of us."

Chapter 30

WHERE TO GO FOR THE ANSWERS
YOU CAN'T FIND IN THIS BOOK

W e're not a nation of letter writers, and if you think talk
is cheap, check your last phone bill. When you can't modify a device
you need (adding dots to the dial of your watch or building a
closed-circuit TV from a Heath kit is out of the question) start
looking for it by asking an agency for the blind or the Talking
Book library. Mustering up a letter or filling out an order form
can be difficult for some people. Drop that dilemma into the lap of
an agency staffer or librarian. Don't stop with the telephone answerer
if your request meets resistance—ask to speak with the agency
director or head librarian. At least those with whom I spoke said
they would see that such paperwork was handled.

Agencies and organizations of and for the blind abound. So you
don't know where to start, the simpler the better. If one of those
listed doesn't market an item you want or can't supply information
you need, a staff person will tell you where to get it.

In case you're compulsive and feel more secure about knowing
everything about everything, I've added a few resource books to
this reading list, particularly helpful to students, professionals
having special interests, and those in work for the blind.

This reading list is admittedly a smattering. If you can't read a
print book, volunteers through your Talking Book library or
Recordings for the Blind will record it for you. The library can

probably locate specific titles. Should you have to cough up a copy yourself, you can write to the publisher or ask a bookstore to order it. Although bookstores deal with national distributors, they will fill special requests, even for privately published works. Independent bookstores probably will fill orders more quickly. You are likely to pay a little more than listed price for this extra service.

When you're looking for a resource within the realm of health and human services, don't forget the United Way or your city or county public health department. Don't forget the librarian's resourcefulness, even for such requests as where to get your cat neutered least expensively or how to have antique furniture appraised.

To find *800* numbers outside your area, call *800-555-1212*. When *800* numbers have been available, I have noted them with business numbers. Sometimes this free service is canceled because of reduced funding.

AGENCIES AND ORGANIZATIONS

American Association of Retired Persons, National Headquarters, 1909 K St. NW, Washington, DC 20039 (*202-872-4700*).

American Bible Society, Special Ministries, PO Box 4835, Grand Central Station, New York, NY 10017 (*212-581-7400*).

American Council of the Blind, 1211 Connecticut Ave. NW, Washington, DC 20036 (*202-833-1251*) (*800-424-8666*).

American Diabetes Association, 2 Park Ave., New York, NY 10016 (*212-683-7444*).

American Foundation for the Blind, 15 W. 16th St., New York, NY 10011 (*212-620-2000*); catalog of products for visually handicapped persons lists resources for other devices, directory of agencies serving the blind in the United States, extensive print library on blindness.

American Optometric Association, 600 Maryland Ave. SW, Suite 400, Washington, DC 20024 (*202-484-9400*).

American Printing House for the Blind, 1839 Frankfort Ave., Louisville, KY 40206 (*502-895-2405*); largest producer of books for sale in Braille, recordings, and large print, sells teaching apparatus for preschoolers through high school.

American Society of Ocularists, Hugh Laubheimer, Executive Secretary, 244 E. Park Avenue, Lake Wales, FL 33853 (*813-678-2737*).

Blinded Veterans Association, 1735 DeSalle St. NW, Washington, DC 20036 (*202-347-4010*).

Canadian National Institute for the Blind, 1929 Bayview Ave., Toronto M4G3E8, Ontario (*416-486-2649*); governmental agency serving the blind of Canada.

Dialogue Publications, 3100 S. Oak Park Ave., Berwyn, IL. 60402 (*312-749-1908*); published in large print, recordings and Braille updates on technology, products and services, education and career opportunities and where to find them.

Direct Mail Marketing Association, Mail Preference Service, 6 E. 43rd St., New York, NY 10017 (*212-689-4977*); eliminates junk mail.

Division for the Blind and Visually Impaired, U.S. Dept. of Education, Room 3330 MES Bldg., 330 C. St. SW, Washington, DC 20201 (*202-245-0327*); administers state and federal rehabilitation programs.

Elderhostel, 100 Boylston, Boston MA 02116 (*617-426-8056*).

Evergreen Travel Service, Inc., 19505 L 44th Ave. W., Lynnwood, WA 98036 (*206-776-1184*) (*800-562-9298*).

Hadley School for the Blind, 700 Elm St., Winnetka, IL. 60093 (*312-446-8111*) (*800-323-4238*); call between 3 PM and 4 PM central time.

Independent Living Aids Inc., 11 Commercial Ct., Plainview, NY 11803 (*516-681-8288*); markets wide variety of aids and appliances.

Lions Club International, 300 22nd St., Oak Brook, IL 60521 (*312-986-1700*).

Medic Alert Foundation International, PO Box 1009, Turlock, CA 95381 (*209-668-3333*) (*800-344-3226*).

National Federation of the Blind, 1800 Johnson St., Baltimore, MD 21230 (*301-659-9314*) Job Hotline (*800-638-7518*).

National Library Service for the Blind and Physically Handicapped, 1291 Taylor St. NW, Washington, DC 20542 (*202-882-5100*) (*800-424-8567*).

National Society to Prevent Blindness, 79 Madison Ave., New

York, NY 10016 (*212-684-3505*); information on sight preservation, low vision, large print, posters, and films.

Recordings for the Blind, Inc., 20 Roszel Rd., Princeton, NJ 08540 (*609-921-6534*) (*800-221-4792*).

Retinitis Pigmentosa Foundation, 8331 Mindale Circle, Baltimore, MD 21207 (*301-655-1011*).

Royal National Institute for the Blind, 224 Great Portland St., London W1, England; national agency serving the blind.

SUGGESTED READINGS

Bierbrier, Doreen: *Living with Tenants: How to Share Your House with Renters for Profit and Security.* $6.95
Housing Connection
PO Box 5536-G
Arlington, VA 22205

Hanninen, Kenneth A.: *Teaching the Visually Handicapped.* 1979. $8.95
Blindness Publications
PO Box 28014
Detroit, MI 48228

Journal of Visual Impairment and Blindness. Available in Braille and on records.
American Foundation for the Blind, Inc.
15 W 16th ST
New York, NY 10011

Kirk, Edith Cohoe: *Vision Pathology in Education.* 1981.
Charles C Thomas, Publisher
2600 South 1st St.
Springfield, IL 62717

Loeb, Gladys: *What, Where and When.* Available on cassette or in large print. $10
Loeb Foundation
2002 Forest Hill Drive
Silver Springs, MD 20903

Lowenfeld, Berthold: *Our Blind Children.* 1971.
Charles C Thomas, Publisher

2600 South 1st St.

Springfield, IL 62717

Raftary, Alice: *Easy Adaptations for the Blind or Visually Impaired Seamstress.* Free print leaflet.

Greater Detroit Society for the Blind

16625 Grand River Avenue

Detroit, MI 48227

Raftary, Alice: *Modifications on Insulin Techniques for the Visually Impaired or Blind Diabetic.* $1 per copy.

Greater Detroit Society for the Blind

16625 Grand River Avenue

Detroit, MI 48227

Smith, Margaret M.: *Getting in Touch with Reading.* Available in Braille only. $8.50

American Printing House for the Blind

1839 Frankfort Avenue

Louisville, KY 40206

Smith, Margaret M.: *Getting in Touch with Reading: Grade Two.* Available in Braille only. $18.20

American Printing House for the Blind

1839 Frankfort Avenue

Louisville, KY 40206

The First Steps. 1982. Large print. $6.50, $1.75 postage.

Peninsula Center for the Blind

2435 Faber Place

Palo Alto, CA 94303

Walhof, Ramona: *Handbook for Senior Citizens: Rights, Resources and Responsibilities.* 1981. Available in large print ($5.95) and on cassette ($10).

American Brotherhood for the Blind

1800 Johnson St.

Baltimore, MD 21230

Weisse, F. A., and Winer, Mimi: *Coping with Sight Loss.* 1980. Available in large print ($10) and cassette ($12). Resource book.

Vision Foundation, Inc.

2 Mt. Auburn St.

Watertown, MA 02172